Love
Never Dies

JEANNETTE YVONNE FERRELL

ADVOCATE HOUSE
A Division of A Capella Publishing
Sarasota

This book is dedicated

in loving memory of my parents

John W. and Drusilla Boyles Ferrell

DESIGNED BY CAROL TORNATORE CREATIVE DESIGN

LIBRARY OF CONGRESS CONTROL NUMBER 2002113743

ISBN 09706576-9-2

Printed in Canada
First Edition
10 9 8 7 6 5 4 3 2 1

Acknowledgments

FIRST, TO JESUS, my Lord, and Savior, Who, through the Holy Spirit inspired me to write this book, sharing with you the last forty years of my life.

Patrika Vaughn, my editor, and Advocate House my publisher, who were definitely God sent. They together went beyond the call of duty in helping me achieve this goal.

Odis G. and Lizzy R. Stephenson gave me nothing but good inspirational advice and kept me uplifted during many moments of misbeliefs.

H. Briant and Frances J. Cotten, who didn't think I was listening at times, stuck by my side. No matter when I called with a question, in the middle of the day or in the wee hours of the night, they always listened and were willing to help.

Etta Mitchell L. Lawrence who took time out of her busy life to read the first three months single-spaced format of the book in its rawest form. Many of her suggestions were taken into consideration and have helped form several of its passages. To you, my friend, I give my earnest and most sincere thanks.

To Rev. Ross M. Marion, the Chancel Choir, the Hand Bell Choir, and the Chapel Bible Sunday school class of Wake Chapel Christian Church, I pray God's eternal blessings. You and the entire church have generously provided your outpouring hugs of love with encouragement and support during my daily walk, and through the many months it took for this book's completion. I earnestly and humbly give you my thanks.

Robin Cotten Photography, with a talented eye for the natural that comes from deep within her soul, produced the photograph that is used on the back of the book.

David McCreary, who took time out of his tremendously busy schedule and formatted the biblical proofing in finalizing this manuscript.

To my aunts, uncles, and cousins, and to all who have been anxiously waiting for the completion of this book, I pray for God's touch and blessings upon you all.

Acknowledgement of all Bible Scripture mentioned within are derived from the *King James Bible*.

Preface

OH, HOW GOOD it feels to be back at my home church again! Folks are warm, friendly, and so full of hugs. It's been a long time since I attended on a regular basis. The only explanation for the closeness I feel toward these dear church members is through the influence of Christ Himself. When I feel down, all I have to do is pick up the phone or get in the car and stop by for a visit. We almost always end up laughing.

In May of 1999, there was talk of a new program to help people cope with the loss of their loved ones. Struggling still with losing both my parents as well as a second cousin, I knew immediately this was meant for me.

By the time the sessions got underway an uncle and his wife had also passed away, bringing the loss to seven family members in an eleven-month period. As the program began, the instructor insisted that attendees write down their feelings in a journal. It could be just a word or two, maybe a few sentences, "Whatever feels right to you," she said.

I carried this thought around for a couple of weeks. Then, one day while out shopping, just by coincidence (*or was it?*) I found myself browsing in a Christian bookstore. Having never done such a thing, I began thumbing through a blank journal with a cover that showed a young girl holding a lamb in her arms. Before realization set in, I was walking out the door with book and bag in hand.

At home, I took the journal out of its pretty enclosure and laid it gently on the kitchen table. Then, not thinking much about it, I carried on with that day's activities. About three or four days later I stopped, pulled out a chair, and slowly sat down, thinking of my once being a lost lamb. I picked up a pen as thoughts began to rise from within.

Dear Jesus, where do I begin? What do I say? Dare I write these thoughts on paper?

Well, before I knew it, nearly an hour had passed, and almost ten pages were filled.

By the end of the program (through the workbook and two written journals later), a few friends rekindled for me a long-ago memory of how Jesus had always been close to our family. Though my parents had, years earlier, suggested that I write about that, writing just wasn't meant to become a reality at that time.

With God's forgiveness, divine leadership and protective shield along with times spent walking and talking, reading and praying, this book came to be. I share it now with you, confessing my young adult years when I drifted away from Christ, and recalling the miraculous event that brought me back into His fellowship forevermore.

$\mathcal{C}$ontents

1

Building Integrity

*I*T WAS EARLY spring of my fourth grade year. Walking home from the bus stop, the air was filled with pleasant smells from the sun-dried clothes Mama had hung on the wooden clothesline that Daddy built a few years back.

Approaching the back yard, I saw my favorite blouse lying in bits and pieces all over the ground. After rushing up the wooden steps and through the kitchen and dining room, I reached the living room and saw the stacks of folded clothes on the couch. Then I shouted angrily, "Mama, what happened to my favorite blouse?"

"Honey, your mother isn't feeling well and she needs to rest," Daddy said with concern in his voice. "How about folding the rest of the wash, putting it away for her, and I'll tell you all about it after supper." I did as I was told, but reluctantly. I was really upset about my blouse being in shreds. *What had Mama done to my blouse?* filtered angrily through my head. Soon my nose began to turn and I began pouting as my bottom lip rolled out.

Daddy looked at me and said, "Jeannette, that's no way to be now. You're growing up and you need to take on some responsibilities. Its not going to hurt you one bit to help out some. You know how sick your mother has been. Now, go ahead and get those clothes put away and then do your homework."

"Shug?" Mama called for me from their bedroom, "There's been an

1

accident and I couldn't help what happened to your blouse. Please forgive me. Our next door neighbor's dog went wild and leaped for my throat. I jumped back and his huge claws dug deep into your blouse, which happened to be on top of the stack in my arms, and it was torn to threads. I'm so sorry, I know it was your favorite."

What I should have said was, "Oh, Mama, I didn't know. I'm sorry for the way I screamed at Daddy earlier," but I didn't. If only I had. All I needed was a hug and someone to say, "Jeannette, it's gonna be all right." Instead, I began to slump deeper and deeper into my own little world — a place where no one was ever sick, ever hurting, ever mistreated — a place I learned to call my little heaven here on earth.

Later that night, Dr. Bean came to examine Mama. Afterward, he called Daddy into their bedroom. I was in the living room when Dr. Bean left and Daddy called for me to come into the bedroom.

"Jeannette," Daddy said in a shaken voice with tears in his eyes. "First, Mama wants to share with you what happened today and then we want to share what Dr. Bean just told us."

Mama got right into it: "Well Shug, in a flash and out of nowhere it seemed, came running toward me was the Smith's bulldog. It began growling and lunged for my throat. I started screaming and struggling as he nearly knocked me down. I can still remember the horrified feeling I had as his huge toenails slid down my arms and I saw your blouse as he shredded it. In the raging battle, I lost one of your daddy's Sunday shirts, too.

"This dog's teeth were right there. I even smelt his horrible breath. I ran the best I could and stumbled up the back steps as I heard his huge paws racing, thumping in the background like thunder. I grabbed desperately for the screen door handle and hurried into the kitchen. Letting the screen door slam behind me, I grabbed the inside wooden door and pushed it against its frame so hard that I heard the glass rattle in the panes. Just as the door shut, I collapsed on the kitchen floor and my armful of clothes fell everywhere. That dog's terrifying growls were intensifying so strongly that again, the windowpanes in the door rattled from his outrageous force. I gathered myself as best I could and pulled up. Holding onto the door handle with all my might, I peeped around the curtain. I saw him slinging his head from side to side, slobbering unmercifully. The growling and snarling he was doing were already frightening. Then he grabbed the other clothes that had fallen to the ground in the battle and his snarling and growling got even stronger. All of a sudden, he must have caught a glimpse of me peeping because he leaped toward the screen door a second time and I nearly had a heart attack!

"I flinched and ran violently into the living room, being scared out of my wits. It seemed like an hour but actually it'd only been a few minutes when I thought, 'Oh my dear Jesus, dare I go look again?' Shaking like a leaf in a windstorm, I crept slowly back toward the kitchen and very carefully peeped around the kitchen door's curtain to see the beast going back into his yard. I said a prayer thanking Jesus for protecting me from that raging animal.

"Shug, I couldn't even leave the house and go get Daddy because that dog was right next door, still unchained. No one was at home during the attack, and there was no one to tie him up. I finally broke in on a party line conversation and frantically asked Brenda to come up and see if she could possibly do something with that wild beast. Shug, Brenda said she was just as frightened by that dog as I was but she'd try and get a man to come over and tie him up. I told Brenda, if it hadn't been for your blouse when that beast attacked me, I'd probably be dead now. I told her I was still mighty shaken and asked her to get your daddy out at the station.

"I was in such a knot that I screamed bloody murder when your daddy opened the front door. After seeing the condition I was in, he went next door and got Grandma to come and stay with me while he went to call Dr. Bean. I was in no shape to go to his office."

I nodded and patted Mama's hand as she finished. Then Daddy said, "Honey, as I said earlier, we have some other news to share. Please be patient as we try and explain this the best we can, okay?" Nodding my head and sitting quietly on Daddy's knee, I listened as he began softly:

"Your mother and I thought you were going to have a little brother or sister before long. But it just wasn't meant to be." Then Daddy began to cry as Mama interrupted, "Shug, Mr. Smith's dog caused me to have a miscarriage. I'm as sorry as I can be about your favorite blouse. I tried so hard and I was so frightened for my life that I guess I overexerted myself to the point of losing the baby. I'm so sorry that this happened."

I could see the disappointment in Mama's face as the tears began streaming down her pale cheeks.

"Daddy and I wanted so desperately to have more children so you wouldn't be alone. We know how lonely you are. Your daddy had five brothers and three sisters and I had five sisters and two brothers to grow up with. Why, there's nothing like having brothers and sisters to help you learn how to get by in this life. We understand that it's mighty difficult for you to say 'no' and to cope. I guess that's why we seem to be over protective at times. Shug, we don't mean to be that way. It's just that we know how the world can be and we don't want you to get caught up into something that isn't right, in God's eyes.

"Your daddy and I are so disappointed about what happened today. All we can do is thank God that my life was spared. We'll just give Him praises.

"No, Daddy and I don't understand why you have to go through life without a brother or a sister, but it is His will for this to be and we have to honor His will and accept His judgements. It could've been another type of accident and I might not even be living. Although I lost a child today, I must believe it was God's will. After all, He always knows what's best for us."

When Mr. Smith arrived home and learned of Mama's loss, he got his rifle and took the dog way down in the woods. As the explosion of the weapon rung through the valleys of the forest, Daddy put his arms around Mama, then reached and pulled me close. From that moment on, we never again rented the house next door to tenants who owned outdoor pets.

2

Faded Love

BEGINNING EIGHTH GRADE in the early sixties felt like walking into a different world. Even the teachers seemed shorter than they were before the summer break.

When Valentine's Day came around, I couldn't wait for English class to end. I had a very special card picked out for Johnny Router. Wearing a blue skirt with a white cotton pressed blouse that he liked, I walked hesitantly toward Mrs. Tanner's homeroom class. Realizing she'd be in the gym and knowing the direction Johnny would walk after his Latin class, I rushed so I could hand the card to him without us being seen.

Oh, the times Johnny spoke of his family. And oh, how he looked forward to running and playing with his neighbor's dog.

Johnny was quiet and gentle. He wore black-rimmed glasses and his eyes were such a royal deep blue, they almost looked black. He kept his black hair short and his skin was olive. Anytime I approached the entrance of a building and Johnny was anywhere around, he'd hasten to open the door — not just for me, but for all of us girls as he shared one of his famous shy grins.

Johnny was special. During class picnics, we would sit together awhile trying not to make a scene because neither he nor I wanted anyone to make fun of us. We were shy in that way. He, too, had been made fun of growing up. Johnny and I shared some short but very special moments. We once spoke of name-calling and the pain we felt down deep inside. He told me that just because he enjoyed reading, learning and studying, some of the classmates made fun of him and called him a bookworm.

"Jeannette, I know I'm different but so are they, and I've never made fun of them, nor will I. My parents make sure I attend church, and I've been taught about Jesus; I know who He is and I've accepted Him as my Savior."

"Johnny, with Jesus, we're gonna be just fine," I insisted as I shared with him my experiences with name-calling and the deep-rooted feelings I had to deal with.

One day, near the end of the ninth grade, I was closing the doors to the library when Johnny appeared saying, "Jeannette, I hope to talk to you while we're out for the summer."

Turning toward him with a smile I said, "Me too, Johnny."

Sure enough, we did see each other — once at the drive-in show, and then when we ran into each other downtown. On one special day he and I were able to attend a movie, along with my parents. It was a rerun of "Old Yeller." During the part where a wild boar had bitten Old Yeller after he had hemmed several of them in the ditch, Johnny looked over and noticed a tear falling down my cheek.

"Are you okay?" he softly whispered.

I just nodded while he gently put his arm around me and pulled me close to give me a comforting hug. While we were driving Johnny home, Mama said the part about the wild hogs always made her cry. Johnny and I looked at each other, our hearts embracing in an innocent loving smile.

Then came tenth grade — special school dances, picnics, annual planning and class projects as we grew in classroom knowledge and also in spirituality and maturity.

On a warm clear day near the end of September, as the sun grazed warmly across the school, I had just left Mrs. Tanner's physical education class and was looking awful. I hadn't washed my hair that day when I showered because of Mama. "Jeannette," she'd said, "don't you dare wash your hair today after Phys. Ed. 'cause you know that fall is in the air and

I don't want you to take a cold. Even taking vinegar doesn't throw off all your allergies."

As I headed toward the high school, I met Johnny heading toward the junior high for his last class of the day. He was wearing a solid light blue button-down cotton shirt, navy blue pants with a brown belt and his proverbial weejun loafers with tassels and no socks. Johnny stopped me in my tracks as I tried to comb my oily hair and straighten the brown dress I was wearing.

"Jeannette, there's a special camping weekend planned with the Scouts. We're going to spend Friday and Saturday nights in tents. Our Scoutmaster told us that the one who tells the scariest story around the campfire each night wouldn't have to cook."

"Well Johnny, you're sure to win that one."

"We'll be back early Sunday morning to go to church. So, I'll see you Monday morning, okay?"

"Okay Johnny. Hope you'll have a good time. Tell me all about it next week?"

"Sure, Jeannette."

"Uh, be careful, okay?"

He nodded continuing toward his last class as I continued toward mine. Being late for class didn't faze me a bit. Getting a late slip to carry home and have signed by one of my parents was nothing, because talking to Johnny was all that mattered to me during that time in my life.

I gave the late slip to Mama and of course, she wanted to know why I had been late for class. I explained about being the last one to shower from Phys. Ed. and how if I hadn't run into Johnny, I wouldn't've been late.

"Jeannette, *you would not have been late.*"

"Yes ma'am," I said. Mama was correcting my English all the time. Although she'd only finished the eighth grade because of staying home with Papa Boyles, she knew when I wasn't speaking properly and didn't mind correcting me.

"Mama? Johnny was so excited about the camp meeting that he stopped me between classes, and Mama, you know how much I like him."

"Well, Shug, I do understand but don't let this become a habit. I'll go ahead and sign this note this once and you know I'll be telling your daddy."

Our kitchen table was used for everything — eating, playing cards, sewing, freezing and canning vegetables in the summer, and especially when there was a problem. Then the surface was used as a conference table. So, after supper was eaten and the dishes were washed, I made myself scarce and told them I had a lot of homework to do. As I tried to disappear gracefully down the hall and into my bedroom, I overheard Mama call Daddy into the kitchen.

Oh no, I'm in for it now, I thought. *I'll probably be grounded, as if getting that late slip wasn't enough.*

"Jeannette?"

"Yes Sir?"

"Conference time."

"But Daddy, can't it wait? I have lots of studying to do."

"No! We need to talk. *Now.*"

Well, I knew when Daddy said *now* he meant *now* and not later. I closed my books, and headed back to the kitchen.

"Have a seat, honey, and let's talk about what Mama told me happened to you today at school."

"Daddy, it was all quite innocent, really."

I went into every detail as I had explained it earlier to Mama.

"Honey, your mother and I do understand. We know you have a pretty good head on your shoulders, and we just wanted you to know that we love and care for you. Your mother and I are not going to ground you in any way. We are not even going to scold you 'cause we know just how fond of Johnny you are, and we would probably have done the same thing you did.

Your mother and I agree that Mr. Jordan should not have given you a late slip, this being your first offense. However, he did, and Mother will sign it with both of our names. She's also written a note for you to give to Mr. Jordan explaining that we both have spoken to you about the importance of not being late for classes."

That night I said a special prayer giving praises to Jesus for giving me special parents.

* * *

The next week, Johnny didn't come to school. Rumor had it that he was sick. I tried to call his home but got no answer. After several tries I told Mama, and she told me not to worry. "Shug, we all need prayers every now and then. Maybe it wouldn't hurt for you to say one for Johnny."

I really didn't pick up on what Mama was saying, I just asked Jesus to watch over my best friend and his family and that His will be done.

The following weekend, Johnny's parents called and talked to Mama. She shared the information with Daddy. Reaching to turn down the TV, Daddy turned toward me and said that Mr. and Mrs. Router were taking Johnny to the hospital because he had a fever and it was continuing to rise. Mama said that we should keep praying because God does answer prayers and miracles happen every day. "Why Shug, just look at your daddy and me. We're living proof of God's healing capabilities." With a ray of hope in Mama's soft sweet voice, I reconciled to accept that God would hear my prayers.

The next Thursday as I began settling into Mrs. Sampson's math class, some of the students began whispering. I didn't pay much attention to them 'cause we, all at one time, whispered about something or someone.

As I headed toward my assigned seat, one of my friends leaned over and told me that some of our classmates had been to the hospital to see Johnny and that he wasn't looking good. Though Mrs. Sampson always smiled and greeted each student as they entered her classroom, this morning, she wasn't smiling. In fact, she was sort of sad looking. When the last student entered her classroom, she closed the wooden door, turned, and headed back to the front of her gray desk.

"May I have your attention please?"

Mrs. Sampson was wearing a white-laced blouse and a straight button-down green skirt with yellow stripes. Her hair was dark brown and she wore black rimmed glasses. Her left arm sparkled as the pretty tiny diamonds around the face of her gold watch glistened in the morning lights. Standing there in the lighted rays as the sun shined gracefully into the classroom, she began to speak.

"Class, I have some unfortunate news to tell you. Johnny Router has encountered a serious viral infection. He went on a camping trip recently and each one took part in the techniques of survival and even drank from a small mountainous stream. Johnny soon began to feel bad and on Sunday afternoon, his fever was getting dangerously high. His parents decided he needed some medical attention and carried him to our local hospital where the doctors, admitted him.

"I've been informed the family was asked several questions including whether Johnny had taken anything unusual by mouth over the last few weeks." Clearing her throat and wiping away a fallen tear, Mrs. Sampson continued, "Johnny needs our most sincere prayers. Let's all bow for a moment and lift up our personal thoughts to our Lord and Savior, Jesus Christ for endurance and guidance as we stand by Johnny and his family during this most critical time."

School was the least of my concerns for the rest of that day. One of the teachers who knew about me and Johnny came up to ask if I was okay. She sweetly offered to lend an ear and even a shoulder. Expressing her concerns, she continued by saying I need not worry about any of my classes, for she understood.

"Jeannette, if you like, I'll write an excused note and you may go home."

"No thank you. I'll . . . I'll be okay."

"Are you sure?"

I tried not to let it bother me. I prayed for Jesus to help me as I somehow managed to continue and tried to understand the terrible thing that had occurred to my best friend.

After lunch, Mr. Preston entered Mr. Taylor's Science class. As Mr. Preston approached and whispered something to him, Mr. Taylor called out my name. A lump formed in my throat, and I didn't know what to think.

"Was it Grandma, had something happened to her? Was it Mama or Daddy, had something happened to them? Why was Mr. Taylor asking me to come to the front of the class and follow Mr. Preston to the principal's office?"

You could have heard a pin drop in that classroom. The other students didn't know the reason for my removal, and neither did I. I could hardly keep up with Mr. Preston. I was tall, but he was much taller. I had long legs, but his legs were longer. I could move quickly, but he moved quicker. Once approaching his office, he asked me to have a seat in front of Mrs. Cuttingham.

"Jeannette, Johnny has been asking for you. As you've been told, he's over at the local hospital and Mrs. Cuttingham is prepared to drive you over there. I will inform your other teachers, and they will excuse you for your next three classes or for the entire day, should you not return to school."

"Uh, Johnny's been asking for me?"

"Yes, that's right, Jeannette." Mr. Preston seemed to understand as he wrote the excuses out and handed them to Sally Ruth for delivery while Mrs. Cuttingham and I walked to her car just across the street.

The drive over was very quiet except when Mrs. Cuttingham told me that Johnny looked different than when I had last seen him. I was nervous and didn't know what to expect, never even having gone into a hospital before. When Mama was in the sanatorium I'd been asked to stand outside, and Mama talked to me through a raised window with a screen between us. She wasn't able to touch me and I wasn't able to touch her. For several months we couldn't even hug, and I didn't even have sense enough to ask why. I was told to just accept it and I did. Mama said that a hospital was a place to go to get well. She told me to look at her and Daddy and remember they wouldn't still be here if it weren't for the care from the nurses and doctors and the Good Lord above.

Arriving at the tan one-story brick hospital building, Mrs. Cuttingham and I entered the waiting room. A nurse, dressed in all white with a tiny cap that sat directly upon her dark hair, came over and asked, "Is this Jeannette?" Mrs. Cuttingham nodded as the kind nurse said, "Please, will you both follow me?"

Mrs. Cuttingham motioned, and we were led quietly down a long, green block hallway. At the end was a wooden door with a sign that read, "Isolation. Put on corrective outer garments and head gear with mask."

I looked at Mrs. Cuttingham. "Yes, Jeannette, Johnny's in isolation. The doctors didn't want him to catch anything that we might give him. Johnny is very, very sick."

We put on the outside paper garments, hairnets, paper shoe coverings and an elastic mask and gloves. All you could see were our eyes piercing over the elastic masks. Even our noses were covered and it was hard to breathe. (I remembered watching Marcus Wellby, M.D. on television wondering how in the world they wore those masks and were still able to operate on people and *breathe*.)

As the nurse opened the heavy wooden door, the first things I saw were tall silver stands with lots of hanging bags and tubes running down into Johnny's body. Then I heard a beeping sound coming from near the tightly-closed window, which didn't allow any sunlight into the darkened room.

Monitors were everywhere. I let my eyes glance over to where they said Johnny was. If I hadn't known who he was, I would not have recognized him, lying there under the webbing that draped from the top of the bed to halfway down his body.

Johnny's body was severely bloated and his eyelids were nearly swollen shut. His face was rough beyond recognition and his fingers seemed all but at the bursting point.

"*JOHNNY?*"

His face lit up like a Christmas tree and he tried hard to smile. As I approached his bed, I pulled my mask down and tucked it under my chin so he could see my face.

"Jeannette, you did come. Jeannette, I'm sorry I didn't see you after the camping trip. I'm sorry. Jeannette."

"Don't talk, Johnny, you need your strength. We can talk later when you get better."

"No, Jeannette, I need to talk now. I want to tell you how much I appreciate your friendship. I want to tell you how much I enjoyed the movie we saw together." Johnny struggled to breathe, and gasped,

"Jeannette, I want to thank you and I want to tell you I really like you, I really do. Jeannette, do you know what I'm trying to say?"

"Yes, Johnny, I do and I like you an awful lot too. Do you understand, Johnny? But, Johnny, I need no apology. Don't worry, Jesus will take care of you. He loves you and, and, and Johnny, *so do I*. Johnny, don't try to talk. I'm here with you and I'll stay with you and we'll pray together."

He once again struggled for another breath, "If I don't make it and Jesus takes me to heaven, we will be together someday forever."

"Johnny, don't say those things. You're gonna to be just fine."

Tears began to flow and, as I tried to hide them, Johnny took his badly swollen right hand and lifted it to my face. Then he slowly swept his feverish swollen fingers across the streams on my cheeks.

I stayed with Johnny as long as the doctors would let me. Dr. Edermon, the local physician, came in and told Johnny that he was going to be transferred to Duke Medical Center where he would be cared for more intensely. This was a facility that was more capable and had doctors with more experience in treating his disease.

"Dr. Edermon? What's the name of my disease?"

Hesitating, Dr. Edermon leaned down and whispered into Johnny's left ear. "Guess you have a right to know, son. You have a viral infection called *spinal meningitis*." Johnny sighed, as if to say that he knew what the outcome would be and turned to me. "Jeannette, always remember that you're my best friend and I love you."

Then he turned his head, closed his eyes, and squeezed my hand. I leaned over, pulled the draped net up and over Johnny's head and kissed his swollen face. A tiny tear flowed down his right cheek.

I placed the mask back over my nose and the netting back to its original position over Johnny's body, then turned and slowly walked out of my best friend's isolated hospital room. After removing my cotton coverings and tossing them into a hamper, I turned and saw Mrs. Cuttingham and Johnny's nurse. Words can't express the sadness etched on their faces. I knew things didn't look good for Johnny.

* * *

One morning about a week later, I was scurrying around the house getting ready for school when the telephone rang. Daddy hadn't gotten home yet from the paper route and Mama was preparing breakfast.

I hollered out, "Mama, can you get the phone?" as I continued to dress and gather my books. I overheard Mama say, "No, I don't think so. I believe Jeannette will be better off being with her classmates than staying home. This way, they can lean on each other and the healing process will begin. Of course her daddy and myself will be here for her during the other times, but for now, it's better for her to be in school."

Then I heard the phone click as Mama put the receiver back on the hook. As I entered the kitchen, Mama said, "That was Mrs. Addie Ruth Pickins."

"Mama, has something happened to Johnny?" She didn't say a word, but the look on her face said it all.

"Shug, I told Addie Ruth that I thought it best . . ."

"Thanks Mama, I'll be just fine at school. Don't worry, okay? Let me eat some breakfast and I'll be on my way to catch the bus. Please, Mama, don't worry. Jesus has my best friend Johnny, and he shared with me when I saw him last that we'd be together one day in Heaven. Mama, I prayed for Jesus to do His will, not mine. He knows what my will was and one day, Mama, Johnny and I will be together."

The day came for Johnny's funeral. The school's flags were flown at half-staff and the doors were closed for half a day so that any classmates who wanted to attend his services could do so. The funeral, for family members only, was held in the adjacent town; anyone could attend the graveside services.

That cemetery hill where they laid Johnny to rest was packed full of people. Cars and buses lined the narrow paths and, down at the pond, several ducks and geese were swimming on that warmer-than-usual October day back in 1960 something.

From that moment until graduation, I often visited Johnny's resting place. I'd talk to him and cry, and tell him of the happenings in school and in my life. I told him of Grandma's sickness. Knowing how fond

Johnny was of Blacky, our family sheep dog, when she passed away, I asked Johnny to look after her until we were together again. I shared everything with him. Then after graduation, there was college and a new public job.

Several months went by and I didn't go to visit my friend. Then, one Sunday after church I asked my parents to ride with me to the cemetery. The three of us scanned the hillside, but never did find him.

The next week I called and asked the secretary of the cemetery if Johnny's body had been moved. The nice lady told me the cemetery had undergone a landscaping facelift. She then told me how to locate Johnny's exact resting place.

With my parents reading my mind, once again after church the following weekend we went to the cemetery. Daddy had saved some breadcrumbs and wanted to share them with the ducks and geese that had taken up residence in the local pond. The secretary had given good instructions. As I approached Johnny's resting place, Mama walked on by to give us some time.

As I kneeled and brushed away some fallen leaves and a few twigs, I gently kissed his head marker while feeling the warmth from Johnny's outreached arms pull me close to him. Wiping away my tears from his tender touch from above, I softly whispered, "Yes my love, one day, we will be together *forever.*"

3

The Hooded Stranger

IN THE LATE 1960s, a fever raged throughout my body. After an x-ray and blood work, Dr. Bean wanted me to see a pulmonary specialist in Chapel Hill for further studies and tests. He said the x-rays showed some unusual spider-like objects that he wasn't familiar with.

I knew in my heart that he and my parents knew best. I just didn't want to leave home. I'd never been apart from my parents except for the time when Mama was in the sanatorium for seventeen months, and I didn't want to ever be apart from them again. "Please, isn't there another way?" I pleaded, to no avail, as they reassured me that this was what God wanted.

Down deep, I knew there was no alternative. The fevers were continuing, and with the abrasions forming all over my legs and face, something had to be done.

The following Tuesday afternoon I told my boss the results from all the doctor visits and of my upcoming hospital admission for further tests. Immediately, Mr. Jones made out a medical leave of absence and said I had nothing to worry about . . . that whenever I was released from the sanatorium, I'd always have a job waiting for me there.

That day arrived too quickly. The wind blew fiercely on this cold, crisp February day as Daddy parked under gigantic bare oak trees. Mama's and my coattails brushed frantically in the air while we held on tightly to avoid an embarrassing moment.

After being admitted and wheeled up to a room, even before changing into my bed clothes, the lab technician came for some blood. Next, in came another to wheel me downstairs for yet another series of tests and x-rays.

It was ten o'clock or so before my parents left on my first night away from home. It was also my first time of being alone. Oh, how I hated to see them go! I don't think I slept at all, as I prayed and filled my pillow with tears I had held back so Daddy could see how grown and how strong his little girl *really* was.

In the wee hours of the next morning, I was startled when a lab technician placed a tray full of clear skinny tubes on the bed next to me. After he turned on the overhead light, I noticed that each tube was covered with a rust-colored cap and each one had a nametag wrapped around it. The lab technician announced he had been ordered to retrieve five vials of blood from me. Laughing while putting the large rubber band around my left arm and inserting a long, shiny needle in the bend of my elbow, he said not to worry because my body would replenish itself within 24 hours. Then three young men in white jackets appeared in the doorway calling themselves interns. They said they were studying rare cases and had been assigned to my situation.

"My situation? *I don't understand.*"

"Well Miss, we need to run some extensive studies to see exactly what you have so we can help you get well. In the meantime, we're going to start you off with some shots of streptomycin."

After nearly three weeks, I began opening up to Mama about being scared. In spite of all the tests and blood work and sputum taken, nothing was materializing and my fever was continuing to rise.

"Try not to worry, Shug, Jesus is going to take care of you. You're gonna be just fine now, you hear?"

I don't know what exactly caused it but after Mama said that I felt warmth inside — it was as if she had touched the raging uncertainties in my soul and left me feeling much peace from within.

Soon after Mama left to head home, Dr. Realm (a very tall man with hair of sunshine and eyes of Scottish blue), the head doctor of the medical center, walked into the room. He reached for a chair and placing it beside my bed, sat down.

"Jeannette? Looks like what we've done so far isn't helping much and your fever is now around 104 degrees. I'd like to perform a technique called a bronchoscopy."

"What's that?" I asked worriedly, not knowing what was coming next.

"Well, it's a slender, tubular instrument with a small, electric light, for examining or treating the inside of the windpipe or the bronchi — or for removing some foreign substance from those areas. We're planning on taking a small biopsy for further testing after checking the monitor and looking around your lung area. It's kind of new, but I believe it will help us determine the right kind of medicine to administer to help you get well."

About seven o'clock Wednesday evening, in walked Mama, Daddy and Dr. Realm. It wasn't long before questions concerning the procedure were raised.

"Dr. Realm, I know Jeannette does not have tuberculosis. She has none of the symptoms. Of course she's weak. It's because of the fever."

"Well, Mrs. Ferrell, I must admit I do tend to agree with you. However, in order to know for sure, I feel it necessary for this procedure to be done. I've scheduled it for one o'clock tomorrow. Don't worry. It's really a simple procedure, and it shouldn't take over fifteen minutes to perform. So," he said, turning to me, "If I don't see you before, I'll see you tomorrow at one, okay little girl?"

"Thank you, Dr. Realm, for stopping by and explaining this to Drusilla and me." Daddy said.

As he turned and left the room, I started crying. "I'm scared."

"You're going to be just fine, honey. Don't worry, Jesus is going to take care of you. He knows you're all we have, and you're going to be just fine." Daddy said.

"Shug, I agree with your Daddy," Mama said, "And you've gotta remember that Dr. Realm said he was going to be right there with you during the entire procedure. You know you can trust him. He's a fine doctor or else he wouldn't be not only the head of the hospital but the head of the sanatorium too."

That was a short night. It seemed like my parents had just arrived when visiting hours were over. "Honey, you sleep good and remember, Jesus is right here with you and you're going to be all right," Daddy reassured me.

Not only does the lab technician like the wee morning hours but the nursing staff does too, I grumbled to myself as concern flowed through me. Here she came, taking my temperature and blood pressure when it seemed I'd just fallen asleep. It wasn't long after she left that I heard a faint tapping on the side of the wall. Turning and slowly opening my sleepy eyes, I saw Mama and Daddy.

All morning long, interns moved in and out of the room. Each one asking the same questions over and over again. I was getting worn out. Out of the blue, Mama blurted, "Haven't you all asked her enough questions? She's having a procedure at one o'clock and she'll be in no shape for it if you keep this up."

"Ma'am, we have our own examinations to do before the procedure is held and they've gotta be done."

"I don't think so. I'm going down to the nurses' station to call Dr. Realm and tell him just how many of you have been in here this morning and see if something can't be done."

"Mrs. Ferrell, Dr. Realm has many patients besides Jeannette, and I'm afraid I can't reach him at this time," said one of the nurses on duty.

"What? Let me tell you something right now. Jeannette is my daughter, and if I don't hear from Dr. Realm soon, her daddy and I will take her out of this center before you can count to three, *is that understood???*" I could hear Mama all the way from the nurses' station. When Mama's feathers were ruffled, *everyone* listened.

Returning to the room, Mama spoke of the nurse's hesitation but dialed Dr. Realm's number anyway. Within a few rings, the angered nurse handed the receiver to her. "Mrs. Ferrell, you're right," the doctor assured her, "How many interns did you say had been in to examine Jeannette?"

"*Only five!*"

"Five???" I'll personally see to it that each will be dealt with. Now, what was the nurse's name who said I couldn't be contacted? I'll deal with her too. Thank you, Mrs. Ferrell. Things should never be conducted this way. We have all the necessary information we need and I totally agree with you. Jeannette is already weak and this extra probing and punching won't do anything but make her weaker. I do pray she'll be able to undergo the procedure. I will come by and check her out before we carry her down."

After that, no more interns came by. The only person who came into the room was the janitor, to sweep and mop the floor, clean out the trashcans and wash up in the bathroom. Around twelve-thirty in walked Dr. Realm.

"How's my girl doing? Is she about ready?"

"Dr. Realm, I'm scared."

"Little Girl, there's nothing to be scared about. The only bad part is having to swallow the tubing. Mr. Ferrell, as I promised your wife, I will take care of those five interns and that nurse on duty. Let's go and get this procedure over with, okay?" Mama and Daddy walked with me as far as they possibly could, both leaning down and kissing me on the cheek. I saw a tear fall from Mama's face. "Shug, we love you and we'll be right here when you get back."

* * *

The room was cold, terribly white, and huge lights hung overhead. They reminded me of the ones at my dentist office back home, only these were bigger. Then I saw a nurse coming toward me with a long, thin clear tube. "Okay, Jeannette, as I push this tubing up the right side of your nose, you start taking some short swallows of water and don't stop until I say so. Do you understand?" I just nodded.

After several tries, the tubing wouldn't go through. I kept gagging and nearly passed out on one occasion. Then finally, the tube successfully entered on the left side. Next I was led to a long, narrow bed and asked to lie down while several interns in white jackets lined up around Dr. Realm. As the overhead lights faded in and out, I heard a lot of mumbling.

What are they doing to me? I can't breathe. Dear Lord, what am I going to do, I can't breathe. I tried to talk and I couldn't. Hey, I can't breathe — can't you hear me? I can't breathe.

No one heard my cries, as thoughts ran frantically through my mind. Then I realized, they really can't hear me 'cause they're too busy mumbling to themselves. *I've gotta get their attention, oh dear Lord Jesus, how can I get their attention? Please, help me. Please. . .*

Seeing the bottom edge of a coat flapping beside my right hand, *dear Lord, please help me grab that coat, please.* It was as though Jesus picked up my hand and yanked that coattail.

"Oh my God, she's turning blue. We've cut off her windpipe. Quick, wiggle the tubing and get air into her lungs. Now!"

Waking later, hearing squeals of rubber pouncing across cleaned floors, I realized the nursing staff was bringing one blanket after the other and placing them upon my ice cold body. I felt like I was literally freezing to death. As the nurses brought the blankets, Mama and Daddy took their hands and pushed each one separately up against me. I was so cold.

Sometime in the night one of the nurses came with a small cup of red liquid, "Jeannette, here. Take this medicine."

Ah! It tasted so good against my parched lips.

"Give me more, please, give me more" I pleaded.

"Sorry, this will have to do."

"No, wait, bring me some more, please?"

"Sorry."

Mama and Daddy continued pressing more blankets up and under my frail frozen body as the fever inside raged. More chills developed as the coolness of my breath from my nostrils brushed against my upper lip.

On into the night as I settled down as best I could, I remember hearing Daddy say, "Mama, I'm going down to smoke a cigarette and get a Coke. Can I bring you one back?" It wasn't long after Daddy left that I stopped the severe shivering and fell into a peaceful sleep.

* * *

When I awoke, I was lying on my back in the dark shadows of the room, stretched out like a dead person. I saw movement out of the corner of my left eye. Turning, I noticed the big brown door slowly opening, and someone coming soundlessly into the room. This figure that appeared to be a person in a brown hooded robe with a tan rope tied around the waist, stood at the foot of my bed and continued to face me, as if staring right through to my inner soul. Although the figure glared, I was not afraid. I felt nothing but complete peace and contentment. I searched intensively with my eyes in the twilight of this night, scanning the darkness deep inside the hooded enclosure — only to find *no eyes, no nose, no face.*

Umm, I guess it doesn't want to be seen. Guess it's just here to pray for me, I thought as a sense of ease flowed through my mind. Turning, this slightly humped figure headed slowly back toward the door and into the silhouette of the hallway, as the door slowly closed. This mysterious visitor seemed to vanish as quickly as it had appeared — out of nowhere.

It wasn't long before I began burning up. Again the door began to open, only this time it was Mama checking on me. Placing her hand upon my forehead, she smiled and began slowly removing each layer of blankets. Daddy did his best to keep me settled by reading the paper or telling about his job and updating me on Grandma's condition in the sanatorium in Raleigh. Mama explained to him about removing the blankets slowly, trying to keep me from taking a cold while this enormous fever was diminishing.

After about five hours, I felt the warmth of being all right. Not only were my pajamas soaked, but also the next three blankets that were removed along with the top and bottom sheets and pillow case—even to the mattress beneath. When Dr. Realm arrived, he said he'd never seen anyone experience such a trauma and l i v e .

Mama and Daddy were filled with joy as Uncle Robert appeared in the small hospital room.

"Where did you come from?" I asked weakly.

"Jeannette, I knew my sister wouldn't have called the police station in King asking for me if it wasn't serious. As soon as I got the word, well, praise Jesus my little niece is going to be just fine."

It took three people, including Mama, to help me up and get me changed into dry pajamas. Then the cleaning crew came in. If I hadn't seen it with my own eyes, I'd never have believed it. There were actual puddles of sweat on the floor. They mopped and mopped and mopped, said they'd never in their entire lives seen anything like it before.

"Shug, I asked Dr. Realm just how high *did* your fever go and he said that the thermometers they use only go up to one hundred and six, and the mercury was all the way to the top. That's all he'd tell us except that your condition was mighty critical. That's when I called Robert. He was here in forty-five minutes, and it's at least an hour and a half trip. He told the patrol it was a family emergency and since he's a Deputy Sheriff, they cleared the way for him and the family. Shug, Jesus was with us all last night."

I slept for a whole day after that. Dr. Realm said it was partially due to the procedure and partially due to the fever; but mostly it was due to weakness. The next night I wanted something to eat. For some odd reason, I had a cheeseburger, french fries and a chocolate milk shake on my mind. Sharing this with my parents, the next thing I knew, there stood Daddy with my request. I raised my head from the pillow. Nearly instantly, it fell back. The strength in my neck muscles was gone.

Daddy cranked up the bed and I managed to take a bite or two of the cheeseburger. I ate only a few french fries and drank about a fourth of the milk shake. Dr. Realm, my parents, and the two nurses in the room held hands, and lifted praises to Jesus for this, His miraculous event.

A few days later, Dr. Realm came in with some good news.

"I think we've stumbled upon your disease and it is not tuberculosis. I almost wish it was, knowing there is a cure. However, what the biopsy revealed was something called Blastomycosis, a rare disease that attacks the lymph nodes in the body. You'll have to take the medication, called Amphotericin B, in a darkened room. The only place we have available is down in the basement. One of the drawbacks of this medication is that we can't let it lie in sunlight due to its sensitivity to evaporation. The liquid is so rare that the United States doesn't even make it. It's only been introduced in England a short time ago."

Not much was known about the disease due to only a few reported cases in England. Dr. Realm continued: "I'll be honest; we don't know any of its characteristics or even if it would cure the disease at all. The only research we know of was from English sources. We'll double and triple-check the sources before giving the go-ahead for treatment. I regard your recovery nothing shy of a miracle, and I want you to start back on a series of streptomycin."

* * *

Two days later I was improving somewhat, so Mama decided to go home early and fix a good supper for Daddy. Laughing, she turned and kissed me on the cheek and waved goodbye after saying, "We love you."

Just as I finished supper, the phone rang.

"Hello? Hey Daddy, I'm fine, how are you? Daddy, we're gonna play some bingo around nine and they're giving out candy bars. Sure hope I win. How's Mama?"

I noticed a hesitation in his voice.

"Daddy, what's wrong? What's happened to Mama?"

"Honey, your mother's all right but she was in a near-miss accident after she left you."

"Please, Daddy, is Mama okay????"

"Shug," mama's trembling voice butted in . . .

"*Mama!*"

"I'm okay but it'll take me a while to recover."

"Recover? Mama, how bad are you hurt?"

"Shug, it's my nerves."

"You're nervous? What's wrong with your nervous" I asked anxiously.

"Shug, while I was nearing the small narrow bridge, I saw a huge transfer truck top the hill. As we both approached, I just knew the truck driver would slow up and let me cross before he attempted to cross. So much for thinking; he was hauling buggy. He didn't slow up one bit. I realized just in the nick of time what was going to happen, and it was as though the good Lord Himself took hold of the steering wheel. Remembering what your Daddy said — if I ever lost control of the car I was to take my foot off the excelerator — that's exactly what I did. With my right two wheels on the shoulder of the road and the two left wheels still on the hard service, I didn't even smile as that stupid truck driver came barreling across. Then, just as quick as the car veered off the road, all four wheels were back on solid ground. I could almost smell the cement odor as the car grazed past the butt of that bridge. Through the grace of the Lord Jesus Christ, I'm alive. No doubt in my mind, His hands were in control of that vehicle. But when I got home, Shug, I was a nervous wreck. Guess it wasn't meant for me to fix that fresh supper I was planning after all. Daddy ended up fixing something for the both of us. Jesus was surely with me today."

"Honey, your mother and I will see you sometime tomorrow although it'll probably be tomorrow night."

"No, Daddy, you take care of Mama. I'm okay and I'll look forward to seeing you Sunday. Before you say anything, listen. You two have been so good to me, coming up here every day. Now take a couple days off and rest, cause I love you and I want you to take care of yourselves, too. As you say, Jesus is looking after us and I'm okay, really."

"Honey, we surely have a fine daughter. We'll see you Sunday morning then."

"No, Daddy, y'all go to church and then come up afterwards, okay? I know how much you enjoy it, and you can tell 'em I'm much better. I'll look forward to seeing you after dinner, okay?"

"Shug, do you have a boyfriend that you don't want us to meet?"

"No ma'am, I ain't got no boyfriend," I answered as we all three laughed.

* * *

Turning to greet my parents one morning, Dr. Realm said, "Mr. Ferrell, looks like Jeannette is better. However, I'd like to give her a few more shots."

Before he could finish his statement, Mama immediately spoke up, "John and I've discussed this matter ourselves, Dr. Realm, and we've come to take Jeannette home — *today*."

"But, Mrs. Ferrell, I don't suggest that at all."

"But, sir, with all due respect, Jeannette told her daddy and me that she didn't think she could stand to take one more shot. She shared with us about the visitor on the night of the procedure. We are more convinced than ever that our daughter has been filled with enough streptomycin and we believe it's high time for just some pure good old down-to-earth rest with no more harsh medicine. We'll take her home, get her on some vitamins and build her strength with some good old country food and she's gonna be just fine."

"Well, I can't stop you. Seems like your mind is made up. But I do insist that you bring her back for a two-week checkup."

"Now, sir, what would you do if it were your daughter, *really?*"

"Mrs. Ferrell, I'd probably do the same thing you and Mr. Ferrell are doing. Thanks to the One upstairs, she is much, much better." Dr. Realm's then turned, kissed me on the forehead, reached and shook Daddy's hand and patted Mama on the shoulder. About ten minutes later he returned with papers for signing.

"Well, little girl, I know you're in good hands. I expect to see you back here in two weeks. No work until I personally release you, understood? Stand up so I can get a good hug. Umm, I'm gonna miss you, you're so special — keep that smile, okay?"

As he turned to leave the room, I called, "Dr. Realm? May God bless you and your family." Then Daddy stepped out of the room while

I changed into the clothes Mama'd brought for me to wear home. I knew I'd lost weight but I had no idea how much. It took three safety pins to hold those bell bottom pants up around my waist. And the blouse — well, you could've gotten two of me into it.

Once outside, I could hardly believe the growth of the trees and the flowers in bloom on this warm spring morning. This was the first time I'd stepped out of the center since I'd arrived two months earlier. Daddy put my things in the trunk and Mama opened the back door for me as I bent down to climb onto the soft cloth seat of their "special" blue Buick. Daddy used to call it Mama's car. Folks said when it was in motion all they could see was two white hands on the steering wheel. Mama used to say that she wasn't tall enough to see over the steering wheel so she had to peep through it to drive.

I sat up as long as I could 'cause I didn't want to miss anything. I felt like I'd been away from home for a year. So much seemed to have changed along the way. Just before we reached home, I was so weak I had to lie down in the back seat. As the music played softly on the radio, I was brought up to date on the happenings of the neighborhood and how happy Spunky, my pet Chihuahua, would be to see me. Soon Daddy turned off the radio, and before long he and Mama began to sing, "Standing on the Promises" and "Love Lifted Me." Tears of joy welled in my eyes. I quietly lifted praises to Jesus for my special parents.

4
Sparks of Tomorrow

"I'M IN MY twenties, Mama, and still not married. I don't even have a boyfriend." I said while crying.

"Shug, don't be so hard on yourself. You have plenty of time for that. One way though, to help it along is by getting involved in church. Have you given any thought to maybe rejoining the choir?"

"Oh Mama, you know good 'n well the reason I quit was because I just didn't fit in."

"I know no such thing. It's all in your mind. You've gotta *be* a friend in order to have a friend. Just look how our church shared their love and support for us when I was in the sanatorium a few years back and when your daddy had those three heart attacks in the late fifties. Not to mention the generosity that was expressed from grandma Ferrell's church a couple of years ago when you were over in Chapel Hill."

"Okay, I'm sorry I said anything."

"Well, you ought to be sorry. If anyone stands up for you when you're down, it's your church family."

"It's just that I feel so different — I just feel so out of place, like, like I don't belong, and I don't know why."

"Sounds to me like you're feeling a little sorry for yourself, Shug. Come help me get supper ready. Papa will be home soon, and we're having fat back with milk gravy and canned biscuits and molasses. You know how he enjoys breakfast once in a while at suppertime. Now, with your help . . ."

We'd just finished putting the meal on the table when Daddy arrived. Our dinner conversation that night was about the upcoming holidays — Thanksgiving and Christmas. We were excitedly looking forward to getting together with the families. Mama's family was always so full of life, just like her. Never a dull moment around 'em. Then there was daddy's family — totally opposite, walking on the conservative side and much more practical in their way of life.

The hustle and bustle of the holiday season found us wrapping presents and writing cards. The aroma of the kitchen included cookies in tins and cheese swirls, placed up and down and all around on paper towels spread atop the counter space. There was apple cider on the stove and warm chocolate pudding in a clear, green bowl while chocolate fudge cooled on potholders on the kitchen table. Ah, such a delightful time of year. As the guests began to arrive, their presence made it all worth while.

* * *

Excitement filled the air as a friend of the family announced some job openings in the adjacent town. With her enthusiasm, a spark ignited in my brain. After discussing it with my parents, I called for an appointment. To my surprise, I was hired right on the spot. Five days a week, eight-hour days with some possible Saturday work. *Thank You Jesus, thank You for opening this door of opportunity and for the healing strength to return to work after that near-death experience.*

The drive was longer than I'd been used to. Although Mr. Jones had done his best to save my previous job, he didn't know of the new management that was being planned just before I entered the hospital and that my previous job had been terminated.

As the months passed with this new position, the initial schedule changed dramatically with increasing hours, requiring an early arrival and a later departure for home. The "occasional" Saturday work that was mentioned on hiring day turned out to be actually having only one week-end off a month. My hospitalization had been just over a year ago, and I was growing weaker. I knew my body was wearing down and a decision had to be made. An interesting ad appeared in the local paper, and the timing seemed right.

Well Jesus, what should I do?

That decision wasn't mine to make. The following week I had been asked to go to the manager's office.

"Jeannette, we're proud of your work. However, you don't have any shorthand skills. Therefore, we feel it is best to dismiss you at this time."

"Sir? Isn't there another position I might be able to fill? Although I'm a business graduate, I don't mind working in another department."

"Jeannette, I feel you should stay with your original vocational skills. You're really not the type of person to work elsewhere." (*I had no idea in the world what he was talking about.*) There had been no previous warning, nothing at all that would indicate termination.

Several weeks later I ran into Sandra, a former co-worker. She and her husband Thomas had become friends with my family. She could hardly wait to tell me what had taken place after I was dismissed. "Jeannette," she said with her green eyes sparkling, "The office became extremely behind and with this stressful situation, two outside women were hired. However, within a single day, it was discovered that neither had any shorthand skills. Boy, was Richard, your former boss upset when they were sent to a technical school to be trained."

I had a hunch there was something more to this conversation and I was right. Continuing with excitement in her voice, "Jeannette, you still haven't met Charles. Remember? He's the one I told you about three months ago." "Sandra, I told you then and I'm telling you now, I'm very satisfied with the way things . . ." Ignoring my comments, she jumped right in, "But, Jeannette, Charles is a wonderful, loving and kind person. But, there is just one small detail. He's divorced and . . ."

"And what Sandra?"

"Well, he has two children."

"Two children? *I'm not interested.* I'm looking for someone who's never been married so we can start a life together like my parents did and like you and Thomas did."

"Oh Jeannette. Get real. I didn't say you should marry him, all I said was I wanted you to meet him. You stay cooped up all the time at home and you need to get out more and enjoy life. You're getting stronger and stronger each day and all you need is someone to go and do things with, like a companion."

"Sandra, aren't you listening to me? I just told you, *I'm not interested.*"

Sandra was just like Mama. One who didn't like taking no for an answer. Not long after, Sandra invited my parents and I over for supper. Although we had already eaten with her and Thomas on several occasions, she just happened to mention that others would be attending as well.

"Mama, I ain't going to Sandra's and Thomas's tonight. I know what she's up to and I ain't going."

"What do you mean you know what she's up to?"

"Well, Sandra's been after me the whole summer to meet this man and he has two children. I've told her and told her I'm not interested, especially in someone who's already been married and already has a family. I know what the Bible says about divorce, and I ain't planning on getting involved."

"Now Shug, you know of no such thing. If Sandra said there'll be other guests it's probably one of Thomas's brothers — after all, he has ten or twelve of 'em."

"Well, you just tell her when you and Daddy get there that I couldn't make it."

"I'll do no such a thing. I've agreed that we'll attend and that's just what we're gonna do, the three of us. Even if it is this man you're speaking about, it won't hurt to have someone to go out with once in a while. There's more to life than work and home. You're getting stronger. Your sickness is a thing of the past. It does a soul good to get out and do things, if its nothing more than eating a hot dog and getting an order of fries and a drink. Or maybe just an ice cream cone. Or maybe a walk in the park. Whatever. It just does a soul good."

I knew it, *I just knew it.* Sure enough, when we arrived at their home, I was immediately introduced to Charles Carlton. Instantly I buckled. Later, he asked if I'd like to walk outside. *Not* wanting too, I agreed. I don't know why as I was against it to start with. But, he was kind of cute and very nice and mannerly, just as Sandra had said.

"Jeannette, have I said something to upset you?" he said boldly. "I've noticed you're a little uncomfortable. Sandra didn't by any chance set us up, did she?" Casting my eyes in his direction when he popped that question was all it took. In the twinkling of an eye, from the sound of his voice and that high school boyish expression, I was star struck. My heart melted and my mouth watered as if I was enjoying a big bowl of my favorite ice cream, garnished with all its glorious toppings. Umm!

"Yes, Charles. It appears Sandra's been doing some matchmaking and we're her targets." As the night progressed I couldn't help but begin wondering, *could it be dear Jesus? Could Charles Carlton possibly be the one I've been searching for all these years? Of course, he'd never replace Johnny — never in a million.*

"Jeannette? Would you like to go to a movie Saturday night?"

My heart began to pound with excitement. "Ah, I don't think I have any thing scheduled for this upcoming weekend (knowing full well *all* my weekends were open; yet I continued to stall, not wanting him to think of me as being forward when we'd just met).

"I . . . I guess that would be okay Charles."

"Good. I'll pick you up at seven if that's all right." Nodding as we walked in the moonlight getting to know each other, I began to feel us connecting.

Saturday arrived. Scurrying around the house making sure my dress was pressed and shoes shined, Mama popped around the corner and nearly scared me half to death, "Shug, you're acting like you're going to the Senior Prom. I haven't seen you this excited in years. Charles Carlton should've come along sooner. Seems good for you to have a pep in your step."

"Oh Mama, I'm so nervous."

"Nervous? What in the world for? You're grown and you know the rules. Just be yourself and don't let him kiss you on this first date or the second."

"Now Mama."

"Well anyway, remember your raising. No kissing at all until the third date and then only a peck on the cheek" I could hear her chuckling as she turned and walked out of the bedroom.

Right on schedule a knock came on the back door. It was Charles Carlton, looking mighty fine indeed. Standing there in all of his six feet two inches with navy dress pants and a crisp (looked like new) blue plaid button-down collar shirt. His wavy golden hair and sparkling Carolina blue eyes simply pierced my soul.

"Hello Mr. and Mrs. Ferrell, nice to see you again. Ah, Jeannette," he said as he turned from shaking Daddy's hand, "there's some special music playing over at the park — with what we talked about at Sandra and Thomas' I went ahead and purchased two tickets. Hope you're not disappointed in us not going to a movie."

"It was nice of you to think of me in such a special way, Charles. Just a moment and I'll get my wrap. And Mama, may we take a blanket to sit on?"

The night seemed to pass quickly and thoughts of the future began dancing through my mind. While enjoying the romantic sky, as it lit up like an enormous electrical explosion, I continued fantasizing about an engagement, then our wedding (nothing shy of impossible) and of being the grandest bride on planet earth. I day-dreamed about the elegance of our honeymoon, which escalated into the ecstasy of our own private island.

Bam, bam, bam, bam. All of a sudden, a giant eruption jostled me back to reality, signifying the end of the musical and firework performances.

As our relationship grew, a more intimate date began to unfold as the Christmas season quickly approached and Charles Carlton popped yet another question.

Driving back from the theater and a delightful steak supper one night, I kept noticing Charles was a little nervous, but I thought it was because of an upcoming job interview. After a brief conversation at my house with my parents, we excused ourselves into the living room for some quiet time.

"Why are you in such a hurry to go to the living room, Shug?" Mama asked. "You've already spent the whole day together. Can't you share Charles with us some?" I mumbled something, grabbed his hand and headed down the hallway. Mama's voice called out loud and clear, "Now you young'uns behave yourselves in there, ya hear?"

We chatted for a while about some presents for the children and his family. Then, out of the blueness of the chilled December night, Charles blurted, "Jeannette, will you marry me?"

"Uh, what? Uh, what did you just say?"

"Will you marry me?"

"Uh, well, uh, uh, Yes! Yes Charles Carlton, Yes! I'll marry you." I jumped up from the couch and threw my arms around his football player's body. He reached for my left hand and placed a beautiful engagement ring on my finger. Hugging, kissing, and embracing each other, happy tears filled both our eyes. Composing ourselves somewhat, we opened the door and walked toward the den. Mama turned sideways on the couch and looked me directly in the eye. "Well? When are you two getting married?"

"Mama? How did you know? Were you eavesdropping?"

"Shug, it's that step."

"There's a certain way you walk when marrying is in the air," Daddy said from his amen corner of the den.

I blushed and answered, "Charles and I did discuss a couple of dates, but we're leaning toward that romantic time of the year. We looked it up and it happens to be on Sunday."

"What day did you say? That's only six weeks away! Oh my, we've got a lot of planning to do and it's just six weeks away. Why the rush? Jeannette Ferrell you're not . . ."

"No way, Mama. You know me better than that."

"Mr. Ferrell, Jeannette and I decided there was no better time to marry than on the most precious loving day of the year."

"I know, son. You planned that day so you wouldn't forget it, right? Believe me, Mama starts reminding me two weeks in advance when our anniversary is coming up."

"Now Papa, you better bet I do. I don't want you to forget it. Besides, I'm worth the remembrance," Mama said as she ruffled her shoulders with amusement.

* * *

Saying our "I dos" brought glorious feelings into my body as Charles placed that little band of gold next to my heart followed by that beautiful engagement ring. It was as though a band of angels was standing in our midst as church bells rang throughout our small community.

I'll never forget that special day when I promised my newly-wedded husband to have and to hold through sickness and in health, till death do we part. I also extended the promise to his children as well as to my Lord and Savior, Jesus Christ. I took each and every syllable to heart as we knelt on His sacred altar, extending our love for each other in anticipation of it lasting throughout our lifetime together.

5
Threading Paths

I<small>T WAS WONDERFUL</small> being a wife and an instant mother. Not having to mix formulas, change diapers or worry about colic in the middle of the night was a relief — although if needed, I'd have stepped right in and done that, too, with the love I had for Charles.

With Henry being just a little over six and Katie just turning four, they were old enough to use the bathroom on their own, to tie their shoelaces, and eat a meal at the table without making a mess. As Charles' and my relationship grew, the children's presence in our home became increasingly enjoyable. Having grown up without brothers or sisters myself and mostly being in the presence of adults, this was *definitely* a new experience. As my life-long dreams had actually become a reality, each day became a new *threading path*.

My, how time did fly. One Friday after school in late April, Henry was just beside himself, telling about a bicycle ride planned for our area the next day. All by himself, he thought of putting up a lemonade stand on the corner where my parents lived. Once Henry made up his mind to do something, it was usually done. His plan sounded good to his Daddy and me, and it was no problem getting Papa and Mama Ferrell's okay.

Daddy insisted on building the stand. With Mama and Katie's help squeezing the juice and making the cookies, we ended up with three gallons of lemonade and three batches of chocolate chip cookies. Charles provided the napkins, cups, and ice along with a few bags of potato chips, and we all took part in the labor. Once Mary Lou, a friend of Katie's found out about their adventure, she wanted in too. Henry's business adventure turned out to be a big success. With the whole block's involvement and a few extra tips, Henry hauled in a hefty twenty-seven dollars.

Katie wanted a new Barbie doll, and Mary Lou said she needed some socks to wear with the new penny loafers she'd gotten for her birthday. Charles knew what his son's desire was as Henry had often spoken of that pitcher's mitt down at Jones' drugstore. I noticed Charles and Henry weren't anywhere around when the clean-up began. About an hour later, they drove into my parent's driveway. Rolling out of the truck with eyes just sparkling, Henry ran to show Papa Ferrell his new catcher's mitt. What a happy time it was.

Our fourth Christmas season was soon approaching. Sitting in the living room just after supper one night, Charles turned the television to the Grand Old Opry. It wasn't long before Henry and Katie both broke out singing right along with those country stars. Just as the show ended, Charles reached in his shirt pocket and pulled out some tickets. As the children carried on their nonsense this Saturday just after Thanksgiving, Charles said, "Start packing."

"*Whaddya mean, start packing?*"

"Honey, I have four tickets for several shows in Nashville. By leaving the day after Christmas, we'll be able to take them all in and get back here before New Year's Eve."

Startled and yet excited too, before I could get a word in edgewise Henry and Katie began jumping with joy all over us. While getting ready for bed that night, I just happened to mention Charles being between jobs. I didn't know if this was the right time for traveling.

"Of course it's the right time to go, Jeannette. Didn't you see how excited those kids were? 'Bout time we all had some fun times together."

"Charles, we give them fun times at the park and at the museums, and there's always fun activities taking place at school."

"Jeannette, you know we've been talking about going one day; and besides, what better time to go than during their school break between the holidays?"

As usual, I put my reservations on the back burner and went along with his plans. Am I ever glad I did. This turned out to be one of the best times we ever had together.

* * *

The following year I developed a low-grade fever. I just shrugged it off, thinking it was an allergy brought on by the fallen pollen from the oak trees as the new leaves began to blossom.

When after six weeks had passed and the fever wasn't going away, I decided to go to the doctor over in the adjacent town. Noticing I hadn't lost any weight, Dr. Cheple suggested I have a complete physical starting the next day, ordering me not to eat anything after six.

Arriving around nine o'clock, the usual blood work and chest x-rays were taken. Since the hospitalization seven years earlier, these x-rays showed scars had developed from the episode over in Chapel Hill, and Dr. Cheple said I'd have to wait from seven to ten days before the blood work report was evaluated.

After a week's wait, I went in for the results. "Strange, indeed," Dr. Cheple frowned as he studied the findings. "Your blood work shows a little increase in your white cells but nothing really to be alarmed over. And you've even gained a few pounds. Jeannette, I'm putting you on some different vitamins and giving you a prescription for some mild antibiotic for a viral infection. Take it all up. Unless you need me earlier, I want to see you in three weeks."

The time seemed to drag by. With my working part-time and Charles preaching at revivals, bringing in just barely enough to stay afloat, he decided to distribute his resumes all over town. Not discussing it with him, I decided to put off going to a doctor, hoping that Charles would find a steady job soon so we'd have some insurance. I let the three-week period that Dr. Cheple suggested become a six-week span. Once the abrasions began to form on my legs, Charles insisted on my going back to see him once more in spite of my unwillingness.

Dr. Cheple was very upset that I hadn't kept the original appointment. He not only scolded me but also charged an extra ten dollars! The fever was still very much present, ranging up to one hundred and one. After asking some personal questions, his next response was not what I'd expected to hear: "Jeannette, I believe your main problem lies between your two ears."

Flabbergasted by his remarks, I told him I couldn't pay him at this time but would pay by the first of the month. He in turn said there'd be an additional five-dollar charge due to lateness. Still stunned at his thought that the fever was imagined in my head, I held back my tears until I got home. *Jesus, I know something isn't right with me, and I don't believe it's lying between my two ears as Dr. Cheple just said. Lord, will You help me . . .* Just then, a tap came on the back door.

"Shug? I saw you drive up. Is anything wrong? Why are you home so early from work?"

Mama instantly noticed I'd been crying. "Mama, really, it's nothing. I just wasn't feeling well and decided to go and be checked out. Without having to drive back to Raleigh, I decided to come on home and return tomorrow. No really, I'm fine."

"I know you pretty good, Shug. It's that fever isn't it? You've been to see Dr. Cheple haven't you? What did he tell you?" Well, mamas are like that, always taking care of their young'uns even after they're all grown up. Don't think for one minute that she didn't give Dr. Cheple a call and a piece of her mind — why, there'd not be a cow left in Texas if she didn't respond.

Once during early summer, Katie and Mary Lou came running into the house just as I'd just hung up from an unusual call. Mary Lou even fell down and started to roll, she was laughing so hard.

"What in the world's so funny, you two? I've never seen either of you laugh so hard."

"Jeannette, you should see Henry's bugs."

"Whaddya talking about, Katie?"

"Come Jeannette, go with us and you'll laugh too." Katie kept going right on and on about Henry's bugs so I just put supper on hold, slung the dishcloth over my shoulder and was led out, with Mary Lou nearly pulling my arm off. Soon we'd popped around the corner of the house just in time to see about fifteen June Bugs having a plum fit. Why, they were buzzing all about and bumping into each other as they slid up and down the clothesline.

"Henry Vinson? What in the world have you done to those poor June Bugs? You go and untie them right this instance, do you understand?"

"Jeannette, we thought it was funny the way they were sliding, we didn't know it was wrong — we were just funning."

"I'm sure it was all done in pure innocence. Your Granddaddy Carlton taught you well how to tie a string just behind their heads and watch them fly. However, I believe you've gone to the extreme of funning this time. Henry, how'd you like to be tied to a clothesline and not able to go about your business? Go ahead now and free 'em and get on with your chores, okay?"

* * *

My mysterious fever kept climbing and soon the abrasions began to spread. In late winter of the following year, even my skin began to burn when taking a mild bath. After rubbing lotions and alcohol on the effected areas did not clear them up, Mama suggested I go see her doctor in Raleigh. Knowing how Dr. Cheple viewed my condition, I made an appointment for the following week.

Charles was able to take a couple of hours off from his new part-time construction job for my first appointment with Dr. Jefferries. On the drive over, we spoke of our wonderful trip to Tennessee and the activities of Henry and Katie's school projects. Then I decided it'd be a good time for us to discuss those disturbing telephone calls I'd been receiving. Charles' response was as normal as any one else's, saying they were probably wrong numbers; however, we both agreed we didn't understand why they always seemed to come in when he wasn't around.

"Honey? I'm probably letting my nerves run wild," I said. "When you don't feel good everything is blown out of proportion. Although I still don't understand the reason behind all that heavy breathing. It's beginning to give me the creeps."

Moments later he became very quiet.

Soon after arriving, a nurse called me into this tiny room. I sat on the edge of a table and Dr. Jefferries entered a side door. He asked to see my hands, then he looked in my mouth, ears, and listened to my lungs. Next, he asked in two of his associates to view my hands as I nervously repeated, "I have a habit of biting my nails."

After taking my temperature, the two associates left the room, and soon Dr. Jefferries joined them. All I could hear was mumbling. This time when the doctor entered, Charles was with him.

"Jeannette, I'm glad you took your mother's advice and came to see me. It appears you are very sick. I'd like for you to enter Rex Hospital next week so we can do some more extensive blood tests and examinations."

Charles and I looked at each other. I knew I was on the sickly side but I had no idea that I was headed for a hospital stay. Looking toward Dr. Jefferries, Charles spoke, "My being an evangelistic preacher and working part-time in the construction field, about six months ago I was hired for a nightly position. However, I'm not sure if my family is covered on my insurance yet."

"Mr. Carlton, it doesn't matter at this point. You're wife is very sick and needs immediate attention. You see, we don't know what's wrong with her, and we feel it best she enter Rex as soon as possible. We'll discuss your personal finances later. Right now, she is more important."

During the drive home, I expressed my concerns to Charles. "Oh dear, Charles, what am I going to do. Who's going to take care of Henry and Katie? How are they going to get to school and Charles, what are we going to do?"

"Jeannette, don't worry. I'm sure you won't be there long and we can manage for a week or two."

"A week or two? It better not be a week or two. Only a day or two at the most," I said as Charles looked at me in a strange way.

Once admitted to the hospital, it was just like Dr. Jefferries said — probing and punching and picture taking. In just two days they knew every inch of my being as modesty seemed to have flown out the window. Then, the first of the next week, Dr. Jefferries told me they'd talked about doing an exploratory surgery to find out what was wrong with me. I'd never been so scared.

"I don't want to be operated on. Oh no, Dr. Jefferries, do I really have to?"

"Little girl." *Oh, Jesus, how I love hearing his rustic voice once again call me by this nickname. Remember Lord, he gave it to me when I came with Mama on her weekly visits back in the 1950s.* Coming back to reality I heard Dr. Jefferries say, "We need to find out your problem so we can treat it; the course you're on now . . . well, it doesn't look good. Don't worry, you'll be in the finest hands Raleigh has to offer and I'll be right there with you during the entire surgery."

No one will ever know my true feelings at that point. Scared wasn't the word. I was petrified. Charles tried to assure me everything was going to be all right. My parents tried to reassure by reminding me of their past illnesses and Daddy's busted appendix when he was only fourteen years old and being here in this same hospital. Papa C and Peg tried to console me with the story of when Peg was operated on for a broken leg. No matter how much they talked, I was *still* scared to death. Since we were between home preachers at the time, there was no one there for my parents except for some church members. They were wonderful, but having to face a major exploratory surgery for their only child and to do it without a preacher was almost unbearable. Although Charles was a preacher, he was also my parents' son-in-law, and it just wasn't the same as having your own *home* preacher.

6

Environmental Factors

I HAD BEEN TERRIFIED of lying helpless while under the anesthesia. Yet, never in my life had I felt such comforting peace, thinking of the good life I had. My loving husband, wonderful step-children and great parents. Falling deeper into the unconscious state, I found myself being drawn toward a tunnel with a huge light that seemed to be filled with fog. Through this mist, I saw what appeared to be people who were gracefully floating in mid-air, as though their lightness was caught up in a ray of genial music, so soft and easy, as I found myself among them. How pleasantly content. I felt as though I was among family and knew them all by name.

Just ahead was another light even more radiant than the one I was in. Focusing into another area, I noticed someone clothed in white.

I felt the presence of God, and somehow I knew I was walking with His Son, Jesus. I felt totally at peace as we strolled side by side in that moment of His glorious grace. I was so content with my surroundings that I literally didn't care if I lived or died. It was just that peaceful and pleasant and serene.

Turning and facing me, He said, "Jeannette, you can come with me now." He spoke in the purist and clearest voice I've ever heard.

"Oh! Jesus! I'd really like to . . . But . . ."

"But?"

"Oh Lord, no human words can express the beauty that lies around; I'd

really love to stay, but what would Mama and Daddy do without me? Especially in later years, how would they manage? Charles and I've already discussed taking care of our parents and . . . "

"Jeannette, could there be something else?"

"Lord, You know me well, don't You. You see, it's just that, well, my dear husband and my parents have spoken often about their experiences while living in the world and always seem to enjoy telling these stories. As some of the events unfold, they begin smiling, and every now and then I might even catch a laugh or two especially from Mama. Jesus, You know that I've, in a sense, been protected from the world and haven't experienced many hardships at all."

"Jeannette, what exactly are you asking of me?"

"Lord, I am so happy although I am very sad too for not knowing why I am sad. Jesus, I've often wondered how can I express heartfelt sympathy to anyone, in any situation, unless I've experienced it myself. I . . . I guess what I am trying to ask You is, would You let me experience a little of the worldly way?"

"I love you, Jeannette Yvonne," He said in a voice that seemed as clear as fine crystal.

In the distance an unfamiliar voice called my name, *"Jeannette, Jeannette, it's time to wake up. Jeannette?"*

The voice became increasingly louder as I snuggled to keep warm under the covers. As melting ice particles moistened my feverish, parched lips, I slowly opened my eyes and peered around the room. The brilliance of the lights was so sharp that it penetrated my eyes like a razor's edge. Feeling the warmth of a cloth on my forehead and reminiscing of the peacefulness of the moment, I wanted so desperately to sleep so I could catch back up with my 'Friend' I had left without receiving an answer.

"I don't like her temp. It's 104 and seems to be rising. Let's get her to ICU immediately."

* * *

Shortly, I was awakened to scurrying sounds of movement as the orderlies hurriedly rolled another person in on a stretcher. The staff rushed over and, with three or four on each side, they grabbed the under sheet and quickly raised and lowered a man onto a bed just like they had done with me. I overheard one of the nurses saying this person was going to be in a lot of misery when he woke up.

Sure enough, it wasn't long until I began hearing some intense shouts from that corner of the room. Whoever it was seemed to be in excruciating pain. His penetrating screams could be heard across the entire unit.

Trying hard to lift my head in the direction of the piercing shrieks, I noticed a young man with black wavy hair lying nearly naked on the bed. A small, white garment covered his privates, but the rest of him hadn't any clothes at all.

"Jesus, why is he so blue and black and purplish all over?"

The screams continued for a long time. He would regain consciousness every now and then. In between, the doctors said they were giving him all the high powered medicine they had and it still didn't seem to help. *Dear Jesus, please help him,* I silently prayed.

No one was able to sleep much due to his agonizing discomfort. There were squeaks and bangings coming from his corner, as if the bed itself was jumping. Later I realized from the conversations with the staff that the severity of his injury was causing him to have serious muscle spasms. Then, early in the morning hours of the third or fourth day, I awakened to hear only the beeps from the heart monitors and the soft swishing from the respirators. Silence set in as only a short while before, the rage of mumbling and sniffles and screams rang out.

Dr. Jefferries reached to pull the curtain. "Nothing to worry you about, little girl. You lie back now and get some rest." The telephone rang and the nurse turned and rushed back to answer it. Just as I raised my weakened body, an orderly pulled a stretcher to the foot of my bed. While glimpsing the imprint of a body underneath the white sheet, my elbow gave way and I fell quickly onto the coolness of the bed sheets that had been previously warmed by my body. As the nurse came back to finish pulling the curtain, I overheard someone say, "Well, he's out of his misery now and not suffering any more. Not many survive with ninety percent of their body being burnt."

Burnt? Jesus, oh dear Lord, that's why he was all those unsightly colors. That poor young man had been burnt. Jesus, please take care of him and, Jesus, please take care of his family and friends too. Let them somehow, someway know that You are there. Thank You, Lord.

* * *

"She's burning up with fever again, we've got to get it down. Nurse, start the ice packs immediately." Turning to Mama, Dr. Jefferries continued, "During the exploratory procedure we removed some of her small intestines and took some tissues from a few other organs. We sent them to the lab for analysis and some went to Duke as well. The infection had already played a major part in the decision to remove her gallbladder and appendix. They were barely recognizable. Other sections of the small and large intestines, along with some of her female organs also had been destroyed. About the time of these drastic findings, we recognized she had only one fourth of the breathing space left in her upper left lobe of the lungs. That's it. The rest has been severely damaged. We even nearly lost her a time or two, Drusilla. Deciding that we'd done all we humanly could, we sewed her up and admitted she was totally in the Lord's hands. Our anticipated three-hour procedure turned out to be an exhausting eleven-hour operation."

On the seventh day, my raging fever began to break, requiring the linens be changed three times in twelve hours. This was a lot like a similar fever that had bedeviled me a few years earlier. Although this one wasn't as bad, it left its mark just the same.

Expressions of love poured in from everyone, even from some folks I didn't know. Lot's of people knew Daddy and Mama because of Daddy owning and operating the Hill Top Service Station for fourteen years, delivering the newspaper for over seven years, having rental houses and building homes all around the area.

After two weeks of slow improvement, Dr. Jefferries recommended that I be placed in a private room. I was sent to room number 27 at the end of a newly constructed hall. I sent word by Papa C and Peg to tell Charles where to find me. Later, I received word that he couldn't get off work. A sense of uneasiness began to creep in, *Dear Jesus, why isn't Charles here? Oh well, when you're working for someone else, you have to do as they say.*

While I was wheeled down the carpeted hallway I asked, "Daddy, do you think Dr. Jefferries will let me have that small black and white television up here so Mama and I can catch up on our favorite soap opera?"

Speak and it shall appear. Dr. Jefferries caught up with us and quipped, "Little girl, I didn't mean to eavesdrop but, if you're interested in that stuff — sounds just like my wife — then I guess you're on your way to recovery." We entered my new room. As I got settled on the bed, Dr. Jefferries pulled up a chair and, glancing over his gold-framed glasses said, "Let's get down to a more serious note. We've discovered the name of your disease."

"Dr. Jefferries, can't you wait till Charles is here?"

"Nope, afraid not! I have other rounds to make, and you need to know about this now. I tell you what, Drusilla, see if you can reach him. Maybe he'll be able to get here before I have to leave."

"Yes, sir."

While Dr. Jefferries listened to my lungs, felt my throat, and checked my arms, Mama dialed the house, Charles' work, and his parent's number. "Sorry, no one is answering the phone."

"Don't worry, Mama, I'll tell him when he arrives later."

"Dr. Jefferries? What is it? We do pray it's curable."

"Well, yes Drusilla, as far as we know it is. However, the procedure we have to follow in administering the treatment is somewhat different. Anyway, the report came in last night from the lab over at Duke. It confirmed our diagnostic conclusions. Jeannette has a rare fungi disease called *Blastomycosis* — any of several diseases caused by certain yeast-like fungi, especially blastomycetes that are contained within the lymph nodes. The only way to treat this once-deadly disease is with a drug called *Amphotericin B*."

"Oh my. This sounds serious," Daddy said.

"It is *very* serious, Mr. Ferrell. The medicine isn't produced here in the States. It's made only in Europe and has to be packed in dry ice, placed in an airtight container and flown here. It's a new drug and has only been used in Europe for a few years. Reports show the drug is highly successful once given properly. However, there are a few known side effects, and there could be others that *just haven't been discovered yet*."

"How in the world did I get such a devastating germ? Where could I have come in contact with it?"

"Jeannette, all we know now is that its origin is in South America."

"South America? I've never even been out of North Carolina!"

"My staff is doing some research on it. Maybe I'll have more information to share with you later. According to the European medical staff, the germ usually attacks men. Only on rare occasions does it attack females."

"Sir? Do you have any idea just how long this process will take? Is this medication to be administered in pill form or will Jeannette be taking it intravenously?" Daddy asked.

"Mr. Ferrell?" Dr. Jefferries asked as he turned and peeped over his gold rimmed glasses, "May I call you John?"

"Yes, sir," Daddy said, eagerly awaiting an answer.

"Well, it seems like Jeannette will be here for at least six weeks."

"*Six weeks?*" I asked with a quiver in my voice, "*but . . . but, why?*"

"Well, the members of the study group in Europe recommend that the procedure begin immediately. However, it will be given intravenously, Mr. Ferrell, and will take from four to six hours to enter her body. And there's another matter of importance: it has been brought to our attention that the medicine is so potent that we possibly will need to cover the container with a brown bag so as not to expose it to sunlight, which could cause an evaporation of the liquid."

We looked at one another with astonishment. We couldn't believe our ears as Dr. Jefferries informed us of this unusual and delicate process.

"Brown bagging? You mean officially I'll be brown bagging in the hospital?"

Dr. Jefferries smiled, then answered, "Since you're on the north side with only the morning sun, we might be able to get by without the bag. We'll just have to wait and see."

"Dr. Jefferries? Well if I have to, I guess I . . . I just have to. I surely do want to get better so I can go home to Charles and the children. You say it's the only medication that's available?"

"That's right."

"So, what you are really saying is that this medicine is still an experimental drug. Isn't that right?" Mama asked.

"Well. I guess you could put it in that perspective, Drusilla. However, to our knowledge at this moment, Jeannette is only the third female in the States to take the series. It holds great odds and, after pulling through the surgery, I see nothing but continued improvement. Now, little girl, don't start worrying about it. You'll be monitored very closely, and we'll chart your progress daily. Should there be even the slightest change we'll immediately hold a conference and be in contact with the medical staff overseas and at Duke laboratories along with their medical scholars."

"Dr. Jefferries? Remember when I was in Gravely Sanatorium over in Chapel Hill seven years ago? This sounds like the same disease that lurked in my body then but wasn't progressed enough to treat."

Dr. Jefferries looked puzzled, so Daddy spoke up, and told him of my two-month stay, of the fever that appeared out of nowhere and about them giving me streptomycin.

"John, let me check those records from Dr. Realm's office. It just might have some bearing on this case." Dr. Jefferries stood, returning his pen to his upper left jacket pocket.

"Shug, Jesus is going to take care of you, and you're gonna be all right. Many are praying, and He knows you are all we have and that we love you so much." (As Mama spoke those words, a light flashed to the request I'd asked of Jesus during the operation.)

Then, Dr. Jefferries reached down and picked up my left hand and reached for Daddy's right hand, "Let's pray," he said. A human chain was formed as I felt the warmth of some heavenly hosts nearby.

* * *

Later that evening, I heard whistling coming down the hall.

"Hi there, Cutie."

"Charles! What a pleasant surprise. How are you doing?"

"It's not how am I doing, it's how're you doing? I'm sorry I wasn't here when you were moved this morning and when Dr. Jefferries came in. With all the balancing of the kids and house work and my job, it was just impossible."

"Charles, you don't have to explain, I understand perfectly. Anyway, my parents were here to lend some support."

"I'm really glad they were. Tell me, how'd it go? What did Dr. Jefferries have to say? Does he know what's wrong with you yet?"

"Honey, he said I had something called, uh, Blasto. Umm, let me see, umm, Blasto something." Looking on the paper lying beside the phone, "Ah, here it is: Blastomycosis."

"What in the world is Blasto — what 'd you say, mycosis?" Charles asked.

"Honey, why don't you stop by the nurses' station later. I'm sure all that information is on my chart, and I know Dr. Jefferries won't mind my husband reading it."

"I'm glad Dr. Jefferries is your doctor. Seems like a good man, and I bet he'll stay on top of this. Sounds like you have nothing to worry about."

"How are Katie and Henry? Seems like forever since I've seen them."

"They're doing really good and said to tell you they loved you and hope to see you real soon."

"Hon? Give 'em a hug for me and be sure they take their baths before going to bed. Remind 'em to brush their teeth, and tell Henry not to forget to wash his neck and behind his ears. And Charles, you be sure and check behind them. They sometimes are fidgety when it comes to their face, neck and ears."

"This mothering is just right for you. You sound like their real mother — always making sure they're clean and behaving. Well, guess it's time for me to leave."

"Leave? You've just got here. It's still another hour and a half before visiting hours end."

"Jeannette, did Dr. Jefferries say what could've caused this Blasto thing? Where did it come from, and how in the world did you of all people get it. You don't deserve anything like that. You're so kind and always thinking of others. How . . ." Before he could finish, I butted in. "There's one other kind of important issue Charles. Dr. Jefferries said they were starting the medication this coming Thursday, just after dinner. Around one o'clock. And hopefully the sun will be far enough away from the window that they won't have to use the brown bag effect. I hope you can be here, honey."

"Maybe I can. We'll see. I've put you on the prayer chain at church, and my parents said they'd probably see you over the weekend."

"Hon, please, thank everyone for me. I'll never be able to repay them all."

"Well, Jeannette, I really need to be going. I know visiting hours aren't over yet, but I need to clock in at eight-thirty, and that only gives me about twenty minutes." Reaching down and kissing me on the cheek, "If all goes well tomorrow, I'll see you about the same time, okay?"

"I love you Charles. And, thanks for the Cho . . ." I whispered as he held his index finger up to his lips and waved while slipping out into the well-lit hallway.

7

Shadowing Respect

TILL IN A weakened state, sleep seemed to come naturally. Oh, how fondly I remember waking to find Mama reading Dagwood or the Family Circle and then breaking out in a loud laugh. "Would you just listen to that! They can come up with the funniest sayings, can't they?"

"Mama? I'm gonna need a blood transfusion. I wonder how much they've already taken from me."

"Shug? I've got a surprise for you. Daddy's making arrangements so he can be here for your first hook-up."

"Mama, you make it sound like I'm being electrified or something. Maybe I ought to charge admission to this rare event," I said, snickering with amusement.

"What's so funny?" Dr. Jefferries asked as he popped into the room. After sharing the inside joke, he said, "In a sense you're kind of a celebrity, being among the very few in the United States to ever contract this unusual disease."

Still on a mostly liquid diet, dinner consisted of a few mashed potatoes, some thin slices of roast beef, and a soft dinner roll. Of course, a meal just isn't a meal without ice cream — but, not today. There was orange sherbet instead. Yuk!

In walked Daddy around a quarter to one. He'd been home and changed clothes. He was now wearing his Sunday best — white shirt, tie, and all. Looked mighty good with his dark brown wavy hair, parted over his right eye as the wave lay gently on top of his forehead.

Turning from shaking hands with Daddy, Papa C. and Peg, Dr. Jefferries assisted nurse Shannah in inserting the needle into my left arm. Recognizing some difficulty Shannah said, "Dr. Jefferries, this doesn't seem to be working. I've tried three or four times and the vein appears to be rolling."

"Move to the right arm," Dr. Jefferries suggested, "and use that device that'll keep you from sticking her so often. That ought to last up to three days — but you, little girl, will have to keep an eye on it, and be sure to notify us should you see or experience any unusual swelling or puffiness, especially should any red streaks appear."

After a smooth insertion, all that was left to do was to turn on the machine and set the drip cycle.

"Now, little girl, that wasn't too bad, was it? I think it's time for you to lie back and take it easy for four to six hours. You can move around some, but only in bed for now. If you need to use the bathroom just ring the bell or send your mother down to get some assistance. Remember, you are *not* to get out of bed under any circumstances! We'll gradually extend your movement as time goes on. Well, I guess that's all I can do. Better go and grab me a bite and head on back to the office. If you need me for anything, just ring for Shannah."

* * *

After supper that evening, Charles came bouncing into the room. "Hey there, Cutie. Thought I'd stop by on the way to work. Sorry I couldn't be here when they hooked you up. Tell me Hon, how'd it go, your first treatment? Any problems?"

"Well, no, not really. Dr. Jefferries came over . . ."

"Dr. Jefferries?"

"Yes. He sure did and so did my parents and yours too . . ."

"Papa Ferrell was here, and Papa and Peg too?"

"Uh, huh. Dr. Jefferries suggested Shannah insert a special needle so they could give me the medicine over a three-day period, so as not to stick me so often. Here, look."

"Well, I'm glad both our parents were with you. With my schedule, I do apologize. However, I know it must've been an unusual ordeal, not liking needles and all. Honey, now you know I would've been here too, if I could've."

"Aw don't worry, Charles. I understand. You have a lot on your shoulders with my being up here and all. I'm sorry I've caused our marriage to be unsettled. I can't help I got sick." Tears began to well. I kept swallowing them back, trying not to let him know how I really felt about having him here. *Lord, You know his and my parents being here just wasn't like having my husband here. Although I am very appreciative of his presence now with love and support, but Lord, we both said those sacred vows and I feel like he should've made a point to be with me, especially this day since it was a new beginning.*

"Charles, Daddy left around two-thirty. Papa C and Peg stayed until around four or so and Mama stayed on until after Shannah came and unhooked me, around four-thirty or quarter to five. See? The machine they used is backed up behind the bathroom door."

"But Jeannette, it's sticking out like a sore thumb for everyone to see."

"Hon, I'll be using it every day for at least six weeks, and the nursing staff didn't see any sense in moving it back and forth."

"Not even on weekends?" Charles asked with an unsettled look upon his round, shaven face.

"That's right, even on the weekends. That's forty-two times in forty-two days, and four to six hours of insertion. I have forty-one more to go. Oh, please, let's talk about something else! I don't even want to think about it. Honey? How are Katie and Henry? Seems like it's been ages since I last saw 'em."

"They send their love and they're looking forward to seeing you over the weekend."

"Charles? You said something about Papa C having some chest pains? He didn't mention it while they were here, and I didn't think to ask. Do you know if he's been to the doctor?"

"Oh, yeah, right. I didn't want to worry you, and I'd forgotten I'd even mentioned it. Peg said the x-rays showed some cold had settled in his esophagus, and that's what was causing his chest pains. Said there was nothing to worry about."

"I sure hope she's right, honey."

"See? That's what I mean. There you go worrying about it already."

"I'm not worried, Charles. I just made a statement. I'm glad you told me so I can pray for him."

"You gonna pray for Papa with all your sickness? I just don't understand you sometimes, Jeannette. Oh, look at the time, it's nearly seven-thirty, and I need to be at work by eight tonight." Leaning down and kissing me on the cheek, he whispered, "I love you."

"Charles, I love you too. Please be careful and, Charles? Thank you for coming and for car . . ." He was half way down the hall before I could finish.

* * *

I had no appetite at all. Shannah came and picked up the dinner tray early to discover I had hardly touched my food.

"Jeannette, I thought you liked mashed potatoes and roast beef. Look, you barely even touched the Jell-O and fruit juice. You need to eat so the medicine will have something to work on and help you get better. You're not eating enough to keep a cat alive, and speaking of which . . ." she twirled around and headed back to get the necessary supplies for the connection.

"Umm, looks like we need to change arms. Your left arm doesn't want to cooperate, but let's try anyway. Here, girl, let's put this band around your arm. Try to make the tightest fist you possibly can. That's right. Now begin opening and shutting your hand like in a fist."

"Shannah? I'm so weak."

"I know, honey. Just do the best you can. Well, it just doesn't want to go and I'm not putting you through any more torment."

Mama had been reading the paper and quietly listening to Shannah's remarks. "How about using a butterfly needle?" Mama asked.

Shannah jumped up and was back in a flash, surprised she hadn't thought of it herself.

Just about that time I felt a sneeze coming on. "Quick, what should I do? I've got to, I've got to, I've got . . . o-o-h, it's gonna hurt. Dr. Jefferries told me to be extremely careful when I sneezed for the first time."

"Mrs. Ferrell, quick, hand me that extra pillow over there. Jeannette, here, let's place this across your stomach so it won't hurt as much. Just grab the pillow when you feel the sneeze coming."

I tried my best not to sneeze. Despite how hard I tried to suppress it, I couldn't. "Ah, ah. Oh my stomach." Immediately squeezing the pillow and holding tightly against those seventy-seven stitches the sneeze was coming with a mighty force.

As I flexed upward from the warm bedsheet and clung to the feather-like pillow across my stomach, the inevitable happened! Ah, ah, ah — C-h-o-o-o-o-o-o! I heard a thump as I tried to slowly fall back against the cooled sheet. It felt like everything on my inside had burst loose. Mama grabbed a cool bath cloth and patted my face and forehead. Then she started laughing.

"It ain't funny, not funny at all. And besides, this pillow didn't help much either," I insisted.

Once over the initial shock of the sneeze, I looked and saw that both Mama and Shannah were in stitches. Tears were rolling down their faces. Mama made a beeline to the bathroom, and Shannah shot out of there like a cannon. "Oh, my stomach!" I don't know why I continued grabbing at that pillow. It didn't help any in lessening the gravity of the moment.

"Mrs. Ferrell?"

"Shannah, it looks like we're gonna be here for some time, so please, call me Dru."

Nodding with agreement, Shannon turned to me and said, "Jeannette, let's try this butterfly needle like your mother suggested." Bingo! With just a slight prick of the skin, the needle slid in without a hitch.

After Shannah left and I settled down to receive the medication, Mama began reminiscing. "Shug, while I was taking those air treatments in Raleigh over at the professional offices, Dr. Brush had problems with my small veins too. I guess that's where you got yours from. At least I gave you something that resembled me." She gazed through her new brown glasses toward the window with a sparkle in her hazel green eyes. "And you do have those little fingers that curve at the tip. Now that's a Simmons trait for sure. Anyway, back to this history lesson. Every time, they'd use the same standard needle in administering those treatments. However, every two weeks Dr. Brush had to take blood and every time he would apologize for having to be so forceful and leaving me all black and blue. After studying my situation, he decided to try a smaller needle. It worked! Although it took twice as long to get the blood than with a regular size needle, it *worked* just the same."

As Mama told of her hardships, which I'd never really realized until now, I began choking back tears, not wanting her to see how weak I really was. Daddy had always said that brave people didn't show emotions, and I really wanted to be brave. I had to do lots of swallowing that day. But that night, when no one could see me, I buried myself and was glad that pillows couldn't talk.

6

Hewing Fate

OUND TEN O'CLOCK on a bright and sunny day in April, Mama arrived bringing more flowers, cards, and the daily paper. "Shug? You'll never guess who called last night. That long lost cousin of yours, Red Darsel from Texas."

"Red? How'd he find out I was up here?"

"Said he was working at the lab when a call came in from North Carolina about a particular test being ran on a patient in the Raleigh area. Said knowing we lived in that vicinity, he looked up the patient's name. Immediately he called to verify it was you."

"Oh, I'd forgotten about him working for that lab. Didn't he start part-time when he was in high school?"

"The Lord works in mysterious ways. I guess it's been four or five years since we've heard from them. Red said his sister was doing pretty good and her husband had recently come through a bad case of the flu."

"Umm, sure would be good to see 'em all again." Reaching to turn up the volume on the TV, I heard the weather man announce a low front that was developing over the southern states. There was a possibility that we might get some snow or freezing rain from it over the weekend.

"Snow? In April?"

"Shug. When I was a young'un I remember it snowing as late as May. With the largest and prettiest flakes you ever did see. Course the

58

ground being warm and all, the snow didn't stick, but it was surely pretty to watch. Why, I even remember one rare occasion it snowed while the sun was shining. Folks talked about it for months. Said that when the sun shined and it was raining, that was a sign of the devil beating his wife — and sometimes she really got a beatin' 'cause it thundered, too."

Wasn't long before Mrs. Gertrude, a big-framed lady with salt-and-pepper hair who appeared to be in her mid-fifties, came in from across the hall. She gave me a large piece of chocolate cake that one of her son's wives had made.

"Jeannette, now that's one of your favorites. Please try and eat it."

"Mama, if you can find me some Coke, I'll try."

"Hey, that's my girl." As Mama swung around and headed toward the nurses' station, I began unfolding the clear wrappings.

"Shug, Rebecca said for you to try drinking this sweet milk instead. Said it'd go better with chocolate cake than a Coke would anytime."

"Well, OK. Thanks." The cake did look pretty good, and chocolate was my favorite. Not finding a fork anywhere, I continued folding the covering back. "Umm, that's good," I said while taking a sip of milk. Mama read the paper during the TV commercials, and we both caught a part of the silence that was in the air. Before I knew it, I'd eaten the whole slice and downed the entire carton of milk.

"Jeannette? You ate it? You ate that whole slice of cake and drank the milk too?"

"Yes ma'am. And I actually tasted the cocoa in the icing."

"Jeannette? Shame on you."

"Ma'am?"

"Eating the whole thing and didn't even save me a smell!?"

"Uh, I'm sorry, Mama. It was so good that before I knew it, it was all gone." Folding her newspaper and laying it across the table, she turned on a dime and headed across the hall toward Mrs. Gertrude's room to thank her for sharing her cake with me. "That's the first time my daughter has eaten anything that she could fully taste since the operation. Thank you, Mrs. Gertrude, and may God bless you for your thoughtfulness."

* * *

"Mama, do you think it really might snow?"

"Never can tell what this month will bring. Just about time for our soap to begin." We were so involved with the show that we didn't even notice until a commercial break that there were three orderlies sitting on the cot and two nurses leaning against the wall in this tiny room at the end of the hall.

"Hello, isn't the show getting good? I reckon you all know a good soap when you see one," Mama said to them.

"Yes, ma'am, we're all caught up in that one. Mind if we watch it with you on our break?"

"Heck fire no, the more the merrier."

After the show, Mama walked toward the metal windowpanes. "Those clouds are beginning to look more and more like snow although the weather man said it was in the fifties," Mama said with concern in her voice. "When Rebecca comes to start your IV, I think I'll go on home before Mother Nature decides to change anymore than what she already has." "You lay back now and enjoy this rest, because when you do get home it's gonna be a different tale." Leaning down to kiss me, she laughingly ruffled her shoulders as she spoke to Rebecca. "Now, you load her up and don't let her loose — no telling what she'd do. Always remember, Shug, Daddy and I love you."

"I love you too, Mama. And, Mama?"

"Mm?"

I watched as she pitched the paper in the trash can beside the bed and placed her navy blue pocketbook over her left arm (just above the silver watch that Daddy and I had given her for Christmas the year before). "*Please be careful.*" Reaching in the left pocket of her burgundy jacket, she pulled out a plastic rain bonnet.

"Mama? It ain't raining, why the bonnet?"

As Mama rolled her hazel eyes over her glasses, I knew I had just spoken some incorrect English. She laughed and said, "Because I don't want to catch a cold. It's probably colder now than it was when I arrived." Throwing the coat over her pocketbook, she beamed me one of her famous smiles, turned slightly, waved, and faded into the tan hallway.

"You have one mighty fine mother, Jeannette. Not many mothers and daughters have the kind of relationship you have. You are very blessed." I just smiled as Rebecca rolled the machine toward the bathroom wall. I asked Jesus to bless her and guide Mama safely home.

* * *

As I lay daydreaming, suddenly the telephone rang. I reached to answer it and heard, "How's my girl?"

"Hey Daddy, is Mama home yet? Have you heard from Charles? He doesn't talk to me much anymore. Except to say that everything and everybody is fine. For me not to worry. But Daddy, I can't help but think about home and about my being here and not being able to be there. Do you understand?"

"Shug, Charles left a note on the door when I got home that said he couldn't get through to your room earlier today and that he was going in early to work to make up some extra time he'd lost last week."

"Make up for time he lost last week? Um."

"Yes, and that he'd probably come by in the morning."

"Daddy, do you know who has the children tonight?"

"I believe they're down at Mr. C and Peg's for the weekend. Don't you worry none now, you hear? They're okay and they'll all see you as soon as the weather breaks. Now, promise me that you won't worry."

"Okay, I promise."

Around seven-thirty or so, I called Papa C's and sure enough, the children were there. They were so excited about the weather and could hardly wait for the first flake to fall.

"Jeannette, maybe we won't have school Monday or Tuesday or Wednesday . . ."

I rudely butted in, "Have you and Katie done your homework for the weekend? Henry, you know you're not to play before doing your homework and your chores. Now, remember to be good to your grandparents and mind your manners, and be sure and clean up your rooms and take your baths and be sure and brush your teeth before going to bed and in the morning too. And Henry, be sure you and Katie say your prayers."

"Yes, Jeannette, we will."

"Henry? I love you and Katie, and I hope you can come up with your daddy to see me soon after the weather breaks."

"Gotta go, Jeannette. We love you too. Bye." I heard the receiver click and the line went dead. I had never spoken to my parents like that. *"Gotta go. Bye."* Why, Mama would've had my hide if I'd talked to them or anyone else in that manner. Before I settled in for the night, I called to thank Mama again for coming today. After conversing briefly, I happened to mention that it was about time for the snack wagon and was planning on getting some vanilla ice cream for a treat.

"My, that sounds good to me too, Shug. I think I'll wait until tomorrow and make a batch of snow cream (if it does snow) and bring you some."

"Oh, would ya, Mama, would ya really? You can make some of the best I've ever eaten. I just hope my taste buds are up to it. Hey Mama, I know you know the recipe right off the top of your head. Please tell it to me so I can share it with Shannah, Rebecca and Janice."

"Well, okay then. You got something to write on? Umm, let's see. I don't fix any for the first snowfall. However, this being our third this season, it's okay. Just tell 'em the reason we don't eat the first snow fall is due to all the dirty particles in the air. It just isn't good for anyone.

"I'll go out and brush off the top layer. Then I'll scoop up the underlying layers of snow and put them into a bowl or a dish pan or a pot or whatever I can get my hands on at the time. Next, I'll open a can of evaporated milk (store brand's just fine) and pour the milk in a bowl and add a teaspoon or so of vanilla, a little more won't hurt, and about a half a cup of sugar, or to taste. Finally, I'll slowly add the snow into this mixture and just guess when to stop, by the texture of the mix."

"Mama, tell Daddy to save some chocolate syrup for me. And reckon you could make some for Charles and the children too?"

"I'm already a step ahead of you, Shug. If it snows, I'm making three batches. One for us, one for Charles and the children, and one especially for you. How does that sound?"

"Good! Oh, by the way, Dr. Jefferries came by and said I'd dropped from a hundred and twenty to ninety-eight pounds. Said to tell Charles and everyone that it was all right to bring me anything I might think I could eat. Daddy, are you still there? Sounds like I'm in prison or something, for you to bring food from the outside. Hey, that includes snow cream."

With whispers of laughter, we said our goodnights with love.

* * *

I felt the stillness of the air as I awakened on this Saturday morning just before breakfast. Noticing the window was partially fogged, slowly my eyes peered through the clearing only to find the ground covered with the biggest, prettiest blanket of fresh snow I had ever seen. There were at least three inches on the ground. Drifts were beginning to form as the wind blew. I could actually hear it howling between the tree branches of the oaks, the birch and the dogwoods. I watched as the young pines swayed forcibly from side to side, seeming to nearly break. It was so peaceful and pure as a few snowbirds, along with a cardinal or two began searching for something to eat. They gracefully pounced across the white, feathery ground close to the corner of the building. At seven o'clock, Janice came in. "Looks like we might ought to change arms. There's a little puffiness around the needle, and we surely don't want any phlebitis setting in."

"What exactly is phlebitis anyway?"

"Well, it's really just an inflammation of a vein. When swelling or a change of skin color is present, usually a streak with a reddish tint is a sign of infection setting in. Of course when there's evidence of some pain around the area, that too is also an indication."

"Janice?"

"Huh?"

"Why did you get here so early?"

"After hearing the weather forecast, my husband suggested I make arrangements to come in. Realizing a couple of the staff members had a lot of the staff had requested the same and for us to be prepared to stay for a double shift. We didn't have any trouble at all. The roads aren't that bad where I live.

"Looks like I don't have all I need to change this tubing. I'll be right back Jeannette, just hang on." Like I was going anywhere.

When she returned Janice said, "Here, hold this gauze tightly where I removed the needle while I move this pole to the other side of your bed." Then she began her dreaded adventure of inserting the needle in my left arm.

"Good girl. You know exactly what to do," she encouraged as I formed a fist and began pumping.

"Your mother is a very wise lady, Jeannette. You can learn a lot from her. Just talking to her these past few weeks, I've learned a lot. I know you're very proud of your parents.

"Bingo." Janice inserted the needle on the very first try.

"Thank You, Jesus."

"Amen," she responded with a sigh of relief.

We looked at each other and smiled as she adjusted the roller on the tubing and started the drip cycle. "Just go ahead and do what you know to do, and I'll be back in an hour or so to check and make sure everything is running smoothly. If you need me before, just press the call button."

After she left, I decided to call and check on things out my way.

"Mama?"

"Hey, Shug. How's Ms. Jeannette?"

"I'm doing really good. Uh, Mama, why don't you and Daddy consider going to church tomorrow morning if the roads are clear? I'll be okay."

"Shug, that's mighty kind of you to consider. Your daddy and I'll talk it over when he returns from his new shop he told you about."

"Oh, Mama. I can't wait to see it. Daddy's eyes just gleamed with excitement. He's so proud. Said he wasn't making any pictures 'cause he wanted me to see it first hand for myself. What's he doing out there on a snowy day like today anyway?"

"Just piddling, but I think there's more to it than that. He mentioned something about building some magazine racks to sell. But, knowing your daddy, he'll probably just give 'em away."

"Mama? You know how prone he is to taking a cold. And you and I both know what that means with his bronchial trouble."

"Shug, you know your daddy. He just has to get out in this weather. Said it helped him feel like a kid again. Anyway, when I saw the smoke from the flue, I knew he was all right. Don't worry now; your daddy's just fine."

"You haven't seen Charles, have you? I've tried to get through to his parents and the operator says all lines are busy and to try again later. I'm just wondering how the children are doing and if, if they're warm."

"Shug, you know Papa C and Peg 'll take good care of 'em and if I know those two, they're having a great time playing in this weather. They've probably got some old cardboard boxes, using them to slide all over those hills down there."

"I just wanna make sure they're okay, that's all. I surely do miss taking care of 'em."

"I know Shug, I know." Never one to end on a serious note, she added, "You best enjoy this 'cause it won't be long until you'll be wishing for some extra rest."

9

Comfort Zone

"CARE FOR SOMETHING special off the snack cart this evening, Mrs.?"

"No thanks, not tonight."

"Are you sure I can't offer you something?"

That voice. Could it be? I slowly raised up and peeped around the bathroom corner.

"Charles! Where'd you come from? You disguised your voice so I wouldn't recognize it, didn't you?"

"Now honey, don't scold. I wanted to see you before tomorrow, and I had an extra hour since I went to work early. I managed to hustle my boss, and he told me to stay as long as I'd like."

"Charles, I've been lying here remembering the times we've shared, you and me together and with the children when they were just young tikes. Oh honey, I'm so glad to see you," I said, reaching out to grasp a hug or two from him. "How're the roads?"

"Pretty bad in spots, but I made it in one piece."

"But Charles honey, you could've been . . ."

"No need to worry, Jeannette. Prayers were answered. Besides, I wanted to be with you. With my odd hours and the time I spend with the kids, I've missed us being together."

"I've missed you too. Along with everything else you have to do, have you managed to finish that job you were working on down south?"

"Oh, I forgot to tell you. You know, that woman was mighty grouchy. I don't think she would be happy if the Good Lord Himself did it."

"*Charles!?!*"

"I'm sorry honey. But, that woman really got next to me. If I'd known of her true attitude when I applied for the job, I'd never have started it to begin with. Jeannette, she was always complaining and finding fault. Why, I even had to tear out one whole section of screening and replace it for her satisfaction. I just simply held my breath when the housing inspector came, praying he'd not notice the re-worked addition. Prayerfully, that's all behind me now — I hope.

"Honestly, I don't know how in goodness her husband stands to be around her. Anyway, the good Lord knew exactly what I needed as I was just before throwing in the towel when Jack and Susan came along. They're just as opposite as day and night. Pleasant and cheerful and . . . Ah, you know the type."

"Charles, has Henry bothered you lately wanting money?"

"No, not lately. But, that boy of mine — ah, I mean ours — is all the time wanting for one thing or another."

"Oh honey, I'm so glad you came over this evening. I've been listening to the weather men, and they talk like the roads might be getting worse as the night progresses."

"Well, you know I can drive in almost anything with God as my pilot, and when I make up my mind to do something, I usually do it."

As we embraced, Charles softly kissed me on the cheek. During the silence of this precious moment, I could nearly hear the heavenly music as it seemed to overflow this small hospital room. It felt so good to be back in the arms of my husband again. *Oh, thank You Jesus, thank You for letting Charles hold me tonight.*

Our silence was broken when he asked if I remembered when those fevers began.

"Oh Charles, can't we just hold each other and not talk tonight?"

"Hon, I was just thinking about how all of this started and thought it'd be a good time to review a little."

"Okay. Let's see. I knew something just wasn't right. Nobody ran a fever like mine and for as long as I did without a reason. Ninety-nine point two. Ninety-nine point four. Like a spiraling effect. Back and forth, up and down."

"Yes, Hon, if only we'd acted on them then, maybe you wouldn't be here in the hospital now."

"And now that you mention it, Charles, I'm still concerned about those harassing telephone calls. At the beginning, when I picked up no one said anything. Then, later there was heavy breathing. Lord, it was plum scary. I still don't understand it. Seemed like every time the calls would be during the day — never at night when you were at home. Reckon someone was watching the house and knew when you were gone? Remember my mentioning it to you and your saying for me to just shrug it off?"

"I haven't gotten any calls since you've been up here. So you see, they were just wrong numbers. I told you it wasn't anything to worry about. You just worked yourself into a dither and probably caused all your nervousness — could even have caused that fever to come on."

"Well, I guess you were right. But, I felt like you thought I was making it all up."

"What makes you say a thing like that? Of course I believed you. Why shouldn't I?"

"Oh honey, it's just that not a single ugly call came in when you were home, that's all. That's why I think we were being watched."

"Hon, nonsense. I didn't mean to upset you by asking you to go over it again. Come here, let's get back to our moment and forget about the past for now, okay?"

Loud and clear the lead operator's voice came over the intercom, *"visiting hours will be over in twenty minutes."* We continued holding each other, enjoying this peaceful serenity. A second time this voice penetrated the stillness: *"visiting hours will be over in ten minutes."* Seemed like the voice had just spoken when a knock came at the door.

"Excuse me, Mrs. Carlton, but it's time for your nine-o'clock medicine."

Jumping off the bed as though something had stung him, Charles said, "Oh my, you mean it's nine o'clock?" The night nurse chuckled watching Charles disengage himself from my tiny bed and jump to the cold hard floor. Hurriedly putting on his loafers, straightening his shirt and grabbing his overcoat he said, "Hon, it's been really good to visit with you and reminisce about the past. I surely didn't know it was this late."

"Mr. Carlton, it's quite all right. You and your wife deserve some time together. I know this means a lot to her, as she's all the time speaking of you and the children. You needn't rush on my account."

"No ma'am. It's just that I don't want to upset my boss, since he's been so good to let me come and stay awhile."

Reaching for his overcoat he turned, leaned down and kissed me on the cheek. I couldn't help but wonder why he didn't kiss me on my lips anymore. Maybe he was wary of catching a germ or something.

"I love you, Cutie. Hope to see you tomorrow if the weather breaks."

"Goodnight honey, I love you too. And thanks for coming. And please, do be careful driving back to work." He waved and vanished into the dim lights of the hallway.

* * *

A couple of weeks later Charles and the children came for a late afternoon visit. After giving me a quick smile, Henry and Katie turned on the TV to watch their favorite cartoon show.

Seeing that they were totally involved, I turned to Charles. "Hon? Is everything okay? You seem a little restless."

"I don't know how much longer I'll be able to continue," he answered hesitantly. "Getting home from pulling those ten-hour night shifts, just as Daddy's dropping the kids off as he goes to work. Then, I fix breakfast and have Henry and Katie wash up a little before catching the bus for school. If all goes well, I get to lay down four or five hours. Then, around twelve-thirty or one, I'm up and rushing out the door to do some odd repair jobs for some folks or another. Then I'm rushing to be home around five-thirty. Either I'm stopping at a local fast food restaurant or cooking a TV dinner for us to eat when the kids come home from Mary Lou's."

"Whoa, slow down Charles. What're you saying?"

"Jeannette, I'm just telling you my daily routine. I've really had it rough since you've been up here. Why, it's almost like I'm not even married — like I don't even have a wife."

I tried desperately to hold back the tears, but Charles noticed.

"Honey. I'm sorry. I didn't mean for it to sound like that. Jeannette, I love you, and I shouldn't have said anything."

"No. It's all right. You need to get it off your chest. I understand perfectly well what you're saying. Don't think for one minute I haven't felt guilty about it. But, do you think I can control this disease? Do you think I like being here instead of at home with you and the children? Don't you know how worried I've been over your having to take care of it all? And when you block me out and don't share your feelings . . . Charles, all I can do is pray."

"He *is* taking care of us. Don't you worry, you hear? We're doing just fine. Besides, it won't be long now. You're improving by leaps and bounds, and you'll be home again in no time taking care of us just like you used to. But for now, my routine goes on — I finish the dishes while the kids get their homework done and gather their clothes so they'll be ready when Daddy comes to pick 'em up and carry them home with him. Then, well, I make my sandwich for work and shower and off I go."

"Charles, I know it's hard on you. I'm so sorry this has happened. I wouldn't have had it happen for anything in this world. I'm doing all I can to get better real fast. But it'll take time. Now honey, please don't consider quitting just yet. At least this job pays for our insurance, and what would we do without it? I just can't think about that right now. I'm so worn out with the medication and all. Please, honey, consider staying for awhile longer, at least until I get home and we get back on our feet some."

"Quitting? How did you know I was thinking about quitting work?"

"Just by the tone of your voice. And your saying that you didn't know just how much longer you could hold on."

"You know me pretty well, don't you," he chuckled. "I'd better be more careful cause you might find out more than you want to know about me."

"Oh Charles, stop your kidding."

"Yeah, well, I guess these headaches are coming from all the stress I've been under."

"Headaches? You've been having 'em more often lately?"

"Hon, I didn't want to add to your worries. Taking care of the kids and keeping the housework done and having to work, too, is a strain. But don't you worry. The doctor told me you shouldn't worry. It's just at times, these headaches seem nearly unbearable."

"Charles, maybe you ought to see another doctor."

Before he could answer the kids turned to us, "Hey, Jeannette, is that bed soft? Let me see." Before I knew it, Henry was climbing up on one side as Katie settled in on the other. Then Charles decided he'd get into the act and stretched out across the foot.

"Well, guess this is what they call, all in the family. Here, let me turn off the TV and let's enjoy this time with Jeannette. But because she isn't up to par yet, we need to honor her by being quiet."

"What's honor?" Katie asked.

All four of us were delicately balanced on the narrow hospital bed, as the children shared their school events and Charles chimed in every now and then with witty remarks. This should have been a warm cozy time. Instead, anger and frustration I didn't know I had harbored engulfed me. Honor? I found Charles' actions disrespectful. I wouldn't have minded the children taking turns sitting and/or lying beside me, but to have all three of them crowding me on this tiny twin bed was thoughtless.

I didn't speak of my discomfort as I tried desperately to follow God's Holy Word and submit to my husband. Taking deep breaths, I began silently praying to Jesus for courage and humility, as my time with the children was short and I had so much missed being with them, taking care of them and mostly playing with them.

"Hey Jeannette, know what I saw coming in the hospital?"

"No, Katie, what?" I asked as her brown eyes grew bigger and bigger with excitement. "The biggest statue of Jesus I ever saw. Reckon He's really that tall in person?"

"All we need now is a big bowl of popcorn" quipped Charles.

"Yeah, a big bowl of popcorn and some chocolate ice cream," said Henry.

"Know what I'd like, Jeannette? Some of your warm chocolate pudding," Katie added.

About seven-thirty, Charles looked at his watch. "C'mon kids, time to get you home and in the bed. Another school day tomorrow and if you don't get your sleep you won't want to get up in the morning. Give Jeannette a hug and a kiss. Honey, we'll try and see you about the middle of the week. And if not, it might be next weekend."

"A whole week before I'll see you again? Well, all right. I know you're doing the best you can."

The children softly pecked me on the cheeks, put on their jackets, and walked out quietly. In the hallway they turned and watched their daddy lean down and kiss my forehead. Then he smiled, reached for the door, and gently closed it behind them as I caught a glimpse of the children waving.

I was so tired that it didn't really matter to me that Charles hadn't said he loved me.

10

Family Reunion

I
T WASN'T LONG before I noticed a burning sensation in my left arm. Immediately I rang the call bell, and soon Jamie came in and began examining me.

"You sit tight and I'll be back in a few minutes."

Now just where am I going? That's the second person to tell me to sit tight.

Dr. Jefferries must've been close by because he soon popped in the door.

"Let's take a look at that arm, little girl. Uh huh, sure looks like phlebitis is beginning to set in. Better pull that needle out and put it in the other arm."

"But, sir, we just moved it yesterday," Jamie replied while charting my vitals.

"Doesn't matter, it can't stay in this arm any longer. It's already getting infected. We need to pack it in ice every other hour until the swelling goes down, and we need to start her on some bacterial fighters for the infection. Little girl, you've really been lucky. Don't you worry none, you're gonna be just fine."

"Dr. Jefferries, will I be able to go home then?"

"Well, let's not speculate right yet. We'll see. Possibly only a couple more weeks and . . ."

"A couple m-o-r-e weeks? You said I didn't have to take this medicine except for six weeks and now you're saying I'll have to continue for two extra weeks?"

"Now, little girl, don't go and get all roused up. I've got some tests ordered for you tomorrow morning. The entire medical staff will sit down and take a long look at everything next week and study where we've been and where we'll go from there."

Please, dear Jesus, please — don't let it be more than six weeks — please, I silently pleaded.

"Dr. Jefferies? I can't seem to get the IV working in Jeannette's other arm. Appears the veins are collapsing."

"Here, let me try. Um, I'm afraid you're right. Well, now, little girl, don't worry." Silence crept into the room as Dr. Jefferies began to feel and search other areas of my body.

"This looks like a good place. I'm going to try and put the medication in one of your ankles, Jeannette." As he spoke, I began to cry. I couldn't help it. I knew how it was going to hurt. When I was admitted, they had stuck my ankle to get a special kind of blood test. I couldn't help it, I just kept crying. "Please, please just allow me one night's rest and try again tomorrow, please," I begged.

"I'm so sorry, but once the medication is started it can't be stopped until the series is completed. I'll be as gentle as I can. I tell you what, I'll even numb the area just before . . ."

"No, it'll be okay. Go ahead."

"I must say you're being very strong for one so weak. Jamie, go and get another pole so we can tie a string to Jeannette's arms. They'll both need elevating tonight. This will help them to be stronger tomorrow. Now, Jeannette, it's only for tonight, as I see it right now."

"Dr. Jefferies, I know you're doing the best you can. Go ahead and do what has to be done. Tomorrow's another day and prayerfully my arms will be better."

"That's my girl."

As Jamie tied my hands to the poles on either side of the bed, Dr. Jefferies found a large vein that seemed suitable. With both arms in the air, I couldn't even grab hold of the side of the bed as the needle pierced that tender part of my body. I tried so hard not to complain — so many were in much worse shape than I was — but it hurt so much that a squeal escaped in spite of my resolve.

"Now, now, that wasn't bad, was it?" About that time, the telephone rang. I heard Jamie say, "Yes, Mrs. Ferrell. But I'm sorry, Jeannette can't talk to you right now. She's all right but will not be able to talk on the phone until tomorrow."

I heard Mama shout, "Whaddya ya mean I can't talk to my daughter until tomorrow?"

"I'll let Dr. Jefferies explain, Mrs. Ferrell." While Jamie handed the receiver across my legs, I heard Mama's loud voice again: "What is Dr. Jefferies doing there?"

"Drusilla?"

"Sir, what's wrong?"

"Calm down Drusilla, it's just that Jeannette's arms are beginning to get phlebitis and I've instructed the nursing staff to elevate them for the night. I've put the medication in her right ankle. Maybe in a few days her arms will be better."

"In a few days? Jamie, he just told me it'd be only for overnight." Before Jamie could reply, Dr. Jefferies said to Mama, "Yes, that's right. Yes, that'll be all right with me. Okay! I'll talk more to you and John tomorrow. I'll be in around eight-fifteen in the morning just before going to the office." He soon finished talking to Mama and handed the receiver to Jamie while continued speaking, "Jeannette, your arms will be elevated *only* for tonight, however, I am going to leave this tubing in your ankle for three days. During that period, the more you use your arms the more strength you'll get and the quicker we'll be able to reinsert the medication back into them. Now, with this new position, all I ask is for you *not* to turn your ankle inward toward the bed. I know this will be uncomfortable for you. However, it's just a precautionary procedure to prevent the tubing from coming out, and we surely don't want to re-stick you in that tender area if it is at all possible."

It was a restless night, not being able to turn on either side or lie in the fetal position that I'd grown so accustomed to. *Oh Jesus,* I pleaded, *please don't let me have to scratch anywhere.* In the wee hours of this unusual night, trying to move as little as possible while lying on my back, I began to hear water running. Every once in a while the staff would use my bathroom instead of going all the way down the hall just to moisten a cloth. Once during the night, I felt movement in the room. It wasn't long before my arms were lowered and the ever-present numbness subsided. On several occasions throughout the night, my arms were wrapped with a cool compact. Assuming Dr. Jefferries had given a nurse orders to do so, I drifted in and out of a sleepy state.

Just as daylight pierced the eastern sky, I notice the linen lady standing just beyond the curtain, where other voices were quietly whispering. I called to her, "Uh, excuse me ma'am, good morning. Was that you who was with me last night?" I asked. With a gentle smile she answered, "No, it wasn't me. Don't you know?" She drew back the curtain, and there, to my surprise, were my parents.

Reaching to give me a gentle hug, Daddy began speaking, "Honey? Charles called us last night telling us what Dr. Jefferries had told you. But, knowing he really needed to work, and since Papa C hadn't been feeling up to par, he wondered if we might give it a thought.

"Shug, he didn't have to say another word," Mama continued, "Knowing how uncomfortable you were, we knew instantly we'd rather be here. It was a mutual agreement to come so you wouldn't be alone during this critical time."

Dr. Jefferries soon bounced into the room. "Good morning. Well, looks as if we need to discuss a few more items. I'm glad you and John are here, Drusilla."

"Dr. Jefferries, can't it wait until Charles is here too?"

"Uh, Drusilla, while I'm refreshing my notes, see if you can contact him. Maybe he'll be able to arrive before I finish."

"Sir, I've called his work, his and Jeannette's home and his parent's home and no one is answering."

With their statements in my mind, *Jesus, it almost seems like an echo effect, as a few weeks ago Mama and Dr. Jefferries had a conversation very similar to this one when I they prepared me for my first treatment. Charles was working then, too, and couldn't be here. Hmmm!*

Dr. Jefferries finished reading his notes and his expressions turned serious. "All of Jeannette's x-rays are showing some improvements, and the sputum seems to be clearing up. However, one of my medical teams thinks we should give her another six-week treatment."

"Another six weeks?"

"Yes, I'm afraid so. Let's see. Today is Tuesday. I'll order some more blood work and instruct the nurses to start the next treatment Thursday afternoon. That's day after tomorrow isn't it?"

"Dr. Jefferries? Are you sure this is the right thing to do?" Daddy asked.

"John, the best we can tell. With the x-rays and the previous blood work, Jeannette still isn't where she ought to be. We all agree that another series should do the trick. However, we will monitor her condition very closely."

"Uh, sir, has anyone ever had two series back to back before?"

"Not to our knowledge, Drusilla. As best we can conclude at this moment, Jeannette will be the first female in the States to take a second series. We have notified all hospitals that might play a significant part in treating this rare disease, including Duke Hospital, John Hopkins, and the hospitals over in Europe. They have each given us implicit instructions and their sincerest attention to this case. The European facilities even told us every aspect to watch out for."

"I see. Well, Jeannette is married, and her husband would be here if at all possible. However, since he can't, it's up to us. She is also our only child, Dr. Jefferries. What would you do if she was your only child?"

Tears formed and ran down his soft wrinkled face. "John, Drusilla, I'd do the same thing you're doing. I'd have questions, as you both do, and my wife and I would pray that our decisions were the right ones for all. We know that Jeannette is still a very sick person, and we feel we cannot release her without trying to help her regain her metabolism to fight the germs that she will face on the outside."

"Well, do what you feel is best, Dr. Jefferries. We'll do our part in helping all we can. And I'm sure her husband and his family will continue helping," Mama said.

"Dr. Jefferries, thank you for coming and talking to us. We don't understand all of it, but we feel our daughter is in the best possible hands this side of heaven," Daddy added.

11

Winding Elements

THIS SECOND SERIES of Amphotcricin B proved to be a good decision. Although I was still having some flare-ups of phlebitis, I was beginning to feel much stronger, actually able to walk to the nurses' station twice a day. Toward the end of the eighth week, I asked Dr. Jefferries if he thought I might be strong enough to go home for awhile. At five o'clock the next morning, even before the sun popped over the trees in the distance, the lab technician was preparing to take more blood.

Just as Mama finished straightening my bed covers around eight-thirty, Dr. Jefferries walked in. "Drusilla, so good to see you. How are you and John doing?"

"Fine, sir. My, you're mighty chipper today."

"Yes, I am. These extra blood samples taken from Jeannette three days ago were sent to the lab at Duke. Yesterday afternoon the head technician called to confirm my suspicions.

"Little girl, let me be the first to congratulate you on your progress. It appears that this second series is exactly what was needed to combat this almost deadly disease. You have improved so much that the test results showed only a trace of the Blasto. A marvelous improvement."

"Praise God, Dr. Jefferries. Praise God! My daughter's gonna be okay." Mama grabbed a paper towel to wipe her tears of joy.

I was speechless.

"So, this calls for a small celebration," Dr. Jefferies continued. "I'm going to give you a pass to go home for a visit. As you continue to improve, they'll become more frequent and the hours will be extended.

"Today, I'll leave you a pass for one hour and thirty minutes. That's nearly an hour of driving time and thirty minutes, give or take a few, for your first visit."

"Gee, Dr. Jefferies. Thank you; thank you so much."

"You're welcome. Now, promise me you'll obey my orders and be back no later than nine o'clock tonight."

"Yes, sir, I promise. Mama, call Charles and ask him to pick me up around seven thirty tonight."

"Isn't Charles working?"

"Oh. That's right. I got so excited that I totally forgot. Well, I guess it won't be tonight then."

"Yes it will. Once I call I'm sure he can make some arrangements to not go in until later. Peg said he'd been putting in some mighty long overtime hours. He's managed to get off at other times, and I'm sure he'll be able to swing this. After all, it's your very first visit home."

Sure enough, arrangements were made. Just before seven, an orderly brought in a wheelchair. With a little help, I slowly sat down as he began pushing me toward the nurses' station. Before we got to the lobby, I felt a bit lightheaded, but being all caught up in the excitement of going home, I just brushed it off as weakness. There he was, right on time, as the orderly pushed me through the door leading to the ramp outside. After handing the orderly a small tip, Charles quickly took over and helped me settle into the car. He seemed overjoyed in this special moment.

"Honey, let me know if I'm driving too fast. After all, you haven't been in a car in over eight weeks."

"Charles, although the sun is setting, it's so bright."

"Yes, I guess you are kind of sensitive to daylight. Here, put these shades on. Maybe they'll help."

As we continued the drive toward home, everything began looking white. "Charles, honey, would you mind slowing down? I . . . I didn't know I was so weak." I began slumping down into the seat beside him.

"Jeannette, what is it? What's the matter? Don't you feel good? Are you alright?"

"Honey, I think we'd better go back to the hospital. I'm weaker than I thought, and I'm getting drowsy and dizzy and very lightheaded. Maybe it wasn't a good idea after all. I'm sorry, Charles. I know I've disappointed a lot of people, but, I . . . I just don't think I'm going to make it." Hesitantly, he turned the car around and headed back. As soon as the nurses saw me, they immediately got a wheelchair and began taking my blood pressure.

"Jeannette, you made the right decision," Charles said. You aren't quite up to going home just yet. Maybe some short trips here in town at first until you get your strength back. Let's see, we'll aim for the ice cream shop in the next couple of days, and then we'll go from there, okay? Let's get you back into bed. You're as white as a sheet."

"I'm sorry, I'm so sorry. Honey, please forgive me" I begged as my head began to wobble and my body went as limp as a dishrag.

"Don't worry. If you're not up to it, then, you're not up to it. I'll call home and tell everyone that I've had to bring you back. Don't worry, they'll all understand." His words were consoling, but his disappointment was apparent through the edge in his voice.

The next morning the nurses noticed a low-grade fever beginning to develop. After making a note of it on the chart, Dr. Jefferries ordered an x-ray and started me on some antibiotics hoping to cure the infection before it totally consumed me.

It wasn't long before the results of the tests came back. "Jeannette, no wonder you aren't feeling good. You have some traces of pneumonia. I've been giving you some medications that were intended for a viral infection. But it's a little more serious than that, so I've ordered an antibiotic that should do the trick. Within a few days, you should be feeling much better."

"Dr. Jefferries, will this effect the Amphotericin?"

"I've already sent documents to Europe for classifications of inter-active medication and they have responded with what to and what not to give. This particular medicine that I'm administering doesn't show any unusual side effects as far as we know, and it should do the trick in clearing up this nasty germ that has penetrated your system."

"Dr. Jefferries, how could this have happened? Everyone has been so careful not to bring anything in. They've even taken precautions not to expose me when a few sneezes were present. I don't understand. Why all these stumbling blocks to keep me from going home?"

"Little girl, I don't have the answer. But with this medication you should be feeling much better soon, and then we'll try it again, okay?"

"Well, I . . . I guess so." Disappointment began to filter through my soul. Dr. Jefferries came over and put his arms around me. He gave me a big hug as he gently kissed me on the forehead. I thanked Jesus for his special touch that I needed so desperately.

Over the next few days I slowly began feeling a little better and even looking forward to the ice cream shop. Charles came for half an hour before he went to work and said he had an appointment with Dr. Jefferries the next day concerning the severity of his headaches.

Early in the afternoon, Charles called with some exciting news. Dr. Jefferries had examined his eyes and suggested he go see our family optometrist. "Oh honey, that's good news. At least we know now those headaches are coming from your eyes. What a blessed relief."

"Jeannette, I love you and I'll see you soon, okay?"

On Saturday Charles picked me up around five-thirty, and we went for some ice cream. We enjoyed sitting and chatting about the children, his work and home life. He seemed to really be happy that I would be released in three weeks.

"Charles, one of the nurses has invited us to her family's place for a small cookout tomorrow night. Do you think we might be able to go? It's just gonna be a few people from the hospital, and she says it'll help me regain my strength."

"Sure, if that's what you want to do. It's okay, I guess. I'll make arrangements, somehow, for the kids. What time did you say?"

"I'll let you know tomorrow. I forgot to ask the time 'cause I didn't know if you wanted to go. I told them I'd be back around eight-thirty, and it's about that time now."

"Okay, I'll take you back *right now!*"

"Charles, I didn't mean to upset you. What's wrong? Why are you so jumpy? Have I said something?"

"No, honey. I'm sorry, I guess I'm just tired. Don't you worry your little head none now, you hear? I'm just tired, and that's all there is to it. Why do you always ask me if anything is wrong?"

I immediately dropped the subject.

Finishing the fifth week into the second series of medication, my veins were nearly shutting down again. Mama just happened to be there when the IV had to be placed back near my ankle. Phlebitis was showing signs of returning and my arms did need a rest. Oh, how they hurt.

The phone rang. Thinking that Mama'd get it, I continued to lay still. When I noticed she was nowhere in sight, I managed to reach across my body and answer it with my right hand.

"Ah, hello?"

"Jeannette?"

"Yes?"

"You don't know me, but I'm a friend of your husband's. I'm an intimate friend."

"Yes, ah, I'm sorry, the connection isn't very good. Please bear with me. Is something wrong? Has something happened to Charles?"

"Jeannette, I just wanted you to know that I am pregnant."

Before I could brace myself to say anything, she continued: "I'm going to have your husband's baby."

"Wait! Wait just a minute. Who did you say you were? And, and what did you just say? You're *what* kind of friend to my husband?"

"You heard me. Charles and I are intimate, and I'm going to have his baby. You hussy you, how dare you treat anyone like you have him."

"Now wait, wait just a minute."

Not even taking a breath, the woman continued, "Charles needs love, and you ain't giv'd him any attention. You say you are sick . . . Who in God's name do you think you are anyway? Not a wife on this earth would treat any man the way you have treated Charles. It's a wonder that you can even sleep at all. Sick? Yeah, I just bet you're sick."

Already feeling guilty about my illness, these words hit me like a ton of bricks. I was stunned. The receiver fell from my hand and clanged against the metal bed rails.

While I stared gazing with astonishment, Mama entered the room.

"Shug? What is it? You're as white as a ghost!"

I couldn't speak. She reached for the receiver, still clanging against the rails and bobbing up and down against the tile floor. As she lifted the receiver to her ear, she heard this woman continuing her horrible accusations: " . . . and furthermore, your husband needs love too. He needs lots of love and attention. You're not the only one who has needs. And his children are going lacking as well. What kind of person do you think you are . . . "

"And, what kind of evil person are you? This is Jeannette's mother speaking. How dare you call here and speak to my daughter in this manner? You are an as . . ."

"Mama? Mama! It's not worth it."

"Shug, it don't matter, I didn't get a chance to tell her what I thought. The phone went dead."

I didn't know how to feel. It had all happened so quickly. Anyway, it didn't matter, since Mama continued to express her feelings in no uncertain terms.

"Why, the nerve of that woman! Who does she think she is, calling up here disturbing you in such a wayward manner? Wait till I see Charles. You just wait. And besides, I'll have her know . . ."

"Mama, don't. I'll handle it. Probably just someone playing a nasty joke, trying to get back at him for some reason."

"I sort of doubt it. He'd just better have a good . . .   Shug, tell me what all she said to you."

After sharing this devastating message with Mama and wiping away the tears I tried so hard to hold inside, my heart felt ashamed of the way I'd been treating Charles. No matter that I was in the hospital, that person was right, I was still his wife. Maybe Dr. Jefferies would let me go home so I could be a wife to him again. The woman's accusations still hadn't really sunk in until that retelling.

"Anyone who'd do that to a deathly sick person has no conscience at all. I'll have her know . . ." Mama ranted.

"Mama? Please, I'll handle it. Now don't go and get yourself all worked up over this. Be careful of your health. I don't want you to end up here, too, with your heart. I just couldn't handle that. So please, Mama, please calm down. I'll talk to Charles when he comes to visit tonight, and we'll get all this straightened out."

"Are you sure he's coming tonight? You know he doesn't always do what he says."

"Yes, Mama, he promised he'd be here around eight. Tell me, what's Daddy been up to lately?"

Understanding my attempt at diversion, Mama took a deep breath and replied, "Well, I heard a racket this morning, and there he was out there hooking up the plows behind the tractor. Well Lord, looks like Papa's got spring fever again, and I know he's heading out to the garden to begin setting the hills for planting another early summer crop. Wasn't long until I noticed peeping out from under the tractor was Paul."

"Paul was there this morning?"

"Yes. Guess your daddy talked to him last night. He talks to so many people I can't keep up with 'em all. Must've asked him to come out and help with the garden cause there he was."

"Mama, now promise me that you won't say or do anything. Promise?"

"Well, okay — for now."

I knew Mama couldn't wait to get home and tell Daddy about this incident, and I couldn't wait to lay back and gather my own thoughts. Had I really heard the telephone ring? Did I really hear a woman say terrible things about my husband? Could it have only been a bad dream?

Dear Jesus, dear sweet Jesus, could it possibly be true? I know Charles has been acting funny lately. Why does he always kiss me on my cheek and never on my lips? I've noticed how sharply his tone toward me has been and how I've been unable to reach him when he said he was at home.

No! I'm just letting my fears run wild, and I'm sure there's nothing to all of this. After all, Charles told me he was a man of the cloth and I believe him. He's very active in church and has been a member since he was a young child. Everyone seems to like him, and I'm sure this is all some sort of crazy joke. A very bad joke, I admit. *But no one in her right mind would call someone in the hospital and tell them such a distorted thing. No one, would they Jesus? Oh Lord, please don't let it be true, and please forgive me for even having these doubts.*

12

A Daddy's Hug

ROUND EIGHT O'CLOCK Charles came bouncing in with two chocolate Popsicles.

"Hi Hon, how ya doing?"

"Well, this is quite a surprise. You're feeling better, I presume?" I asked coolly.

"How could you tell? Yes, I know I've been treating you kind of bad lately, and I thought this ice cream might make amends."

"It was mighty kind of you to think of me, honey."

"Of course I think of you. What makes you say a thing like that?"

"Charles, I have something to ask you, and please don't get mad."

"Mad? What are you talking about?"

I described in detail the phone call I had received earlier that day.

"Why, I can't believe in God's green earth that someone would actually do such a disrespectful thing. You mean to tell me she actually called you today and said those things. About me?"

"Yes!" I answered, not knowing whether to laugh or cry.

"Who did you say she was, Jeannette?"

"I don't remember her name. What she said was so devastating that I went into a traumatic state. If Mama hadn't been here . . . "

"Um, your mother was here?"

"It isn't true. Right, Charles?"

"Honey, just hurry up and eat that ice cream before it completely melts and gets all over your night clothes. Don't you worry none, I'll take care of this."

"But how, Charles? You don't even know this woman."

"And you say you don't remember her name?" asking a second time.

"No, sorry."

"Well, I didn't tell you this because Dr. Jefferies didn't want you to be upset. Remember that lady down south? Now she might be responsible for this whole thing. I told you she never smiled and was all the time complaining and how glad I was when I finished those repairs."

"Now Charles, don't go and fall into a trap and accuse someone of something they might be completely innocent of. You of all people ought to know better."

"Do you think I'm that stupid?"

"Charles, calm down. No need to talk like that. But maybe you need to talk to our lawyer and ask his advice on how to handle a situation like this."

"No, like I said, don't worry. I ain't gonna do nothing stupid, but I will see if I can't get to the bottom of this."

As I finished the ice cream, he began talking about the ball game he'd taken the children to on Sunday before he took me to Janice's party. He said he taught Henry how to whistle through his front teeth.

"I hate I've messed things up for you, not being able to take care of the children and all. But it won't be long now and we'll be together, as a family ought to be. Right Charles? Oh, honey, I can hardly wait to be a wife to you again."

A noticeable silence oozed through the room as I spoke, "I'm looking forward to it, aren't you, Charles? Nearly twelve weeks is a long time to be apart."

"Uh, what? What did you say, Jeannette?"

"Never mind, it wasn't anything important," I answered as my mind filtered back to his *not* giving me a straight answer about my phone conversation with that woman. I was gathering more pieces of this unusual set of circumstances as I continued to wonder what he meant about taking care of it. He acted as though he knew whom to contact.

Please Jesus, please forgive me for thinking this way. Please help me get a good night's sleep and start fresh and clean tomorrow.

"Well, Jeannette, I guess it's that time, once again. I'll call you tomorrow, okay?" he said while leaning down and giving me another peck on the cheek.

"*Charles, why do you do that?*" I asked bluntly.

"Do what?"

"You know, kiss me on the cheek. You haven't kissed me on my lips in nearly two months. I'm not contagious, you know." He shrugged, not seeming to know what to say.

"Ah, don't mind me," I mumbled. "You just don't want me to catch any germs from you that might keep me up here longer, isn't that it, honey?"

"Yes," he replied immediately, as though I'd given him a reason. Maybe I had.

* * *

During the next couple of days I began to feel much better. Mama came up on Thursday, and I was to go home with her after receiving the medication. I wanted so desperately to leave early so I could stay longer. So, when she left the room to get some fresh water and more cups, I reached over and upped the flow of the IV. Sure enough, it wasn't long at all before the medication finished. When I pushed the call button, the nurses couldn't believe what I'd told them.

"Are you sure, Jeannette, the entire packet has emptied? It's only been three and a half hours. Must be something wrong with the machine. Well, ok, I'll be down as soon as I can," said Teresa, the substitute nurse.

In about ten minutes she came in to disconnect the IV. "Where's Janice and Shannah?" I asked. "Janice is training and Shannah is on break.

"You're looking forward to visiting home today, are you not?" Teresa said in her Swedish accent.

"Yes ma'am."

"Well, let me hurry and free you from these tubes so your mother can help you." I changed into a bluish blouse and my favorite bell-bottom polyester pants (the same ones I wore home from Chapel Hill a few years back.) To my surprise, they nearly fell off as they did back then. I, again, had lost a lot of weight. "Mama, if you don't mind, please go and see if the nurses have any safety pins."

My excitement was growing, but I began to feel queasy and light-headed. *Um, maybe if I splash some cold water on my face, I'll feel better.*

I slid off the bed, managed to grab the door handle, and swayed into the tiny bathroom area. As I turned on the faucet and reached for the water, my head began to spin. All of a sudden, I became very weak. I braced myself between the commode and the inside wall as I slid down onto the cold tile floor.

"Jeannette, where are you?"

"Mama?"

"Shug, what's happened since I've been gone?" As I began to explain Mama said, "Here, let me call for some assistance. I can't get you up all by myself. You've lost weight, but you're still too much for me."

Teresa came in with Joe, the floor janitor. They put me back into bed, clothes and all. I grabbed the side rails and held on tight. "Stop! Please make it stop," I shouted.

"Stop what?" Teresa asked.

"The room is moving so quickly, and I'm very dizzy." Just about that time I began trembling. "Mama, I'm scared. What's happening?"

"I don't know," Teresa and Mama said at the same time. As my entire body began shaking severely, Teresa and Mama laid their hands on my legs trying to calm them. "Mrs. Ferrell, press the call button over there."

"Yes, may I help you?"

"William, call for Shannah and Janice and also for Dr. Jefferries. We have an emergency in here, and we need further medical assistance immediately."

"Yes, ma'am."

It wasn't long before Shannah and Janice both came running into the room. Shannah said William had reached Dr. Jefferries' answering service. It appeared I was having some sort of reaction to the medication, and they didn't know what to do. I began complaining about the light hurting my eyes. "Um, must be really bad 'cause you never complain."

Hearing this, Mama closed the blinds and the bathroom door. I began shaking worse. Someone said, "I wonder if she's going into convulsions."

"N-n-n-n-NO" I sputtered as the trembles got worse. "M-m-m-y ma-ma-ma-ma-mind is okay. I-I-I-it's just I ca-ca-ca-ca-can't st-st-stop tre-mbl-in.'"

"Muscle spasms are getting really bad, too," Teresa said.

When the tremors hit, I felt like I would jump off the bed. Three nurses and two janitors were trying to hold me down, and at one point the bed actually began jumping. Mama continued putting cold cloths on my forehead and wiping my arms with cool compresses.

"I just ca-ca-ca-ca-can't be-e-e-e still."

"Jeannette, listen to me," Janice said, shouting. "Try to take deep breaths. Very deep breaths."

The harder I tried, the more severe the trembling became. Short, very shallow breaths were all I could muster. Finally, Dr. Jefferies arrived. He couldn't believe his eyes. He immediately placed a call to Europe. Shortly afterwards, he came back into the room with a needle full of a white substance. I didn't ask any questions, and he didn't volunteer any answers. The next thing I knew he'd popped my hip full of it. Within a few minutes, I began to calm down.

"Dr. Jefferries, I have never known the medication to go into her so fast. Jeannette called me at three-thirty and said it was all gone."

"Uh, huh!"

"Jeannette, you didn't by any chance have anything to do with it, did you?" His stern voice and his piercing blue eyes seemed to penetrate my inner soul. I hung my head.

"You don't have to say a word. I know how much you looked forward to going home with your mother today, and I had a feeling you might do something like this. I won't scold you because I think you've learned a valuable lesson."

"Yes sir!"

"Jeannette, you know you know better than to mess with the IV," Mama said.

"I . . . I do now!"

"Shug, you could've . . ."

I rudely interrupted, "Mama, I was so excited about going home with you that I could hardly wait. I wanted to spend more time with Charles and the children and you and Daddy . . . I guess I just wasn't thinking clearly." I was so embarrassed by my selfish stunt, I could hardly wait for everyone to leave so I could pull the pillow over my head and pretend it never happened.

"Well, little girl, I might have done the same thing," Dr. Jefferies said. After all, you've been here for nearly ten weeks. I'm surprised you didn't do this before now. I would have."

"Me too," chimed in Shannah. "Me too."

"You've really been a trooper, and we're all proud of you for the way you've handled yourself. I don't know if I'd have been as pleasant through all of this. Drusilla, you and John have one sweet and considerate daughter, of whom I know you are both mighty proud. Why, she's as close to me as my own daughter. Now, that's enough of that," Dr. Jefferies said, as I saw a tear fall from his cheek.

"Little girl, I know you're exhausted after that episode. You just lay there and get a good night's sleep, and you'll be okay to go home tomorrow."

"Thank you for understanding, Dr. Jefferies, and I'm sorry I caused you all so much trouble and worry. Mama, I'm sorry."

"Shug, don't worry about it. I'm just thankful you're going to be all right. You had me scared to death! I didn't know what to do, and I didn't know how to act. Don't you ever scare me like that again, ya hear?"

"Don't worry, I learned my lesson. I'm glad you were here, and I'm sorry for scaring you. It won't happen again. And, please, do be careful driving home. I love you, Mama."

As the Carolina blue skies began to darken, the hospital room also began to lose its bluish colors. Only the light from the hallway filtered into the area. I let my mind drift back into the past, visualizing just the three of us, me and my parents at home together, not so long ago. Back when time seemed to nearly stand still.

Oh dear Lord, please help me to get better so I won't be a burden on my husband. Dear Lord, please help me to be a good wife and a good stepmother. And, dear Jesus, I give You thanks for helping me through that outburst of emotions earlier today. I pray it won't be long till I can be released and go home to stay."

Lying there, in the darkness of the night, I slowly felt the presence of another human being. I felt great peace as this person embraced my back and gently gave me a hug. I slowly turned to see who this wonderful person was. To my surprise, it was none other than Daddy.

I reached and hugged his neck as he continued to hold me. Nothing was said. Nothing needed saying.

13
Walking in Time

URING THE NEXT eight days at home, no matter how hard I tried, things just weren't as they had been before my illness. One obvious change was Charles' scolding me in front of the children, about my "inability" to correct them properly. I confronted him about his treating me like a stranger in my own home. Charles spoke as though nothing had happened.

Then, unexpectedly, he said, "Hon, I'm sorry, but I can't stay with you today. I have something I have to take care of in town. It's very important I get it done today."

Jesus, what is going on? What have I done to be treated like this? Please help me to understand.

"Jeannette? Did you hear me?"

"Uh, yes Charles. I heard you loud and clear. I don't understand why you would scold me in front of the children in any such manner. All I asked them to do was to wash their hands before eating the ice cream you bought for us. Please, please tell me what I've done to make you so angry. And, can't you wait and take care of this business some other time? I don't get that many chances to come home, and I'd really like for you to stay. Let's talk about this thing that's bothering you."

"Bothering me? What ever gave you that idea? Nothing's bothering me. I'm sorry if I upset you earlier. Maybe I didn't understand your instructions to Henry and Katie. Anyway, let's just drop it. You've been wanting to visit with the children, and so I thought it'd be best to take care of this business today and not put it off. Besides, it'll give y'all a chance to get better acquainted and help them get used to you again. After all, they, too, have suffered."

"Now wait just a minute. Is this what it's all about? My getting sick? Are you blaming me for our nearly three-month separation? Charles, I could very well be dead! Guess that's what you wanted in the first place . . . you didn't expect me to live, did you?"

"Honey, now let's don't talk that way. You know good 'n well I love you and prayed every night for your recovery. Now, let's just both calm down. It's not doing you any good to get all roused up. Remember what Dr. Jefferries said, 'Don't get upset — walk away'."

"You don't have to remind me. I remember all too well. Anyway, I guess you're right. Go ahead to town Charles, but try not to be gone long, please."

About twenty minutes later, the telephone rang. The children and their next door neighbor and Henry's classmate friend Mary Lou were in the living room coloring.

"Want me to get it, Jeannette?"

"That's real sweet of you Mary Lou, but I'll get it. I need to gain my strength back." I pushed up from the couch and walked into the small hallway to answer it. When I said hello, no one spoke. The strangest feeling came over me.

Again, I said, "Hello. Is anyone there?"

Just before hanging up, I heard heavy breathing coming from the other end. It scared me so much that I immediately hung up and returned to the living room. "Who was that on the phone?"

"I don't know, Katie. Probably a wrong number." Then, four or five minutes later, it rang again. "I'll get it, Jeannette."

"No. That's okay Katie. Thank you, anyway." I managed to once again rise and walk toward the rumbling noise.

"Hello?" The line was still open. "Who is this? Can I help you? Maybe you have the wrong number." Again, there was silence. "Please, tell me what you want!" The breathing got even louder as devilish laughs arose in the background. Slamming the receiver down, I hurried back to the living room and told the children plainly not to answer unless their daddy was at home. No matter what!

"Katie? Henry? Have you gotten any unusual calls lately?"

"Whaddya mean, Jeannette?"

"Have any calls come in with no one saying anything when you picked up?"

Shaking their heads, Mary Lou spoke up and said her mama received a call like that one time and she had their phone lines tapped.

These calls, who could it possibly be? I let my mind replay another telephone call not so long ago.

"Hey Jeannette," Mary Lou remarked, "maybe you ought to have this one tapped too."

 The phone rang again. Hesitantly, I managed to answer it — again, meeting silence.

All of a sudden, I heard someone knocking at the back door. I nearly jumped out of my skin. I hung up and peeped around the corner, thinking it might be Charles and that maybe he'd locked himself out of the house. I walked slowly and saw through the curtain that it was Daddy. I opened the door.

Daddy was almost as good as Mama at interpreting my expressions. "What is it, honey? Why the look?" I began to spill my concerns. "Daddy, I don't know who that was."

"Who, who was, honey? What are you talking about?"

"I've just had three telephone calls and no one said anything. All I'm getting is this frightening sound of heavy breathing, and in this last call, I heard an evil laugh in the background. It's scaring me, Daddy. Henry and Katie say they haven't gotten any calls that were different lately. I keep telling myself that it must be a wrong number or something."

"Where's Charles?" Daddy asked, reaching for a leftover french fry.

"He had to go to town and said he'd be back in a little while."

"What was so important that he couldn't stay with you, just an hour or two?"

"Now Daddy, don't go and read anything into it. Charles said he had to take care of something, and now was a good time for the children to start getting used to me being around again. After all, it's been nearly three months since I've been home."

"Well, he's right about that. But looks like he could've taken care of this matter at a later time. How are you getting back to the hospital?"

"Charles said he'd only be gone half an hour and that when he gets home he and the children would take me back."

"Jeannette, I want to go with y'all, too," Mary Lou said.

"Is this the first time the calls have happened since you've been home?"

"Why, I believe it is, Daddy, why do you ask?"

"I'm just a little concerned, that's all."

"Ah, Dad, don't be. Like I said, probably just a wrong number or something."

"When will Daddy be back from town?" Katie asked.

"Shouldn't be long now. He said the matter would take about thirty minutes or so. Is there something I can help you with?"

"No, you ain't been here for weeks, and Daddy's been helping me with some school projects. I'll just wait till he gets home."

The phone sounded from the hallway again.

"You better let me answer it this time." Daddy rose from the dining room table with another french fry in his hand.

"Hello? Who is this?" No answer. "Honey, I believe it was the same person you just described. As soon as they heard my voice, they hung up and the dial tone came on."

"Daddy? You know Mr. Smanks down at the telephone company don't you? Will you see if he'll put a tap on this line for me? I'd like to get to the bottom of this before I come home to stay. Not only for myself, but I don't like the children being exposed to something like this."

"Sure, honey. I'll do it tomorrow."

"I'll tell Charles when he gets back so he can listen out for them too."

"NO!"

"No? What do you mean by that, Daddy?"

"Not that you can't tell your husband, but don't you think the fewer people who know about this the better? Besides, should it be a pest after Charles, he won't know it and will be safe. Understand?"

"Yes, I believe I do. It wasn't all that long ago when Charles told me about a woman who he'd just as soon never have any dealings with again. That she was so hateful and cruel and she never smiled or had a kind word to say about anyone or anything. Yes, what you said does make sense. Okay, I won't say anything to anyone. I don't care to keep secrets, especially from my husband, but in this case it could prove to be beneficial."

"That's my girl."

"Papa Ferrell? Will you come and color with me and Katie and Mary Lou?"

"Henry? Tell you what. I'm afraid if I get down there on that living room floor I might not be able to get back up. How about you coming in here to the dining room table, and I'll see what I can do to help you in that department."

"Gee. Thanks, Papa Ferrell."

Then, next thing I knew, the children were gathering their books and crayons. Henry wasn't going to have Daddy all to himself after all. Soon Charles came through the back door. "Hi Papa. Doesn't Jeannette look really good?"

"She sure does, son."

"Where's Mama Ferrell?"

"Oh, that's right. I nearly forgot why I came out here in the first place. She's home baking some homemade biscuits, and she's gonna put some of that country ham we cured in them so you can take some back to the hospital with you for a (midnight) snack, honey."

"Oh gee, thanks Daddy. Bet I know the *real* reason you didn't want to tell me. You were trying to save 'em for yourself, isn't that right? Charles, I'm glad you reminded him cause we all know Mama. We wouldn't've heard the last of it if we'd left and she hadn't given 'em to me, with all the hard work that goes into making 'em."

* * *

Two days later I asked Charles to see if Papa C and Peg could come up for a visit. He said they were delighted at the request and looked forward to it. But when we arrived home, Henry and Katie weren't there. "I thought it was understood that I'd be visiting with them as well as your parents," I said.

"I'm sorry, Jeannette, I forgot to tell you. They'd already made plans to go home with one of their classmates, so I told them that I'd go down and pick them up when we arrived."

"Okay. But that means I'll be alone until you get back or until your parents arrive."

"That's right. You're much stronger now, and I have all the confidence in the world that you'll be just fine. Besides, your parents are just a block away, and you can call on them if you should need anything, right? Now, I won't be gone long. Daddy and Peg'l be here shortly, and you can visit with them until I get back with Henry and Katie."

"Please don't be gone long. I'm still sort of shaky. Now, you did tell your parents it was today that I was coming home, didn't you?"

"Sure did. They'll be here soon. Just lie down and rest until they get here, okay?"

Charles hadn't been gone ten minutes when the phone began to ring. I hesitated to answer because of what happened during my last couple of home visits. *I wonder if Daddy got up with Mr. Smanks yet.* I didn't want to get upset, and no one was here but me. It stopped after the third ring. *Must've been another wrong number.* I turned on the radio and listened to some country gospel music while waiting for Charles' parents to arrive, "*Oh no, there it goes again. What am I to do? Dear Jesus, what is happening to me?*" This time it continued to ring, five, six, seven times until I finally got so antsy I decided to answer it. Just as I reached for the receiver, Mama knocked at the back door and entered with another batch of homemade buttermilk biscuits. "Shug?"

"In here, Mama, fixing to answer that telephone again. It keeps ringing and ringing and ringing. About fifteen minutes ago, it rang three times and then it hushed. Now it's ringing off the hook. Mama, I'm scared. Who is it that keeps doing this to me?"

"Let me go back to the house and call Mr. Smanks and tell him you're receiving those annoying calls again. Don't answer it until I get back, you hear?"

"*But, Mama . . .*" She was gone before I could say there might not be anything to it. Finally, the rings stopped. And just as she got to the doorway, it started back again. It rang and rang and rang.

"Answer it, Shug," Mama said. "Go ahead, it's okay. I'm here with you now, and Mr. Smanks is having it taped. Go ahead, answer it. But, remember, if it's that mysterious caller, keep them on the line as long as you can so the telephone company can get a good connection for the trace."

I nervously picked up the receiver and said hello. As expected there was heavy breathing on the other end. I held on, listening as long as I could stand it, and then, I held the receiver out toward Mama so she could hear it too. It didn't take her but just a few seconds to handle that situation. She reached in to the right front pocket of her shorts and pulled out one of the whistles I'd won at the state fair when I was a young'un. She began blowing it as loud as she could. It nearly burst my eardrums it was so loud. Instantly the heavy breathing stopped, and we both heard a clicking sound.

"That'll teach 'em to call here in any such a way. Shug, I wonder if it could be that woman up to scaring you. You know, the one who called you a few weeks ago."

"Oh Mama, don't get carried away. Like Daddy suggested, it could be someone who's trying to pester Charles in some sick way."

"You're right there. It's some sick manner all right. They're crazy and need to be in a mental institution."

Ten minutes later the phone rang again. Mama knew I was very shaky by this time. "Here, let me answer it," she insisted. As she whirled around the dining room corner.

"Hello?"

Mama nodded, indicating that someone had actually spoken on the other end. After hanging up she had the strangest look on her face, "Shug, wonder why Peg didn't ask to speak to you? She said they'd promised Charles they'd come up and visit while he ran his errands in town and picked up the children. But his father wasn't feeling good and they decided not to come up today . . . Said to tell you that they'd see you soon, though, maybe when you came home to stay. Then she thanked me for relaying the message and hung up."

"Mama, what's with that look of yours?"

"What look?"

"You know good'n well what look I'm talking about. I can see those wheels in your head just a turning. I don't know if I should be asking you that question cause I think I'm fixing to get a really good answer, right?"

"Well, if you ask me . . . Now, Peg said she promised Charles that they'd come up here today and sit with you till he got back from town. So that tells me he asked them to come up."

"Yes, so? I told Charles I wanted to visit with the children and his parents the next time out and that's exactly what he did — he made arrangements for our visit, together."

"Oh, you told him this?"

"Yes, Mama, why? What are you thinking? There goes that look again."

"Uh, Shug, just be careful. That's all I'm going to say right now. Just be careful."

"What'd ya mean, just be careful? I don't understand."

"*You will.*" I just shook my head, thinking Mama was way off base here. Although I did wonder if Mr. Smanks had been able to get a connection with that last harassing call before that whistle was blown.

Charles finally came in around six-thirty. The children were in a hurry to hug and kiss me and then be off to Mary Lou's. "Henry, Katie, wait. Aren't you going to stay here and visit with me some? I have some questions for you. Please, catch me up on your school activities. What about what's happening at church? Have you learned any more Bible verses?"

"Sorry, Jeannette. We really need to talk to Mary Lou about tomorrow's play at school. You'll be home soon, and we can catch up then. Can't Katie and me go now, huh? Can we please?" Henry asked.

My heart softened to his big brownish eyes and I agreed. "But, don't stay too late. I'll call her mother and see if you two can stay with Mary Lou while your Daddy takes me back to the hospital."

"Oh, gee, Jeannette, thanks. We love you." And out the back door they fled.

I looked at Charles, "What took you so long, Hon?"

"Oh, I had a few errands to run, and time just got away from me."

"Good to see you, Charles."

"You too, Mama Ferrell. Is that freshly baked biscuits I'm smelling?"

"It surely is, and I don't do this for everybody, you know" Mama chuckled as she turned to open the back door. "Well, let me get back to the house, and I'll try and see you tomorrow, Shug."

"Okay, Mama. Thank you for coming out and for those buttermilk biscuits. Yes, I'll be having everyone's mouth watering tonight. That's for sure."

Again, I turned to Charles. "Honey, I don't understand. You never mentioned anything about having errands to run, and I was hoping I'd get to enjoy the children some on this visit. I only get to see 'em about once a week as it is. Looks like you didn't want the children here.

"Oh, I forgot to tell you."

"Tell me what?"

"I'm sorry, honey. Katie and Henry have been invited over to Craig's tonight, and they'll catch the bus tomorrow for school with his children. I've made arrangements to pick them up tomorrow afternoon."

"Charles! I knew it'd be past their bedtime, and I've just made arrangements with Mary Lou's mother for them to stay there until you returned home after taking me back to the hospital. Why wasn't I informed of this before now?"

"Honey, I'm sorry. I'll call Craig's parents and have them pick the kids up at Mary Lou's house. I just didn't see the point of getting you all upset. I didn't think you would mind so much. What's the big deal anyway? I thought that seeing some different scenery would help. All they've seen for the past ten weeks is home, school, their grandparents', and the hospital. Besides, my headaches have started back. I've even noticed some pain in my ears, too. I didn't think it was necessary to tell you cause you just wouldn't believe me anyway."

"Of course the kids matter to me. Honey, let's make sure they have a clean change of clothes. I didn't see them carry their homework with them. Headaches? Aren't you wearing those new glasses Dr. Jones prescribed for you?" I asked. "Charles, this is the first time I've heard about your ears bothering you. Maybe you should get an appointment with Dr. Jefferies and have them checked."

"See, here you go worrying. No need. Their homework is to be finished at school, and their bags are already packed for their overnight stay at Craig's. See, no need at all to worry your little self. No need at all. But just to set you straight about one particular thing."

"Yes honey, what is it?" Finishing folding the bath towels and placing them beside the other folded clothes on the couch, Charles reached in haste. He quickly snatched them up and hustled toward the hall closet leaving words behind that stunned my entire system.

"From now on, you will use the term 'children,' not 'kids,' when referring to Henry and Katie. Don't you know that kids are goats? And I'll have you to know that Henry and Katie are not goats."

Dear Jesus, what's the matter with him? I asked silently, as thoughts ran through my mind. *Kids is just slang, and I've heard him use that word a zillion times.* Silence prevailed as I mustered up enough energy to see what was in the cupboards. I needed to fix for supper to go along with one or two of Mama's buttermilk biscuits.

Charles asked, "What are you doing? You need'nt fix any supper. Let's go out. I got a bonus this week, and the children aren't here. When we leave for the hospital, we'll stop by one of the steakhouses. Whaddya say? My parents didn't stay long?"

"Surprisingly enough, honey, with all the commotion I forgot to mention Peg's call. She said Papa C wasn't feeling well and that they'd wait and come up when I came home to stay."

"Did she say what exactly was wrong with Daddy?"

"No she didn't. Just that they'd see us later," I answered while gathering a few clean gowns and slippers to carry back to the hospital.

14

Fallen World

"TO WHAT DO I owe this visit?" I asked my parents as they entered my hospital room on a bright and sunny May morning.

"Honey, we need to discuss something with you," Daddy said, reaching for the green leather chair near the bathroom while Mama straightened the bed sheets and turned off the television off. She seemed to make a special effort to sit near me instead of settling into that dark green recliner as usual. Mama had a distinctive way of showing her nervousness by clicking her long fingernails with her thumb and index fingers or by biting her bottom left lip with her teeth. This morning, she was doing both.

"Shug, Daddy and I are here on a matter that needs immediate attention."

"Sounds serious. What is it?"

"Honey, Mr. Smanks (as soon as Daddy spoke this name a sinking feeling rushed down to the very pit of my stomach) called your mother yesterday and wanted to come by for a visit."

"Shug, we were so concerned about what the news might do to you that we've asked Dr. Jefferies to come by."

"What's Dr. Jefferies got to do with it?" I quietly asked.

Speak of the devil, and he'll appear. "John, Drusilla, good to see you both again. Hello, little girl." Dr. Jefferies spoke as he reached for the only chair left in the room. "With what you told me over the telephone, I came as quickly as I could."

"Sir, looks like we might have some personal matters to discuss before Jeannette is released from the hospital. She's been receiving some harassing phone calls lately when visiting home. Mr. George Smanks, a lifelong friend of mine who works at the telephone company, was asked by Jeannette to tap her line due to these calls. He came by yesterday and shared with Drusilla and myself some disturbing news. Here, take a look for yourself." Daddy handed him several pieces of paper.

"Jeannette, we love you and would do anything for you. That's why we asked Dr. Jefferies here today. To be with us as we tell you who's behind those terrible calls."

"John, you tell her. I just can't without losing my cool." Mama's face began to turn red while her eyes glared with anger and her nail popping increased.

"Honey, to your mother's and my sadness, we are very heartbroken to learn of it being your husband, Charles."

"What? You're saying that Charles is behind it? No way! NO, I don't believe it. Come on Daddy, tell me it's not true."

"He's the one, and only one, who's been harassing you. The only thing your mother and I can come up with is he's been trying to make you crazy."

"It seems to us he's been having a good time while you're here, and he doesn't want you home. Once you're discharged, he won't be able to continue his rendezvous, and his possibility of becoming a daddy again is also an issue of importance . . ." Mama spoke with bitterness in her voice. "I know you questioned my thoughts a few days ago. However, I knew I was right all along, I just knew it."

"No! No, it can't be Charles. No, I won't believe it."

"Here, read the findings, honey. You'll see that all those calls came the exact date and time Charles wasn't with you. It's all there. Look at the pattern and remember the excuses he gave about running errands that he hadn't discussed with you. And the pictures. They have a special way of stamping a recorded date and time."

"Pictures? You have pictures too?"

"Yes honey, George went a step further and asked for all types of documented proof, including photographs."

"Dr. Jefferries, you understand our point in having you be with us?"

"Yes, this is a very serious matter — one which needs considerable attention. I'm grateful you considered me close enough to ask me to join you in this very delicate matter. I'll be more than glad to help in any way I possibly can."

"We're not asking you to break your confidentiality with your patients, Dr. Jefferries. However, we are asking you for your most dedicated and expert advice in handling this issue.

"Drusilla, John, let me deliberate over this for a while and I'll get back with you. In the meantime, Jeannette's welfare is my greatest concern. It looks like we'll be discharging her within a few days."

"Thank you for coming, Dr. Jefferries."

"You're welcome, Drusilla. John, till we meet later." Just before leaving, Dr. Jefferries came over, put his big husky hands on my arms, bent down and gave me a gentle kiss on the forehead. Then he turned, nodded, and excused himself.

"Well y'all, where, what, how, to be sure. I just can't believe such a thing." I let my mind drift through this episode of misbeliefs and confusion. *"I married him for life. We exchanged very sacred vows that were to last till death. How could this possibly be? Why would he do such a thing, to anyone? Here's absolute proof of it being Charles, my husband. This is the most cold-hearted disgrace of my life. I don't know what to do. I don't know what to say. I just don't know how to handle this matter with him."*

"Shug, you know I call it like I see it, and although he's your husband, I've had a funny feeling, way down deep, for a long time. With your being sick an' all, I didn't see the point of giving you any extra worry. You had enough on your shoulders. While you were recuperating from surgery, Dr. Jefferries held a conference with Charles and us, stating that it was very important to keep you as free of worries as possible. He said that over in Europe the doctors noticed a big difference in patients who were under stress when taking the medicine versus those whose worries and frustrations were omitted from their lives. Well, your Daddy and I did our part. Shug, Charles was quiet during the entire meeting. He'd pipe in on occasion, but mostly he didn't speak. Then, just before closing, Dr. Jefferries said that quietness was one of the reasons he'd placed you down at the end of the hall of this new wing. He said he knew you were mighty sick, even to the point of death. He and the other medical doctors felt it best to keep you away from as much stress as possible. He knew that the staff would have to tend to you with more aggressiveness, but he thought it best to do it just this way."

"Y'all, I'm scared. I don't know which way to turn. Please, do you have any answers? If so, please, please tell me what to do."

Tears began to flow down Daddy's rugged face. "You're a miracle. God's given you back to us, and now this has happened. I don't have the answers, and neither does your mother. Honey, all we all can do is pray."

"Well, is that all?"

"Yes! The Lord will help us out. He always has, and He always will. Just trust Him."

"I guess you're right, Daddy. I surely wish I had your and Mama's wisdom."

15

Depressed after the Storm

I LAY QUIETLY WHILE the medication flowed slowly down the tubing and into my tender veins. *Dear Jesus, what am I going to do? Please help me, please. I love Charles. Dear Jesus, how am I going to handle this? I know I haven't been a good wife these last few months. Looking back on Mama and Daddy's life, they too had some very serious illnesses in their relationship. But they made it through and are now so strong in their faith. So, what happened to mine? Charles said he was a man of the cloth and I believed him. But when I asked to see his certificates and diplomas he said they were at his parents' house. You know something Jesus? I never did see them. Because he doesn't have any? Could he have just pretended in order to please me into marrying him? Could all this just be some kind of sick disguise? Lord, could I have been so blind that I just ignored my friends when they told me to be careful? But how did they know? How could they have possibly known his true identity? I don't know where I went wrong in lacking judgment of character.*

Jesus, I guess this is Your answer to my request about living a little in the world isn't it? Now I guess I'm on my own and have to handle it the best I can. Lord, please don't be too far away so I can talk to You every now and then.

* * *

Thoughts of my husband's unusual behavior kept haunting me. Him not wanting to kiss me on the cheek, failing to tell me of his continued health problems, and his not even sharing the children's home or school activities. He would just shrug the subject off and tell me not to worry. He kept saying he had everything under control.

After supper one evening, I decided to walk down to the nurses' station. Hearing my name called, I looked, and to my surprise, here came Charles prancing toward the desk wearing his favorite melon pajamas and canary robe. He was holding his head high as thoughts of dismay danced through my head wondering why he was here and wearing his nightclothes.

"Charles?" I asked abruptly not realizing it wasn't a whisper, to the point the nurses stopped what they were doing. "Why are you dressed in your pajamas?" Without finishing the sentence and seeing the stunned look upon my face, he immediately intervened before I could continue.

"Now, Jeannette, don't go and start worrying. Remember those neck, shoulder, and leg pains I've been having? Well, I took your advice and made an appointment with Dr. Jefferies over a week ago. I didn't tell you because I knew you'd worry." As Charles continued talking, thoughts began filtering through my mind. *Oh Jesus, I was concerned about his pains, but I had no clue about the extra burden he was carrying.* "So, after some x-rays and blood work, Dr. Jefferies' staff called yesterday and asked me to come to the hospital for further tests. They suggested I'd be in here no more than three days."

"Three days? Oh my, honey, who's going to take care of Henry and Katie?"

Sensing someone other than us in this conversation, Charles turned to see, followed by me. The entire nursing staff immediately lowered their heads and started shuffling some paperwork. Turning back and facing me square in the eye for a second was a warm feeling of the man I fell in love with, Charles said, "Jeannette, c'mon. I think you need to lie down." *Thank you, Jesus, for letting Charles' spirit see that I am a bit tired and our brief conversations belong to us, not the hospital staff.*

Once I settled back on the bed and Charles stretched out in that old squeaky green recliner, he continued telling that Papa C and Peg had the children and all arrangements had been made for school and even the weekend, if it should come to that. As I lay listening and praying Dr. Jefferries would find the problem and release him before then, I began to notice some unusual comments coming from him.

"Jeannette? I've been involved with all sorts of tests today, *just like you.* Lots of blood work *just like you* and many x-rays *just like you.*" Instead of directing my question to my husband, my thoughts flowed upward, "*What does he mean, Lord, just like me?*" Oh well, at least he's sharing.

An overnight stay was all it took. Around one o'clock a tap came on the door, and with a big smile on his face Charles was beaming. "Guess what, honey? Dr. Jefferries said those x-rays yesterday showed I had a hidden torn ligament in my lower back. That's what's been causing all my trouble."

"That's wonderful, Charles. I see you have on your street clothes."

"Yes. Dr. Jefferries gave me prescriptions for some pain medicine and some liniment and said I should begin to feel better soon and should be able to return to work on Monday." Before closing my eyes for that night's sleep, I said my prayers and especially thanked Jesus for His touch in helping the doctors pinpoint the cause of my husband's painful shoulder problem.

* * *

A few days passed, and the daily medication continued. Resting and thinking became a daily routine as many flashbacks began to occur of my teenage years growing up. *Jesus, this one particular event stands out in my mind. I pray when Henry or Katie gets to this age, Charles and I will be able to render wisdom as Mama and Daddy did for me.*

I'd never been around anyone who drank before Lord. You know that. Even in high school, I was either thirteen or fourteen when some of the older classmates decided to have one of those parties. Knowing my parents' biblical upbringing, I kind of knew I'd not be allowed to attend, although I had already said I would. After telling Mama and Daddy after supper of this upcoming party and suggesting I'd like to go, the war was on. *Oh dear Jesus, do I remember this event.* Instead of my winning, I ended up arguing severely with them, pouting, and running to my bedroom.

Angrily, I turned to shout back at Daddy, "I don't know why I can't go!" while slamming the door behind me. Instantly, I grabbed a Winston cigarette and puffed as hard and as fast as I could to let out some of the frustration. Although I ended up feeling dizzy and nauseous, that didn't stop me from pulling and puffing, as if I was in a frantic rage.

It wasn't long until I heard a soft pecking sound at my bedroom door. "Jeannette? Come in here and let's talk about it," Mama said. "Besides, you shouldn't be smoking in that room. We have ample ashtrays in the den, and it could be dangerous for you in there with all the things you have lying around. You know we'd rather you smoke in front of us than behind our backs."

I was being scolded again. Although I knew it was the wrong thing to do, I went ahead and let some evil thoughts filter through. *One thing's for sure, Lord. They can't control my mind. When, when are they gonna stop blaming me for everything. First it's the party, and now it's smoking. Just wait till I get grown and move out on my own. Huh, I'll show 'em what I can and can't do, and they won't have anything to do with it.*

After several minutes of fuming and fusing with myself, letting out much anger and forming a fist just before pounding the bedspread beneath, I noticed my doll Dicey lying right where my fist would've hit. Instantly, I reach and picked her up and gave her a big hug. Tears began falling from my eyes. Slowly calming down, soon I reached and opened my bedroom door, only to hear Mama's footsteps clapping against the hardwood floors as she headed back toward the den.

I slipped hesitantly into the hallway, cigarette in hand. Trying to act grownup and yet, still with a semi-loud voice I said, "I don't wanna talk about it. I just wanna go to the party. I never go anywhere except to church and school, and I stay here at home the rest of the time. I don't understand why I can't go."

"Jeannette, that's enough. You heard what your mother said, and I totally agree with her. You are *not* to go to that party and . . ."

"Shug," Mama said with a kind voice, "I have a pretty good idea what goes on, and your daddy and I don't want you involved with it, that's all. You're a decent person, and you have morals to uphold. We don't want to see you fall, and we strongly disagree with your attending."

"But Mama, what will one little party hurt?"

Anyway, I wasn't allowed to go and that was that. *Oh, Jesus, do you remember what happened at school on Monday?* Umm! Was I ever glad my parents didn't allow me to attend. As soon as I stepped off the school bus, SallyRuth and BrendaLeigh came rushing to greet me. "Jeannette, are we ever glad you didn't go to Timothy's party on Friday."

"What are y'all saying?" I replied with astonishment.

"I told you BrendaLeigh, Jeannette didn't know. Aren't you glad we met her? Anyway, Jeannette, it's been said that eight of our friends had to spend the night in jail. And, they not only have to face the judge but also Mr. Preston's gonna suspend them for a whole week. And Jeannette, some of their parents were on vacation and had to be rudely interrupted because of their disruptive behavior."

Needless to say, where our minds were the rest of the day, and when I arrived home from school, Mama'd already found out about the incident. "I'm not gonna say. 'I told you so'."

I wished I'd put my arms around her and said 'I love you and thanks for caring,' but I didn't. Instead, I just hung my head in shame for the way I'd acted and rushed to my room. Lying across the bed, I wept and asked Jesus, *"Lord, they'll never let me go anywhere without them ever again, because of my immature nature. Jesus, I'm trying to be a grown-up and yet, I'm still so foolishly wrong. How did they know, Lord, how did they know? When am I gonna get to be as wise as they are?"*

* * *

The telephone rang, pulling me back to the present. I picked up the receiver. A dial tone. I remembered five weeks ago when . . . *Jesus! Oh no, that telephone call from that woman. Could it possibly be true? Did Charles have a relationship with her while I was here in the hospital, and could he truly be the father of her child? Was Charles really behind those harassing calls I received when visiting home? Oh, Jesus! Please, please help me to sort through this horrifying mess!"*

I must have drifted off to sleep when I heard someone calling my name. I opened my eyes to see Charles standing there with a solemn, stern look on his rounded face.

"Hey honey, to what do I owe this visit? Shouldn't you be home resting for tonight's work?" I asked.

"Jeannette, I wanted to come and talk to you."

Dear Jesus, what's wrong? Charles always calls me honey and now he wants to talk? I don't understand the urgency. Please, as he continues, please help me to . . . "What is it? All these weeks I've asked you to do just that and praise God, you're actually here. Please, go ahead. I'm listening."

"Please don't interrupt until I've finished, okay? I don't know how to tell you this. It's just that . . . well, when you were told of my having a relationship with this woman . . . well, it isn't true. This woman is out to get me because I borrowed some money from her, and she says she'll get even with me one way or the other. I've been wrong in putting her off. I know now that I should've nipped it in the bud in the beginning, but I didn't. I thought she was just bluffing. That's why I didn't tell you the entire truth when you asked. You see, I did some work for her and she paid me in advance. And I also borrowed some extra money because the job I had wasn't paying enough to cover our expenses, with you being hospitalized. I didn't want to bother my parents with this, and I surely wasn't going to bother your parents either. I felt ashamed to borrow from the bank cause I already owed them, and anyway I just didn't see how in the world I could even make their monthly payments. I didn't want to borrow from my friends cause I already owe them way too much. Guess I really got myself into a bind, and just didn't know what to do or where to turn. Guess I turned to the wrong person."

"Charles! Why didn't you come to me in the first place? And what about those bonuses you kept telling me you were earning from working extra? Oops, I promised I wouldn't say anything."

"Jeannette, Dr. Jefferies said for you not to be disturbed with any worries . . . said that the medication was really strong and that they didn't know much about its side effects and that you were to stay as worry-free as possible. That's why I didn't say anything, and that's why I didn't come around you much cause I didn't want to feel guilty for not sharing with you."

"I know you're trying to come clean, Charles. You're trying to clear your conscience of any wrongdoings. And I believe you are really telling me the truth, the way you have experienced it."

"Whaddya mean the way I have experienced it? There's no other way I could've done it! I did what I thought was right, at the time, and since that day, that terrible day when she called and upset you. I'm very sorry she caused this conflict between us. I'm very embarrassed over this whole situation. I know I should've been more honest with you in the beginning. That day you told me about her call, I realized she'd called my bluff."

"Yes, it would have helped Charles. But, is this all you're owning up to?"

"Whaddya mean is that *all* I'm owning up to?"

"Well, are you sure there's nothing else you 'd like to share with me concerning anything, anything at all?"

"Um, no. Nothing I can think of."

"Honey, are you sure? Are you absolutely sure?"

"Uh, yes, why're you asking? What's with all these questions?"

"Well, we have another matter to discuss. A very important matter that could possibly turn our lives upside down." *Dear Jesus, please help me — I need You—now!*

"Jeannette, what on earth are you talking about?"

"The last few times I've been home on visits, I've had some harassing phone calls. I never did receive a single call when you were there."

"I remember you mentioning something about someone breathing heavily. Tell me more about these calls. Do you have any idea who it could've been? When did they happen, and where was I at the time?"

He never let on that he knew anything about it. He even had me doubting Mr. Smanks, the documents, the dates and times and the pictures of him holding the receiver. Oh, he was a smooth one. A true con artist.

As I began describing the circumstances, my dear, sweet husband's face turned as white as a sheet. You could've wrapped one hundred blankets around the room, as the temperature became colder than ice. "I even asked the children if they 'd received any ugly calls when I wasn't there. So, maybe I was wrong in not informing you of my having our line tapped. I didn't tell you this because I thought it would be better for you not to know if someone was trying to pester you for whatever reason. And, if this was the case, we would resolve it with Mr. Smanks, once and for all. "Earlier today I learned the truth behind those nasty telephone calls. I was totally stunned — even more than I was when that woman of yours called.

"I didn't want to believe it. How could this be? I asked myself. No! No, I won't believe it, I insisted. But I had no choice. The evidence is not only in black and white, but in color, too.

"Charles, we said sacred vows on the Bible in front of God and our families and a church full of people. I said those vows with a sincere solemn oath, an oath on God's Holy Word till death do us part. Hon, I did the best I could with our marriage. I did the best you'd let me do with the children.

"We might as well get it all out in the open. One other thing's been pressing on me for several years, something you just shrugged off. You said while we were dating that you'd been preaching over at one of the larger churches in Durham. That you'd held revivals there and were scheduled to preach at other churches as well. Even after we were married, you'd insist I stay home with the children while you attended several revivals. Honey, you never did show me your ordination papers nor did you ever let me go with you to those revivals. Was that just your way of getting into my family? Do you think I fell in love with you because of your preaching? All I wanted was a loving, trusting, honest husband, and I thought I'd found that in you.

"Remember? We had fun together, up until the last fourteen months or so when I first noticed small changes in your behavior. It began gradually with my not having any real say in correcting the children. I didn't understand why you were being so abrasive with me all of a sudden. Your

"You began raising your voice, coming in later and later, and leaving earlier and earlier. I believed you when you told me the company was short-handed and you were needed for extra work. I believed you when you told me some co-workers' vehicles broke down and you needed to stay with them until someone came to pick them up, or when you would volunteer to drive them home yourself. I believed you, honey! And now, just a few short weeks ago I asked why you couldn't come by for a visit before going to work, and you said you were too tired.

"Then there was the time I asked why you didn't call me more often, and you know your answer. Something about working overtime and being too exhausted to call anyone. Oh, I'll never forget the times you even brought the children and how you didn't really seem to mind my discomfort. Then there's that other telephone call—the one you're telling me that she called your bluff. The one you never gave me a straight answer on.

"Here, take a look at these documents. It's all there. Time, date, photographs—it's all there."

Charles appeared stunned. "Wha— where did you say you got this, and why? How dare you have me followed any such way!"

"Followed? No, Charles. For the last two weeks when I visited home, you know yourself that you've managed to come up with all sorts of excuses to leave. I began to notice when you weren't there that I'd get some mighty ugly telephone calls, consisting of some vigorous heavy breathing. Seemed like these calls were disturbing me only. Knowing that Daddy knew the manager of the phone company, we asked him for a favor. Mr. Smanks called and confirmed my request, and the tapping began almost immediately. Yesterday, he brought these documents to Mama and Daddy and they showed them to me this morning."

Charles lifted himself from the green metal chair beside my bed and tried to look into my eyes (without success). He then turned and began pacing the floor in my small room. After several minutes, he came and sat back down on the chair.

"Being afraid of what this news would do to me, Mama and Daddy asked Dr. Jefferries to also be present."

"Not only your parents but Dr. Jefferries knows too? When were you told of this?"

"Just this morning. I don't understand why you didn't come clean about this matter, too. It's proof that you were at a pay telephone booth at the exact times and the exact dates I received those nasty calls. Furthermore, the pictures show some type of cloth draped over the mouthpiece. And, if that isn't enough, this particular booth, downtown on the corner, also recorded that our telephone number was dialed at that exact time."

I paused to catch my breath, hoping against hope that he would chime in and just say something, anything, on his behalf. "I'm beyond shocked. When I first saw this, I couldn't believe my eyes. Not Charles! Why would he? Why is he? Why did he? You knew this all along and never, never once shared anything with me.

"I know I haven't been much of a wife to you over the last few months. But I couldn't help it. I can't help that I got sick and couldn't be with you. I thought our love was so strong that we could work through anything, that we'd become survivors like our parents have. I love you Charles, with all my heart. Miraculously, you led me to believe that you loved me too. I never thought you'd lie to me. I never knew you'd dishonor me in any such way. I thought our marriage was based on Christian beliefs. Charles, don't you have anything at all to say?"

It seemed like an hour went by in complete silence. Charles got up from his chair, walked to the window, and glared out as though he, too, was in a daze.

"Talk to me Charles! Please, tell me the truth. Are these documents wrong? Was that woman telling me a lie, or was she telling the truth? Those bonuses you received from work — were they really bonuses or were you out rendezvousing or borrowing from Peter to pay Paul? Talk to me, honey. Now is the time. Not later, not when you get home, but now. I have all the time in the world. I'm not going anywhere. All I'm asking of you is to tell me the truth. In Jesus, Holy Name, please tell me."

I slid from the bed, grabbed my housecoat, and walked slowly out of the room and down the hall. As I strolled, a few of the nursing staff said they were glad to see me up and feeling like walking. If only they'd known what was inside my heart and mind at that moment. I wanted to shout to the rooftops that my husband had deceived me, had destroyed my innermost respect and literally torn our world apart in the ugliest way imaginable. But I just put on a fake smile and nodded and continued strolling down that lonely hallway.

Minutes passed as I waited patiently for my husband to come and say "they" were wrong — that the documents were false, all was fine, and that he couldn't wait to take me home to be with him and the children to stay. He did not appear. After visiting the small chapel at the end of the hallway, I managed to gather what strength I had and walked back to my room. I found him sitting at the foot of the bed. Clenched in his hands were the photos and documents. His chin lowered to his chest, I watched in amazement while he wept.

I didn't approach him with empathy. I couldn't. There are no words to describe my feelings at that moment. I didn't know how to act. I didn't know what to do. No words formed in my mind. This was the most devastating moment of my entire existence. After standing and staring at him for several moments, I finally broke the silence.

"Charles? Do you have anything you'd like to say?" He said nothing, just continued weeping.

"Honey, when Dr. Jefferries releases me in the next few days, (the good Lord above had to have been speaking through me — there's no way I could've ever said those words that came next) I can't go home with you under these circumstances. My going to our home would only cover up these distorted lies which I cannot and will not tolerate.

"I need time to think and sort through this mess. I had no idea that you, the one I trusted my total life to, would treat me this way. I'll be released from the hospital after nearly three months with no job and no money. I guess I'll be going to my parents. I don't have anywhere else to turn. If you want to talk to me, you can reach me there."

* * *

The silence finally broke as Charles asked, "Jeannette, what am I going to tell the children?"

"Ah yes, the children. All I know is just to ask Jesus to help you be honest and to remember very vividly our current situation caused by your dishonesty. Start today being an honest person. Don't lie to your children, to your friends, or to God. Learn to practice what you've preached."

The following few days were filled with mixed emotions. I was happy to be discharged from the hospital and yet sad that I wasn't going to Charles' and my once happy home.

As Daddy drove into the yard, standing there on the chair looking out the picture window was our little pet, Knottroot, a black and tan Chihuahua. Just as soon as I entered through the den's door she began jumping and twisting all around as her tail nearly wagged off. Still in a weakened state, I moseyed over to the couch where she followed. Jumping, licking, and loving me all over. She was so glad I was home, home to stay.

Oh, how good it feels, Jesus, I never thought I'd ever get to come home again, I thought as tears began to well in gratification.

* * *

A few days passed. I went down to the little home that was once Charles' and mine. I guess I was curious to see if Charles had come home without contacting me. As I put the key in the back door keyhole and turned the doorknob, a foul odor greeted me. The kitchen floor cracked as I stepped inside, as if no one had walked across it in a while. There was a noticeably musty smell. I walked slowly toward the living quarters and throughout the small house, back into the kitchen I opened the refrigerator and found. Spoiled and rotten food. Grabbing a plastic bag from the pantry, I pushed in the unsightly items. For a long while, I stood still and let my mind drift to the lovely sounds of children playing nearby. I actually caught myself calling out for Henry, then realized it was only my imagination playing tricks.

I let my tears flow across the countertops. *"Oh Jesus,"* I cried when I discovered Charles' two door keys lying on the divided bar near the refrigerator. I folded my arms, lowered my head, and wept. After a while, I composed myself and found some extra strength as I walked through each room again. Sure enough, Charles' clothes were gone from our closet. His shaving materials had been taken from the medicine cabinet in the bathroom, and his favorite chair in the living room was gone.

Yes. There was explicit evidence that he had been here, gotten his and the children's things without as much as a word to me. All that was left was an old thirteen-inch black and white television he'd bought at a yard sale for about five dollars. (He was going to fix it up and give it to the children for their Christmas.) The rest of the things in the house were mine — furniture that we'd purchased together and some small items I'd brought into the marriage.

As the first few days passed, I clung to a false hope. Then weeks and eventually months came and went. There was *never* a call, *never* a visit, *and never* a *response* from my "beloved" husband. Nothing! To me, this proved his guilt. But the guilt I felt for myself was nearly unbearable. Thoughts continued to torment my mind of how I had stood on sacred ground and said those vows in front of Almighty God, Himself.

16

Promises in Motion

ETTING SETTLED AT my parents home was different and at times
difficult. Slowly regaining my strength from Mama's home
cooking, it wasn't long before the doctor's appointments grew further
apart. Over a course of seven months, I was allowed to slowly begin doing
some light housecleaning.

Among the seven rentals my parents had, one had recently become
vacant. Daddy asked if I'd mind helping he and Mama prepare it for
another move in. There were cabinets to be washed, shelving to be
replaced, and carpets to be vacuumed. Windows needed washing, cob-
webs needed knocking down, and areas around the sinks and under
the cabinets needed spraying. Daddy had to replace some caulking
around the windows and the bathtub. He also had to stop a leak from the
kitchen sink and do some painting in one of the bedrooms.

"Jeannette, I've been praying that God will send someone, this time,
who will become friends with you. I know how lonely you must be, and
I believe getting out more would help. It's not good for you to stay home
all the time."

"I'm fine, Mama. No, really, I'm okay."

"Uh huh, I know. I know how fine you are."

"Now Mama, don't go and read something in that's not there. Being
with you and Daddy has helped me a lot. I thank Jesus every night for you
and your love and support in helping me get on with life."

But as I reassured her, I wrestled through thoughts of what to do with those things that kind folks had given us at our wedding showers. What do I do with the fine china that Mama and Daddy had given me and Charles? And what do I do with this diamond wedding ring that had been slipped on my finger from supposedly the most wonderful person in the world. Sacred vows had been spoken in God's Holy Church and in front of family and friends. Yes, Mama knew me. She knew me all too well. I tried to hide my true feelings and thought that for the most part I was doing a pretty good job.

Just before the weekend, a couple called from Raleigh about the rental. They said it sounded just like what they 'd been looking for, and they'd be out around seven.

"Won't you put that ironing up before they come?" I begged Mama.

"No, Shug. If they ain't seen nobody iron before, then its high time they did. Besides, tomorrow's Sunday, and I've got to get your daddy's shirts and pants ironed for next week. Don't forget to polish his shoes, Jeannette, and get the dust off your heels and mine. Wouldn't hurt for you to get out what you're gonna wear and make sure it's clean."

Shortly after their meeting, Daddy brought the couple up to the house for the interview and to meet Mama and me. The man stood six feet tall but had the shortest chest I'd ever seen. He looked like a basketball player: tall, slender, and nothing but legs. The lady was red-headed and wore a pair of white shorts. What caught my eye was her hose. I'd never seen anyone wear hose with shorts before. I didn't think it was proper to be dressed like that when interviewing for a place to live, even on a hot day in June, but hose?

To their surprise, the young couple fell in love with our small hill top community. The man also discovered the community wasn't too far from his work. The young woman said they'd never lived in a block home before, and she launched into lots of questions. "Does it have a dishwasher? Does it have a garbage disposal? Does it have many spiders?"

Mama started laughing. "Have you always lived in the city?"

"No, ma'am, I was born and raised in the mountains and, my husband is from the Midwest. But Henry George and myself have become accustomed to these luxuries, or, may I say, to these finer things in life."

"Well, I hate to disappoint you," Mama laughed, "But there's *no* dishwasher, there's *no* garbage disposal, and you might even find a spider or two in early spring and in late fall. Now, Papa does all the maintenance work, including keeping the yard cut and trimming the shrubbery. He also sprays (reaching for her spitcan) for those, as you say, crawly things in both spring and fall, so you shouldn't have any trouble. However, should you happen to see some of 'em, just get you a can of bug killer and spray — unless you don't mind using a flyswatter. Now remember, you shouldn't see any, but if you do, most roaches come from paper bags you get from the grocery stores. So, be careful not to keep 'em stored up too long. You can't see 'em, but the eggs usually hibernate in the corner of those bags and once you get 'em home, they'll hatch and that's how they get started. So, I can't stress enough to just be careful."

Once the young woman told mama that she was from the Pilot Mountain area that's all it took. Mama was born in Rural Hall and raised in the King area. They struck up a conversation and discovered that Shadow Creek wasn't all that far away. She and Mama took to talking, and before you knew it they were huggin' and laughin' and telling all about mountain doings. The young woman even pointed out that mama'd get along real good with this lady's grandpa — dipping snuff and all.

The young man, on the other hand, was all involved in Daddy's work. They too, hit it off. Mama continued ironing and dipping her snuff. I was embarrassed. *They* were having such a good time that I excused myself. I couldn't care less about any of their conversations. I knew nothing about mountain life growing up or about building, except that Daddy would leave about seven-thirty in the morning and get home about five in the evening.

I went to my room and left the door partially cracked, then slumped down on the bed, thinking of how I didn't belong. *Jesus, that young couple seems so happy. Why, dear Lord, why did my marriage end in divorce? Why did Charles do me that way? Jesus, why?"* Envy and jealously was etting in big time. I was feeling low and very sorry for myself and didn't understand why. I couldn't break away from all the feelings of despair that were locked deep inside. *I pray for guidance, Jesus, as I find myself asking what the Bible says about divorce?*

After the couple left, I returned to the den.

"Jeannette, you should've stayed in here. Henry George and Henrietta seem like very mannered folks. You would've enjoyed talking to them," Daddy said.

"Maybe I should've Daddy, but I figured you all had business to discuss, and so I left you alone to do it."

"Honey, you didn't have to leave because of that. You're our child. You're always welcome, and don't you ever feel like you don't belong, ya hear?"

Dear Jesus, how do I tell Daddy how I really feel? Oh Jesus, the guilt and shame I feel for being the only person on both sides of the family to ever experience a divorce — the anger and all the hurt — dear Lord, how? I cannot, I don't know how! How do I express to him my third-wheel awkwardness? There they are, he and Mama, this woman and that man. There are always gonna be couples. I'll always be an oddball and will never, ever fit in again. Oh dear Jesus, how can I ever tell this to Daddy without him or Mama feeling pity for me? I don't want that. I just want to be left alone.

My heart yearned for someone to reach out and hug me. That's all I wanted, and yet I knew even if someone had tried, I'd have just pulled away because of my strong, stubborn nature.

17

Venturing into the Unknown

EARLY TEN MONTHS had passed when Dr. Jefferries said it'd be okay for me to do some light work, possibly a secretarial position. He graciously reminded me that I wasn't physically able to lift over ten pounds and initially could only work half days.

My parents knew how upsetting it was for me having to go through this divorce, and they offered some friendly advice. Accepting their request, I asked Daddy's lawyer for help. What a blessing Mr. Rouph turned out to be. Not only did he help with initiating the beginning paperwork, he also helped in a spiritual way by asking me to read and study a certain chapter in the Bible, Matthew 19. In following through with Mr. Rough's suggestion, it wasn't long before it turned out to be a treasure chest full of information that I've kept close my entire life.

The pain that raged within my soul from this divorce was so great that I began to pretend there was never a Charles, never a Henry, and never a Katie in my life. With my parents and Mr. Rouph's help, I was trying so desperately to put this divorce behind me and look toward a new beginning. I literally threw myself onto the pavement searching for a job. Going from one interview to another, each time Mama encouraging me with these famous lines: "Don't give up. Don't ever give up. Someone, somewhere will hire you. If they knew the kind of person you were and would just look beyond that health insurance aspect, they'd hire you in an instant. Discrimination is what it is — you're just a poor risk. But regardless, keep trying — *never give up.*"

Day in and day out, two to three interviews a week. "Sorry," the letters would say. "We can't hire you due to your recent illness."

"But what about my résumé and all my job experience and the years worked?"

"Sorry. We just can't take a risk on this unknown disease."

"But, sirs? The good Lord has healed me, and I'll never have that disease again."

"Ma'am, you really don't know that and neither do we. Nope. Just too much to risk."

On the way home from a birthday celebration in King, I talked to Mama about my applications at over thirty companies. "Am I ever gonna find a job? I've prayed and I've searched everywhere I know. Am I always gonna be dependent on you?" I cried.

We continued down this dual-lane superhighway and noticed a dark cloud ahead. Immediately we were caught in a terrible downpour. Then, just as Mama began saying something about not giving up — to keep my chin up and keep smiling, that something would give — something interesting happened. We'd never have believed it if we hadn't experienced it ourselves.

We noticed a large, brilliant golden light that seemed to never end. Daddy continued driving, and it felt as though this enormous light kept following us. Then, out of the blue Mama had the explanation.

"Papa? Jeannette? We're riding in a rainbow!"

"Mama? Do you feel it?"

"Yes, Papa, I feel it — what about you Jeannette, do you feel it?"

"Feel what? What are you two talking about? What's there to feel? Just a bright golden light following us as we drive, and we're all traveling together in it! Even the southbound side of the road is in it, too. Look, the whole area is caught up in this gigantic golden light, even the trees and the land and the ponds and the animals — everything."

"It's an angelically magical moment sent from Heaven above. No doubt about it, it's a touch of our Master's Hand," Mama declared.

Turning and gazing out the side window, I had no problem seeing this huge glowing light. But for the life of me, I didn't feel what ever it was they were talking about. *Oh well, Jesus, maybe one day I'll feel as they are feeling. Maybe one day.* I was so caught up in my own situation that I couldn't see God's love. Instead, the smoldering ashes that had begun to kindle deep within like an infected boil distracted me.

"Shug. That's your answer."

"*Uh?*"

"Yes, you'll soon be hired. I don't know by whom, but you're gonna be hired pretty soon."

"Mama, how do you know that?"

A long pause, then Mama and Daddy began singing, "Open Your Heart and Let the Sunshine In." In the middle, Mama broke off to say, "Jeannette? Have you given any thought to selling? Both sides of your family have experience. Maybe that's your talent, too. Never can tell unless you try."

"Selling? I've never done it for a living. You and I've had some Stanley shows and one or two Tupperware parties but other than those I've never had any sales experience."

"Well, just a thought. Think about it. A little is better than nothing."

Reckon Mama could be on to something, Jesus? Maybe it could be an outlet for me. I'll check the paper when we get home tonight and tomorrow's paper, too.

* * *

The Raleigh paper had an ad for an Avon representative. I clipped the ad, dialed the number, and began speaking to the area's district manager. After she'd asked a few questions, she scheduled an interview for Thursday at Mama and Daddy's house.

Mrs. Taylor arrived promptly on Thursday. Daddy had told us earlier that he had some unfinished business to do at the shop and that he wasn't needed anyhow, because Mama was good at knowing whether folks were on the up-and-up. I brought out some refreshments, and Mama soon joined in giving her approval of this lady.

After a phone call to the home office, I was accepted on the spot to be a representative. The hours were extremely flexible, giving me the opportunity to either work part or full-time.

In no time I had a clientele of fifty-plus customers. However, I began to notice I was putting as much back into the business as I was getting out of it. Neither of my parents could make me understand my faulty tactics. I worked many hours from the telephone, using word of mouth, and walking door-to-door showing samples. I even felt the need to give samples away, no matter how much they cost. In my mind, this was brilliant advertisement. Mama and Daddy continued to talk, but I still didn't understand.

The winter of the following year, I got a tip from a neighbor that a lady in a nearby subdivision was looking for a representative. After a four-month acquaintance, she wanted to know why I was out selling and not holding down a full-time hourly job.

"Well, it's like this, ma'am. Selling Avon is the best I can do. I've applied all over everywhere for a job, and I'm always told I'm too a high a risk for their insurance. This job doesn't pay all that much, but I don't mind. At least it gives my parents some extra relief."

She began telling me about the plant where her husband was the manager. Asking if it was okay with me, she said she'd like to mention my situation to him.

Upon arriving home, I burst into the door and shouted, "Mama, guess what? Could it be?"

"Never can tell. I'm sure if it's the Lord's will . . ." she picked up the dish towel lying on the countertop and continued scurrying about while fixing supper.

"When will Daddy get home?"

"Now Shug, don't go and get your hopes up too high."

Soon Daddy walked into the den. He removed his khaki hat and placed it on the oak coat rack behind the door.

"Hey Daddy?"

"Hey honey! Hey Mama!" he shouted into the kitchen where Mama was stirring some snap beans on the stove.

"Dad? I got some mighty good news to share with you."

"Wash up, Papa! Supper'll be ready when you get in here. Jeannette, you go and wash up too, and finish setting the table. There'll be plenty of time to tell Papa your news."

I started to fill one of the glasses with ice when Mama said, "I don't want any ice. Jeannette, you know better. You know I don't drink tea. Just put some water in my little snuff glass over there and only one piece of ice. You're so excited about that news that you're not paying attention to what ye'r doing. Am I right?"

"Yes, guess so, Mama. After all, it is kind of exciting just knowing someone cares enough to try and help. I'm sorry."

"What's all the commotion about in here? Um, sure smells good, Mama. I'm starved."

"Daddy? Mama's fixed all your favorites and some mashed potatoes, too."

"Papa? How 'd your day go?"

"Nope! Not this time, Mama. You go first and tell me about yours."

"Shug? While you're still up, check and make sure I turned off all the eyes on the stove, and open the door to the oven so it can cool from the biscuits . . . Not much to tell. Such a purr'ty day. I did manage to get some washing done and finished planting those bulbs that Kathryn gave me Monday. Then I decided to have a vegetable supper and laid out a package of corn and okra and tomatoes and thought, wouldn't some strawberry shortcake be good for a change? So, I took out three slices of that pound cake that Delma made for your birthday last week and thawed some of those strawberries I won over at the park last month."

"Mama, let me tell you something, you couldn't've fixed anything any better than this. It sure looks good, and I can hardly wait to dig in," Daddy said as he reached for some butter beans.

"Now it's your turn, Papa. You're smiling for some reason. Please tell us."

"Well. Before I tell you, let's hold hands and say the blessing. We bowed our heads as Daddy prayed: *"Dear Jesus, thank You for this day, and Lord, thank You for this food that's been prepared for us, and I pray You'll bless the cooks and all future cooks, too. Amen."*

Dipping several spoonfuls of butter beans onto his plate, Daddy asked, "You remember Stacy, don't you? The young fellow that just moved here from Ohio, and he and his wife are in the family way?"

"Daddy? Whaddya mean in the family way," I asked.

"Honey, you young folks probably don't know our expressions of long ago. Stacy and his wife are expecting a baby."

"Oh!"

"Well, as I was saying, he was already on the job when I arrived this morning and said he'd been there about thirty minutes."

"Seven-thirty? Gee, what's up, Papa? He must really need to work to be there that early."

"There goes your curiosity again, Mama. Well, you're half right. You see, Stacy asked if he could possibly leave early. Maybe around ten or so, due to his wife expecting their first baby anytime now. I would've excused him anyway, especially with a little one on the way, whether the others were there or not."

"Papa? He must've suspected it being near."

"Evidently so, honey. Well, I went ahead and let him off and then around two-thirty here he came back. And was he ever beaming. I knew the answer before he even told me. Said he and his wife were proud parents of *twins*. Honey, just brought back a few . . ."

"Papa, I know. I think about it too — at times."

Mama looked at me with a deep concern in her voice, then turned to Daddy, "And anyway, tell us the rest of it."

"Yes, Daddy, please. I have something to share with you too."

"Well, after hearing this, there's no way I could let Stacy stay. I knew in my heart that he'd rather be with his wife and newborn babies. So I went ahead, let him have the rest of the day off and told him not to come back until his wife felt comfortable with him being gone. Honey, you should've seen his face."

"You don't have to explain. The answer is written all over yours."

"Jeannette? Now what's this about your having some news to tell me?"

"Oh! Daddy! You'll never guess in a million years what happened to me today."

Of course, it *never* fails. The darn telephone had to ring just as I began to tell Daddy about my conversation with Mrs. Jonks while delivering her Avon order.

"Honey? It's for you. Some lady by the name of Mrs. Jonks?"

Taking a swallow of tea, I reached across the corn and taters for the receiver, cleared my throat, and felt kind of guilty for thinking that ugly thought about the telephone, especially when it turned out to be for me.

"Ah, hello Mrs. Jonks."

"Jeannette?"

"Yes?"

"Could you come over after supper, let's say around seven-thirty? My husband would like to talk to you about your situation."

"Yes, ma'am, I'm looking forward to it. Thank you for calling, and I'll see you then."

"Honey? What was that all about?" Daddy asked looking over his dark brown eyeglasses.

"That's just what I was fixin' to tell ya when the phone rang. There's a possibility I might have a job."

"A job?"

"Yes, Mrs. Jonks is one of my Avon customers. Well, it turns out her husband has something to do at a local company and might be able to help. She asked if I could come over around seven-thirty tonight."

"Shug? Sounds to me like you've got yerself a job."

"Mama, how do you know that? I haven't even had the interview yet."

Daddy, looking over his glasses, wiped his mouth with a paper towel and said, "Ah, your mother's a smart one, and she just knows some things, honey.

"Mama, that was the best meal ever. If I never eat another, you can sure bet I enjoyed this one."

Scooting his chair back on the vinyl floor, Daddy began to rise. He picked up his glass and tossed the ice cubes into the sink. Then, before leaving the kitchen, he bent down and gave Mama a kiss on the cheek.

As he turned and patted me on the base of my neck, I scooted my chair up closer to the table so he could squeeze between the countertop and me as he made his way back to the den. Then Mama said, "Jeannette, let me go and enjoy a cigarette and get a dip of snuff. Go ahead and rake up the scraps and stack the dishes, and I'll be back to wash 'em after awhile."

"Nope, not tonight, Mama. You go ahead and enjoy your thing, and you and Daddy can watch the news together. I've got an hour before I go over to the Jonks's so I'll do the dishes. After all, that supper was delicious, and you've been in this kitchen all evening. The least I can do is clean up."

Oh how good those firsts few puffs of Mama's cigarette smelled as they penetrated the kitchen area. It wasn't long before I, too, was enjoying a few puffs before washing the dishes.

"Shug? I do wish you'd quit smoking. After all you've been through with the illness and all, don't know why you even started back. You were doing so good, quitting before entering the hospital, and then you had to go and start back just before Christmas."

"You know why I started back, Mama? I didn't think I'd really been hypnotized."

"But you were, weren't you?"

"Yes, ma'am. I just didn't think so at the time."

"What're you two talking about now?"

"Daddy, you remember Mama going with me to Raleigh last month?"

"No, can't say I do. Which time was that? You two are all the time going somewhere. Refresh my memory."

"You remember my telling you about Jeannette wanting to quit smoking and that she'd heard about this man at the Professional Building that hypnotized folks?"

"Okay Mama, maybe it does ring a bell now that you mentioned it. Go on, Jeannette."

"Well, in his baritone voice he pronounced my name, 'Mrs. Jeannette Ferrell.'"

I said, *sir? That's Ms.,*" as I rose to shake his hand.

"Honey. You don't have to go into the exact details. Just get to the point. Where is this leading?"

"Be patient, Papa! There's a lot to be said here, and she's telling it the only way she knows how — exactly how it all came about her smoking again."

"I am being patient. But she needs to get to the point and stop beating around the bush."

Feelings of sadness began to creep into that moment. I was trying to be as precise as possible. All I wanted was for Daddy to get the whole picture, to not leave anything out. Whenever Mama told something, she was very detailed about it and no one ever asked her to stop and get to the point. I wondered why Daddy was saying this to me! *Jesus, help me to hurry up and finish this insignificant story. It doesn't really matter anyway.*

"Okay, Daddy, okay. Anyway, as I began reciting the alphabet backwards from the letter G . . ."

"Honey? You didn't think it worked and that's why you lit that cigarette, isn't it?"

"*DADDY!*" A sinking feeling of hurt and humility came over me, making me want to run and hide and just forget this whole thing. I knew I needed to finish whether he wanted to hear it or not, but feelings of discomfort boiled down deep within my soul.

"Papa. Let her finish," Mama said, rolling her green hazel eyes in his direction.

"Yes. That's right, Daddy. You're right."

"See? I knew that's what would happen. That's all you had to say. You didn't have to go all the way around the mulberry bush to say what happened."

"You're right, Daddy, I didn't."

"By the way, how much did this cost you? Ah, let me say it this way. How much did you lose in order to find out that you *hadn't* been hypnotized?"

"Daddy, we won't discuss that part."

"Well. You've been so detailed in everything else. Don't you think I should know how much this all cost you, too? Honey, I agree with your mother. Please try and not smoke. Cigarettes will do more damage to your lungs, and you know what Dr. Frate told you. Even Dr. Jefferies said that smoking was definitely against you."

"Well, you and Mama both smoke, and Mama even dips snuff too. Now, that's one habit I don't have."

"Shug? I'll give you a dip anytime you want it. Besides, dipping is much better for you than smoking is. Anyway, that snuff that Grandma Ferrell used to give you — remember?"

"Yes ma'am. Now that was g-o-o-d snuff."

"Remember when she would get her a dip and offer me a dip and you and Donna wanted a dip too? So, she'd get up and go to her tiny kitchen. Then she'd get cocoa and sugar out of the pantry and gather two cups from her china cabinet. She use to say that no china was too good for you as she'd laugh and continue making the snuff mixture."

"Umm! To this very day, it brings back so many wonderful memories."

Leaving the house at seven-fifteen for the Jonk's, I mumbled, "It cost me a full one hundred dollars for the hypnosis treatment," then I pushed the storm door behind me and hurried to the car so I wouldn't have to deal with Daddy's forthcoming remarks.

Mrs. Jonks greeted me at her back door. "My husband will be in soon after he finishes speaking on the phone. Would you care for something to drink? We have juice, coffee and tea."

"No, thank you. Hasn't been long since supper."

"Hello. Jeannette, is it?"

"Uh, yes sir." I rose to shake his hand.

"What's this my wife's been telling me? You can't get a job because of your recent health condition?"

"Yes, that's right, sir. That's why I'm a representative of this cosmetic line. Just to make some extra money. I feel like I need to help out my parents. After all, I am living with them, and I feel I need to pay my part. They tell me that I don't have to, it's just that I want to, sir. It's not right for them to carry my extra load by themselves."

He paused before speaking again. I noticed he was a tall, slender man with grayish hair. His silver-framed glasses brought his soft, Carolina blue eyes into focus. They appeared to be the same color as Mrs. Jonks' baby blue fine china, which was displayed gracefully in her white kitchen cabinets. Also noticeable was the straightforward way he expressed himself.

"Jeannette, here," he said, reaching across the kitchen table and picking up some pieces of paper that were clipped together.

"Sir?"

"It's an application for employment at the company. If you're still interested, that is."

"Interested? Yes sir. I'm interested, I'm very interested."

"Just fill the pages out and bring it back to me, *personally*. I'll review the application and talk to the managing supervisor to see if there's a chance that we might be able to help you in some way."

"Ah! Gee! Sir, thank you! Thank you so very much."

"Don't thank me just yet. Give me about a week, and if you haven't heard from me by then, please feel free to call."

"God bless you, sir, for your kindheartedness. Yes, I'll fill these out tonight and return them to you tomorrow." I turned and thanked Mrs. Jonks for calling and left, lifting my heart to the heavens and thanking Jesus for His opening a door of opportunity. My head was so full of excitement that I could hardly stand myself. As I drove up in our yard, I noticed Sam nearly wagging her tail off while coming to greet me.

I opened the car door and jumped out, and I do believe she was smiling too. She ran with me toward the porch, and we both rushed into the house. Mama and Daddy were sitting in their usual places. Daddy was in his brown leather recliner near the television and Mama was settled on the couch with her snuff box on the end table near the fireplace and reading the daily paper. Neither one looked up nor did either even as much as raised an eyebrow.

"When do you start to work, Jeannette?"

"Well, first I need to fill this application out and then . . . Wait a minute, Mama? How did you know I might have a job?"

"Honey? Remember our talk at the kitchen table just a while ago?" Daddy said, trying to rattle my brain. Looking up, I noticed the grins on both their faces, as they, too, seemed happy for me. Mama even got up and greeted me with one of her special hugs while Daddy asked me to come over (with his breathing, he wasn't able to get up) so he could give me one of his special kisses on my cheek.

The next day, I received a telephone call from Mr. Jonks.

"Jeannette?"

"Yes, sir?"

"I've been instructed to call and inform you of a position that is opening soon. This position calls for someone to work a shift schedule, and I'd like to know if you'd be interested."

"Interested, sir? Yes, I'm interested. Sir, are you sure the insurance you have will cover me?"

"I've explained your situation, and the application is being forwarded to the proper departments. The insurance company has assured me that all you need to do is work for this company for one year. After that time, providing there's no recurrence of the illness, then yes, this insurance will cover you. We do have percentages, which we'll discuss when you come in tomorrow morning. Be here at eight sharp and ask for me. We'll go from there."

"Sir, I understand some companies let women wear pants. Will I be allowed to, or will I be working in the office, and should I wear Sunday clothes?"

"You will *not* be working in an office, in spite of your previous jobs. We do allow casual dress codes and you may wear jeans and a T-shirt. Be sure and wear thick socks and shoes with rubber bottoms."

"Mr. Jonks?"

"Yes, Jeannette?"

"Thank you! Thank you so very much for helping me."

"There's no need to thank me. I was just doing my job."

"Sir? You reached out and helped when no one else would. I promise, sir. With God's help, I'll do the best I can to never let you down."

"Shug, did you say that was Mr. Jonks on the phone? Papa, please turn that TV down so I can hear her. Now, what time are you to be there tomorrow?"

"Mama. How did you know I was hired?"

"I keep telling you, I just know. When are you gonna get it through your thick skull?"

"You know what I mean, Mama. Anyway, he said the job required my lifting up to ten pounds and said I'd be assisted with the twenty-five pound products."

"Shug, you know what Dr. Jefferries told you. Please, please don't over do yourself. This or any other job isn't worth a relapse."

"Mama, now you know I know better than that."

"Yes, I do know you, and I know you don't know how to say 'No,' too."

"How much will you be making, honey, and what about vacations?"

"Mr. Jonks said I'll start off making minimum wage, and after a year I'd be entitled to a week's vacation. Said as the economy increases, my wages would increase. Instead of getting a lunch hour, I'll be taking two fifteen-minute breaks and one thirty-minute break a day with this swing shift schedule. Sounded confusing, but I guess once I get involved I'm sure it'll clear up. I don't much like the idea of working on the weekends, especially on Sundays, but after all, it is a job."

Mama and Daddy reached for my hands, lifted up thanksgiving to Jesus for His sheltering arms of love, and asked for guidance as I ventured out into an unknown world.

While saying my personal prayers later, I asked, *"Jesus, what did Mama mean when she asked Your protection for me in this unknown world?"* I was too happy to worry about it. I soon closed my eyes and fell asleep.

18

Glimpses of Home

I'd NEVER BEFORE worked in an atmosphere where there were so many people of all lifestyles and cultures. I'd always worked with Christian folks. About two months into this new job, everyone was discussing a movie that had been released a few months earlier called *The Omen. How awful*, I couldn't help but think. How in the world could anyone sit through such a mind-boggling motion picture, and how about the actors and actresses? How could the writers even create a movie of this sort and be able to sleep at night with a clear conscience. And how could the producers have children playing such devastating parts?

As the weeks passed, there was more talk about this movie. I caught myself actually starting to listen to this nonsense, even though I had never had the inclination to go to such a harrowing movie. Then I began noticing an interesting and a persistent concern from my coworkers about my living at home.

One coworker even had the nerve to say, "Jeannette, you are grown, you can do whatever you like. You don't have to ask your parents' permission."

"Oh, but I do. I live there, and I respect their rules. I would never do anything against them or their beliefs about maintaining a home."

"Jeannette, you just don't get it. Why, you have it made! Living at home, no responsibilities, able to keep your paycheck, able to buy anything you want when you want it. You're just not using your head. Go out! Live a little! Besides, going to a movie by yourself ain't gonna hurt. Haven't you ever gone to a movie alone before?"

"Uh, no."

"Where have you been all your life?"

"Like I said, I'm living with my parents, and we're just fine. I'm the happiest when I'm with them. They aren't just my parents, you see, they're my best friends."

"Huh. Well, my parents surely aren't my best friends," she spoke with hostility.

"Something is *wrong* with you. Have you absolutely *no* desire to live *your* own life? To do things the way *you* want to do them?"

"No. Like I've told you, I'm happy just the way things are. If a movie is mentioned, we go see it together. If a trip is mentioned, we plan it and travel together. If a garment is needed, we plan and shop, together. If groceries are needed, a list is made — together. And if I'm not helping a cousin or a neighbor, I'll go with my parents to the store. If someone new comes into our lives, we visit them together as a family. I'm happy, I'm very happy the way things are, and I don't foresee it ever changing. Unless Mom or Dad gets sick and then we'll take care of that situation, with God's help, *together*."

It seemed like it was getting tougher to work with a few of the people. The job was wonderful. The convenient distance from home to work was great. The work was enjoyable, except that some of my co-workers constantly made comments about my living at home. At first I just went along with them and tried not to let it show that their innuendoes bothered me.

And then one day, yet another approached me with, "Haven't you ever thought that your parents might *rather* you have a place of your own so they can enjoy themselves without having you around all the time?"

"What are you saying to me?" I cried, stunned at their remark.

"Look. Your parents aren't gonna tell you to move out. But I bet if you tell them you are moving, they won't stop you. As a matter of fact, I bet they'll appreciate you more and will even make plans to help you move."

The more I thought about this, the more I *allowed* myself to listen. These foreign questions and statements slowly began filtering into my mind. Not in a disturbing way, but rather in a quiet, seeping way that weakened my mental state and made me unsure.

"Could this person be right, Jesus? Could some of the others also be right? Do You think Mama and Daddy would rather I have a place of my own, even though they've never mentioned it?"

After a few months, I got the impression that maybe, just maybe my co-worker's were right after all. As I listened, my heart began to value their words more than the words of my parents. As positive feelings rushed through my veins of actually being well enough to live and maintain myself, I began looking for a place of my own, without my parents knowledge.

Some of the workers led me to believe that finding a place without my parents' assistance could be a difficult task. However, these co-workers kept reminding me that I was a grown woman who was working, and had a steady income and was able to make my own decisions. They even brought up the issue of Mama and Daddy being proud of me once I started making more of my own decisions. My co-workers' words of life sounded much better than the life I was accustomed to. The more I listened to their wonderful, fun-filled adventures that even included some church parties, the further I slid into a path that eventually led me astray.

After many days and nights of mental wrestling, I finally convinced myself that surprising my parents was the best way. *This will be fun. Oh, how I'm looking forward to fixing up a place my way.* And yet, somewhere deep in my gut, I knew they would *not* approve.

At first I just made small excuses so I could be gone longer than expected to the grocery store. As anticipation grew, so did my excuses. I started telling them there were lots of new stores in the area that I wanted to check out.

"Shug? What about trying to find one of those old-timey oil lamp burners in some of your browsing? I've been looking for several years now and haven't found one yet. Maybe you will." Mama was smart, but I don't think she suspected anything.

"Okay, Mama, I'll be on the lookout for you. Show me what it looks like. Maybe one of the antique shops will have one. If not, they tell me over in Cameron there's a store with all kinds of early-American products."

Well, what have I got myself into this time? I reprimanded myself. Here I am trying to find a place to move to, and now I've told Mama I'm just out browsing in new shops. Dear Jesus. I'm really getting into a mess. Oh well! I'll be able to keep it all straight. I'm sure there's nothing to worry about.

I spent many days searching for just the right place. Part of my criteria was a place within fifteen miles of home and work. I was looking for a unique housing area that included such options as a swimming pool, tennis court, yard and utility maintenance and a house or an apartment that had friendly neighbors, and all within my budget.

"Mama? Was that Tracey on the phone?"

"Yes, Shug. She wants me to go by the grocery store and get her some canned goods and a bottle of her favorite wine. Said for me not to forget her favorite ice cream, too."

"Mama? When does Tracey want this?"

"You know as good as I do. When she calls, she wants it yesterday. I've noticed you've been preoccupied with some shopping of your own these days. By the way, I have a few tomatoes that need juicing and a few ears of corn that need freezing. Being you like shopping so much lately, how about going and getting these things for her? I'll get started on the canning and freezing while you're gone, and when you return you can help."

Agreeing, I got some extra money from Mama. Of course, I couldn't go to just any grocery store. Tracey had her favorite. But thank goodness the Clixie was on the way to her house. I raced to the store, anxiously gathered the groceries, and searched for the emptiest checkout line. Racing through town, not a single stoplight caught me. Time was on my side, and everything was turning out smoothly, giving me time to check out a really cute apartment.

I told Tracey I had some other errands and could only stay a short while. But she had other plans for me. Not only did I help put away the groceries, she even asked me to replace a light bulb in the hallway. Then I had to roll the plastic grocery bags in a certain way, put a rubber band around them and place them a certain way in her special drawer. Next, she asked me to write down her doctor's name and telephone number — in large print.

"Sure Tracey, I'll be glad to help you," I said, thinking all along that I mustn't linger due to the appointment I'd made earlier that day. I'd already fibbed to Mama about browsing, and now I had only two hours to play with. *Oh Lord, I've got to be calm and collected or Tracey'll detect something in my voice. Like Mama, she is very perceptive.*

"Tracey? Now, that that is all done, do you have anything else for me to do before I leave?"

"No. Don't think so. You be careful, and I'll talk to you soon. And, Jeannette? Thank you for helping me today. I'll pay you back one day."

"Pay me back? What're you saying, Tracey? I do this to help you, not to get anything back. I love you, Tracey. We're family. We don't do things to get anything in return. We do it because we want to."

"Shush now. Run along. We'll discuss this later. See ya."

I finally excused myself, and off I went.

WOW! The place was much better than I'd ever dreamed of. It was located in the country near the outskirts of town. Rolling hills and pretty landscaping with dahlias and pansies, and roses all in bloom. After speaking to the manager, I saw one of the apartments. I fell in love with it immediately. It had all the latest appliances and even a built-in trash compactor. All rooms were fully furnished, and there was a second bedroom with a hide-a-bed. All maintenance was kept up by the complex. *This apartment is just what I'd been looking for. Thank You, Jesus. It is perfect. Wait 'till I get home and tell Mama and Daddy. Oh, how excited they'll be. Once they see how happy I am, this'll make them happy too.* I went ahead, signed the year's lease, and was so *happy!* I even sang on the way home, so delighted I'd finally done something on my *own.*

Pulling into the driveway, I saw Mama at the mailbox. Sam came running to greet me. As I opened the car door, Mama said, "Jeannette, why did it take you so long to go to Tracey's and back?"

"Mama, I'm sorry, I didn't realize," knowing I was telling her a story.

"I called Tracey to ask you to stop by the grocery store on your way back home, and she said you'd been gone over an hour. What could you possibly be doing? Had you forgotten about the canning and freezing chores to be done? I needed some more bags and some lids."

Yes, I had forgotten about that stuff — freezing and canning was the last thing on my mind. I didn't know why we had to do it anyway, since my co-workers had pointed out that it was much cheaper to buy it rather than go through all that hard work. But here at home, the garden was Daddy's pride and joy, and Mama had to follow suit once harvesting time approached. Living in their house, I had to abide by their rules. After all, they had been good enough to take me in after the hospitalization and were there for me throughout the divorce. According to my co-workers, I would always be their little girl. *I* so desperately wanted a place of my own and to do the things *I* wanted to do, as they did when they were younger (although deep down *I* was very satisfied with the way things were).

"Jeannette, where's your mind? Did you hear me at all?"

"Oh, I was just browsing," I answered, hoping she would just drop the matter. Not Mama! Once she began, her inquisitiveness got stronger and stronger.

"Where did you say you'd been?"

"Oh, just browsing."

"Browsing? There goes that word again. Browsing for what? I hope you were looking for that oil burner I asked you about. Anyway, these chores are more important than your so-called browsing."

"I was just browsing here and yonder, Mama." I knew I shouldn't be stretching the truth, especially to Mama. She knew me like a book.

"Now Jeannette, don't lie to me. You know I can tell when you tell me a story cause your nose begins to turn sideways."

"Okay, Mama. After supper tonight, I'll share something with you and Daddy."

"You'll do what? Whaddya mean you're gonna share something with us? Tell me right now. I insist."

"No ma'am. After supper, 'cause you will both be delighted to hear about this exciting news."

"Jeannette Yvonne, your daddy and I have noticed for weeks that you've been acting kind of funny. Our conversations haven't been as open as they use to be. What is it, Shug? What's going on?"

"Oh, you and Daddy are going to be so pleased."

All day long, Mama kept popping up with remarks about my not being open with them. Every now and then, "Don't know why you're being so secretive. We've always shared things together. Don't know what's in that head of yours that you haven't shared with us for weeks."

Oh, what a supper! Snap beans, cut-off corn, fried okra, hush puppies. There was even fatback with some pieces of country ham, Covington molasses and some red-eye gravy to sop.

"Ok, Jeannette, I've waited long enough. Now, tell us what's going on with you."

"Well, Mama? Daddy? I've decided its time for me to move out. I'm much stronger, and Dr. Jefferries has given me a clean bill of health. I'm so thankful for your help during these past few years. I can never repay your kindness."

"*Move out?!?*" Daddy said.

"Whaddya mean, *move out*? Aren't you happy here?" Mama's eyes began to bulge.

"What've we done to make you decide to move, honey?" Daddy asked with a disappointed voice.

I was stunned, "Why do you seem so disappointed? I don't understand. I thought you'd be happy for me, and besides, I've already found a place, and it has great features."

"No, wait. Let's get to the bottom of this, and let's do it right now," Mama insisted.

"Get to the bottom of what? I thought you 'd be happy and excited that I'm able to move out on my own and have a life of my own. Jesus, I don't understand."

"Don't you use Christ's name in that manner!" Daddy shouted.

144

"What manner? What are you talking about, Daddy? What you are telling me?"

"Jeannette, what is happening to you? You've changed since you started working at that company. You're not our sweet little girl any more. Those co-workers of yours have been filling your head with the wrong kind of stuff. We are your family. We love you. Your mother and I'd thought you could share anything with us. We don't understand why you'd want to move. What have we done to cause you to decide to do this? Please, please tell us, and we will do our best to make it better for you. Honey, we just don't want to see you destroy your life."

"Destroy my life? I'm not going to destroy my life just because I move away from home. And besides, I've already found the perfect place. I've already made a down payment along with the first month's rent."

"You've done what???" Daddy exclaimed as his eyes bulged.

"Yes! I'm sorry you don't feel the way I thought you would. I'm sorry you're not happy for me. I thought you'd be excited, that you'd even help me pack and move to this really great place. I just don't understand you. You are both all the time saying that you want the very best for me, and yet when I made a decision, you look as though you could bite a ten-penny nail in two."

"Jeannette, what has happened to you? We don't know our own daughter any more."

"Well, I've decided to move, and that's final."

"Final??? What do you mean that's final?" Mama said with her hazel eyes just a dancing.

"Like I said, I'm going to move, with or without your support."

I jumped up from the table and hurried down the hall to my bedroom. Daddy called my name. Then I heard Mama say, in her firm voice, "No, John. No! Let her be."

The next day I shared this news with my co-workers. They were so excited about my decision that they even offered to help me move.

"Hey, Jeannette, we'll throw a big party for your moving out on your own. Wait till you see. You're gonna have a ball. You're gonna be responsible for your life, and nobody else's. Oh, how I envy you. You're gonna be so busy having fun that you won't need your parents at all. They're gonna be so proud to see your progress. Have you decided to go and see that movie yet?"

"No! But, you know, I just might decide to do that, too. What can it hurt? As you say, I'm a grown person, and I can take care of myself. What could a simple movie do to a person anyway? Yes, I'll see it this weekend."

"Good girl! Oh, I'm so proud of your decisions. You're really acting like a grown up now," with statements from both Fred and Lucy as they each gave a high-five salute to the others in the break room.

Things happened so fast that I caught myself enjoying being at work more than being at home. Home wasn't too pleasant. Mama and Daddy were giving me the silent treatment. As hard as I tried to converse with them and tell them of my daily activities, they ignored me as though I wasn't even there.

Dear Lord, what have I done that's been so horrible? Jesus, I love them so much. But, Jesus, I need my space too. I need a life of my own. Lord, I haven't forgotten that You healed me, and I haven't forgotten the request I asked You either about letting me live a little in the worldly way. I guess this is all part of it, isn't it?

* * *

The next Sunday afternoon, I told Mama I'd decided to go see that movie all my co-workers were talking about.

"Well, you're grown and are making decisions. We just wonder if you're making the right decision to see this kind of movie. Oh well, be careful." Uneasy thoughts arose as I walked out the door. *Jesus, I just don't understand their viewpoints, please help me to, please?*

On the drive over, I let some positive thoughts enter my mind. *Yes, I am grown, I can go, and I can do whatever I please, when I please. I don't need . . .* when a little tiny voice, deep from within began to say, "*watch it, Jeannette. Be careful before saying what you don't need. Jesus is listening, and He can and He just might grant your wishes. Just be careful.*"

Where in the world did that come from? Did I just drop off in a daze while driving? Did it come over the radio? Was it my guardian angel or, *could it really be You talking to me, Jesus?* Letting my mind think it was Him, "*Oh, how good it is to finally hear from You. By the way, You never did answer my mid-seventies question about whether I could live a little of the worldly way, Lord.*

Guess I'm the first one here. The parking lot is nearly empty. From what my co-workers said, I thought the lot would be full of cars. Oh well, I'll just park over near the entrance so I won't have to walk far when it's over. "*And, Jesus? I'm glad to see the sun way up high in the sky on this warm Sunday afternoon. Maybe it'll still be shining after the movie. I don't care to drive at night, and besides, Mama and Daddy might be worried.*

Somewhere, in the inner depths of my soul, I didn't want to see this movie. But I had to show my co-workers, and I needed to prove to myself that I was a strong person.

"Only one?" The ticket lady asked. Faking a slight grin, I turned and went through the glass entrance door that led into a small lobby. I canvassed the area: there were five brass poles with swags of wine-colored ropes neatly placed to form two rows, a concession stand on the right and the restrooms on the left. In front were two heavy drawn drapes that seemed to be the entrance into the theater area. Not particularly enjoying crowds, I decided to go ahead and purchase a drink, a candy bar, and some hot, buttered popcorn.

As I approached the main area, a young man was standing just outside of one of the draped curtains. I couldn't help but notice him looking at me in a most unusual way. Reaching out his hand, he spoke with a soft voice and said, "Only one ticket?"

"Yes. That's right. Just one."

He took the ticket and tore it in half. "You hang on to this other half, ma'am. We'll have a drawing at intermission, and you might just win a prize. It'll also come in handy should you need to come back to the lobby. You see, you'll need this stub for re-entry."

"Thank you, sir." The young man then pulled some cords behind the drapes. As they opened, he motioned me to walk through into the movie area.

"Oh my!" That uneasy feeling approached from within once again. The room was totally dark. Not a light of any kind. Then, just behind me I sensed someone's presence. Not being able to see, I heard a familiar voice.

"Ma'am?"

"*Uh, yes sir?*"

"Please, follow me. I have a flashlight, and it'll help in finding a good seat."

"Thank you sir, for your kindness."

The young gentleman escorted me to the upper middle section and asked me to sit on the outside chair. He said doing so I'd have easy access to the lobby. Still not picking up on these remarks, I tried to settle down and get comfortable.

"Ma'am? Please pardon me for saying this, but you just don't seem like the type to be watching this kind of movie."

"Sir? I must admit I do feel kind of out of place. But some co-workers of mine said this was a fantastic movie and suggested I see it."

"Ma'am? With all due respect, it can have a very penetrating message if one isn't really careful. And the truth of the matter is, someone like you shouldn't be watching it alone."

"I appreciate your concerns. Please, please don't worry. I'll be just fine." He nodded, turned, and walked back up the isle.

I settled into the cushioned seat. I had my drink on the floor, a candy bar in my purse, and the hot, buttered popcorn in my lap. I was all set. Finally, I let the remarks of that young man and the lady out in the ticket booth, penetrate.

Jesus, they seemed so concerned about me. Why? And, why did that young man say I shouldn't be watching this movie alone? My co-workers hadn't said anything about that. Lord, I just don't understand what all the commotion is about. Why are Mama and Daddy so insistent that I not move out, and why are they so against my watching this movie? Several people took seats to the right of me, and I had to move my drink and scrunch my legs to one side, praying I wouldn't spill any of that expensive popcorn. My mind raced, wishing someone was with me. I didn't like being there alone. I thought back to only a few weeks ago when we had a more happy time at home. *Jesus, I just don't understand.*

Suddenly, loud music surrounded the theater. Heavy drums roared, a tremendous outburst of thunder, and clasps of brilliant white lights flashed across the auditorium. My eyes were wide open, staring toward the "center stage" of total blackness. Next, the huge black curtains opened and previews for upcoming attractions blanketed the large screen. Almost immediately, several fierce looking Doberman Pinchers appeared on screen. I was terrified, and glued to my seat. I soon discovered that the music would swell just before a traumatic scene was shown. I quickly covered my eyes. Then, I'd catch myself peeping through my fingers and closing my eyes so tightly, they would hurt. I remember trying to reach around to clasp my earlobes, desperately attempting to shut out the horrific sights and the tumbling sounds of terror. *Oh, Jesus! Why? Why did I think I could . . . ?*

As soon as the thundering began, it stopped. Just then the house lights came on and an announcer appeared on center stage. "May I have your attention please?" His husky voice reverberated over the squeaky microphone. "It is now intermission and there will be three drawings for a nice prize. If you'll get out your stubs, I'll read off the six number sequences and would like the winners to stand and continue standing until the drawing is over."

Stub? What stub? I was dumbfounded. I did not look for the stub. I did not stand because I could not move. This movie was the most unbelievable film I'd ever encountered. *What was I thinking, coming to see something of this magnitude all by myself? If only Mama was here. She'd have some off-the-wall remark that would have me laughing, and I'd be able to put this thing in its right place. But Mama isn't here and would never, ever come to a movie like this. Dear Jesus, I wonder if it'd be alright if I left? No, I promised my co-workers I'd see the movie, and since I'm here, I might as well see it all.*

"Attention! I have called out this third number and no one is responding to it. Once again, if you have this number please stand up." He repeated the six number sequence. *Please, Jesus, please don't let it be mine — please.* I just wanted to shrink into a size one and slip out of that awful place, pretending I'd never set foot in it.

"The last three numbers are six sixty-seven. I repeat, six sixty-seven are the last three numbers."

I hesitantly lowered my head to see the ending numbers and began praising God. My stub did not match the numbers I had just heard.

After the short intermission, the second half began in the same manner, loud and startling. As the plot unfolded, I couldn't believe my eyes or ears. Learning of this child's demonic overtones was nearly impossible to witness. *Dear Lord Jesus? What in the world has possessed these producers and screenwriters to promote such a movie? Oh, how I wish, and I know it's a sin to wish. But right now, I do wish someone was with me.* Everything this child did in the movie was deliberate. He caused tempers among adults to fly and trouble among children. The child appeared to be totally filled with an evil spirit. No good came out of his soul. Only harm was established through his eyes that revealed strange mystical powers. The Doberman Pinchers were among his weapons, and they seemed to act on demand just by the way the child looked at them.

I quietly discovered that I was not at all prepared for what appeared at the end. As the hair was parted at the crown of the child's head, there it was — imprinted as plain as day — three consecutive sixes. Without another spoken word, the movie ended with these written words at the bottom of the screen quoting God's Holy Word, the Bible. "Here is wisdom. Let him that hath understanding count the number of the beast: for it is the number of man; and his number is six hundred threescore *and* six. Rev. 13:18."

At that point, I had the most eerie feeling. It was as though I was trapped in a cave. The atmosphere was musty, and the air seemed clammy. People slowly got up and began to leave. I sat stunned, feeling like I was still glued to the seat. Those last few lines were embedded in my mind. I felt frozen by the most shocking movie I'd ever seen. Too scared to move, I sat still and waited until the theater was nearly empty. Finally, I mustered enough courage to get up and walk. With my knees wanting to buckle and my eyes focused only to the front of the theater, I began a slow pace toward the lobby.

The auditorium lights weren't as bright as they had been during intermission, and I didn't see that young man anywhere. I could have used his guidance then. No one said a word. There was complete silence in the lobby. Everybody who saw The Omen must have been in the same startled as me. Finally, I was able to see the light from outside. *What a blessed sight. Thank You Jesus.*

As I went through the big glass door, I noticed the parking lot was full of cars, trucks, and people. *Jesus,* was all I could muster in my thoughts as I headed for the car.

I quickly unlocked the door and jumped inside as though someone or something was after me. Waiting to exit the parking lot, I noticed people yelling and shouting at each other as they slowly left the area through the traffic jam that began to form. As I approached the parking lots only exit, a kind person stopped the line of traffic and motioned for me to come out. I turned to throw up my hand in appreciation and realized it was that young man who had seated me in the theater. He smiled graciously and indicated the peace sign with two fingers.

While driving home, the sign of the beast was all I could think about. *Dear Jesus, how could anyone make such a movie and be able to sleep at night? Please protect them, I pray. And Lord, thank You so much for the sunset shining across the land, and for allowing me to get home before dark. Oh Jesus, what am I gonna tell Mama and Daddy???"*

I was still shaking when I got home. Coming to greet me, as usual, was our faithful Sam.

"Sam? Sister has just seen some mighty unusual things and she's frightened. What about giving me a big hug? I can use one along about now. I don't know how to tell Mama and Daddy about this scary experience."

As though she knew exactly what I was saying, she jumped up and licked my face and snuggled her body close to mine. I felt warm, as if Sam was saying, "Jeannette, I love you unconditionally."

After our "talk," I was able to gather some energy and go inside. Almost immediately, with a stern look on his face, Daddy asked, "Honey, how was the movie? Did you enjoy it?"

"There were some scary parts, but I managed to get through it. Let me change into some shorts and I'll be right out." I rushed through, hoping he wouldn't notice my trembling body.

I guess I'd stayed too long because a knock sounded on my bedroom door.

"Shug? Why do you have the door closed? Are you all right in there?"

"Yes ma'am. I just couldn't decide exactly what to put on."

"Well, come on out when you do. Your daddy and I want to talk to you."

Mama knew something was wrong, because I never closed my bedroom door unless I was upset and didn't want to talk to them. I didn't realize I was sending out signals of distress by closing my door.

"Sorry I took so long. Sure is a warm night, isn't it? Did you see Sam come and greet me just awhile ago? She is surely a special one," I chattered.

* * *

"Shug, your daddy and I have been discussing this matter of your moving."

"Mama? You just won't leave it be, will you?" I said while giving thanks to Jesus for them *not* mentioning the movie.

"For this last time, neither your daddy nor I will mention it again. I'm asking you once more. Please tell us what we have done, and we will do our best to fix it. *We love you. You* are a part of our family. We don't know what has happened to our daughter. Won't you please be honest with us? What have we done wrong to make you hate us?"

"Hate you? I don't hate you. What kind of a question is that?"

"Honey? Your mother and I have been wracking our brains to figure out your sudden interest in moving out. We understand your wanting to have a social life. We understand your wanting to get involved with people your own age. What we don't understand is your wanting to *leave* to do it. We know, too, that although your health is better, you still need looking after to a point. Especially until you are a *lot* stronger. There are lots of singles at church who would love for you to associate with them. There are also all kinds of activities at church they would love for you to be part of. We've brought you up in the best way we know how and yet, you want to leave this home and start anew all of a sudden? No. We don't understand the urgency."

"Mama, you know why I don't get involved with those church members. You know I feel out of place, especially with my being divorced and all. None of them are or have been through a divorce. I'm the only one in that church that it's happened to. You and Daddy both know how devastating it's been, and you both know that they don't even have Sunday school classes for divorcees. It hurts to admit that Charles used my sickness as an excuse to betray me. I know I'm looked down on for not staying with my husband and trying to make a go of it. I know what they all think of me. I see the look on their faces, and I'd just rather be alone than to be reminded that I don't fit in."

"Shug, they're probably expressing their love to you," Mama said.

"Love? Yeah, right. You go on believing that if you want to, but I know better."

"Honey, I probably shouldn't say this, but with your attitude lately, you're probably taking their cares the wrong way."

"The wrong way? Daddy, keep it coming. I know you and Mama both blame me, and it isn't always my fault. I can't help that my marriage ended in divorce. You know the love I have for Charles and the children. And to think he didn't even have the decency to let me know of the children's move to Virginia with their mother. If it hadn't been for his cousin and my cousin's conversation last week, I'd not even know that. As far as his whereabouts, they hadn't seen him since we signed our divorce papers."

Mama and Daddy kept quiet as my heart continued to overflow. "I still love him, and I always will. It's just that I can't help feeling like an outsider, especially when the church folks turn and snicker behind my back. I see them looking at me, and I feel their distance when I approach. It's as if I'm infested with the black plague or something."

"Shug! You know of no such thing. You're just assuming people are snickering. You don't even go enough to get involved. There you go again, letting negative thoughts enter your mind. Your daddy and I are proud of you and the way you've handled yourself. Besides, you're doing what the Bible says to do. Yes, Charles *is* the one who betrayed you. He *is* the one who caused your marriage to split, and he didn't even have the decency to talk to you when you came home from the hospital. It wasn't anything you could help. He's the one who broke it up — *not you*."

"But Mama, when I was married, there were two of us. Then when the children arrived, that made four of us. With you and Daddy, there were six of us, and Papa C and Peg — that made eight of us. Can't you see? It was always pairs. Now, it's just me again. And I make number three. And, everybody knows that two is company and three's a crowd."

Tears began to swell but *I* was determined to suppress them. I had to be brave and not show any emotions. I couldn't let them see how torn I really was inside. *Oh Jesus, please, I pray for Mama and Daddy to live a long, long time. I just couldn't bear living without them. Please Jesus — don't take them, too — please.* My heart nearly burst with the deep emotions I swore I'd never share with anyone.

"Shug? Why don't you start going to church on a regular basis? And if it's the Lord's will, *you* can start a singles Sunday school class yourself."

"Oh Mama, now. You know fully well that I can't start anything. I'm not like you. I don't have the charisma you have. I'm not a people person. Although I've come back home from my broken marriage, that doesn't give me the right to mingle among the singles or the married ones. You don't know how awkward it is. It's as though I'm out in left field. So, I'd just as soon stay home. Besides, my schedule calls for me to work a lot on Sundays, and I've found some friends at the company to hang out with. Seems like it doesn't matter to them if I'm a divorcee or not."

"We love you, honey, and we just want the best for you. Please, try to start back to church and get involved with those wonderful people. If you try, I promise you it won't be like you think it will."

"Sure Daddy, keep believing that if you want to."

"Shug? Give them a chance to help you. You might be surprised."

The more Mama spoke about the church and its people, the more aggressive I became. Trying to avoid Mama's request altogether, I found myself struggling endlessly, it seemed, against an urgent feeling to come clean. A part of me wanted to blurt it out, while another kept pushing it back into my soul.

Then, all of a sudden, my mouth flew open, and out came these words: "Well, if you must know about this change in me . . . But, but . . ." I said while hanging my head and clearing my throat a time or two. "Those people at work . . ."

Startled at what I just said, and before I could continue, Mama spoke openly, "I knew it. I just knew those people were behind your unusual actions. I'm sorry, Shug. Go ahead and share with us what you started to say."

"Daddy, I didn't know what to do. They kept telling me that you and Mama had rather I leave and that I was grown and that something was wrong with me because I didn't want a place of my own to tend to and to fix up and . . ."

"Honey, you don't have to tell us word for word what they have been brainwashing you with. I think your mother and I can figure the rest of it out on our own. You see, I told your mother that I was afraid something like this would happen. You are so vulnerable to everything, mainly because we've sheltered you from the outside world. We have had experiences in the world and you haven't. This was something *new* to you, and as I predicted, you fell head over heels for their conniving ways."

"What do you mean, Daddy, conniving ways?"

"Honey, not that I'm blaming anyone. It's just that in the world some people haven't had the upbringing that your mother and I have had,

155

and we've tried to raise you in that same God-fearing manner. We've been through some mighty tough times. The depression was bad enough, and then World War II. And, honey, I didn't, and I'm sure your mother didn't know it at the time, but we were really poor. God was looking after us then, and He's looking after us now."

"Shug? Do you have anything else you'd like to share with us now?"

"Well? Yes," I said still with shyness as realization dawned on me. "This is also why I went to see that terrible movie. My co-workers kept nagging at me about being an adult who should be able to handle anything life had to dish out. I, uh, I really didn't want to go. But, when you both were totally against it, then I became totally for it. Yes! The grass was greener on the other side. A side I'd never in my life experienced. I liked what I saw. I enjoyed being independent, and I even enjoyed being around folks who seemed to like me."

"Honey? Aren't there others up there that are church goers?"

"Yes. But, they work mostly in the office areas. And yes, I'm close to these office employees, but we don't associate much due to our working schedules."

"Shug, you just keep on being that sweet person that God made and keep on trusting Him and praying for guidance and everything will turn out just fine."

"I'll try and do better, Mama, but how am I to treat these co-workers? I can't avoid 'em. I work with them on a daily basis, and we even have break together."

"Honey, just treat them the way you always have. Just don't let yourself agree with their views. Even if it means eating by yourself. It's better to be alone than to be influenced in the wrong direction. What seems right can sometimes be deadly wrong."

"But, Daddy? How can I know if I'm being influenced in the wrong direction?"

"Now Shug, I can answer that one for you. You know how you've been brought up. Church, reading the good book, focusing on God's Word. When these people begin talking about other matters and they don't express it in a Christian manner, then you'll know. You can almost always spot one."

"Mama, you can spot 'em miles off, but I can't. I believe what everybody tells me. I've never been able to read people the way you and Daddy have."

"Honey, when you have doubt about something, trust the Holy Ghost. He'll always be there for you. And, if it can wait until tomorrow, bring your questions and problems home. We're always here to help you. We won't tell you what to do; we'll just advise you as to what we'd do. Now, that don't mean that we have all the answers. Each of us in our own way will continue to read the Bible, pray over the matter and the answer will be brought to us. It always has and it always will."

"But Daddy, what am I going to do about the apartment? I've already signed a year's lease and made a down payment along with a month's rent?"

"Shug? The grass isn't always greener on the other side. We're glad you decided to come forth with this. Those co-workers of yours really played a number on you, didn't they?"

"Mama, I'm sorry."

"Shug? Where is this place, anyway?"

"It's that new subdivision off highway 14 A, called Coeler's Place. You know it, Daddy. It's the one that Buddy helped plan the landscaping for."

"Honey, we have time. C'mon, let's go over there now and talk to the manager. I don't foresee any problems once we tell 'em the truth."

"Truth? You mean I've gotta tell him of my immaturity?"

"I think we can come up with a better business way of handling this matter than showing your childlike mistakes, honey. Leave it to me and your mother. We'll show you the correct way. I haven't been in the store business, and we haven't rented all these years without learning some tricks of the trade."

Sure enough, Daddy handled it like a pro. I was so proud of him and Mama. The apartment manager returned my payments in full and even shook Daddy's hand and sent us off with well wishes. I learned a lot from this situation. If only I'd listened to my conscience to start with, this would never have happened. But, if it hadn't happened, it would not have been a lesson learned.

19

A Sheltering Touch

"SHUG, HAVE YOU put your name in the pot yet for your company's upcoming seminar trip to Cincinnati," Mama asked me.

"Yes, the first of the week. But there's no way I'd ever win something like that. There'll be at least three, maybe four hundred entrants. I don't stand a chance of winning."

"You stand just as good a chance as the next person. Don't be so hard on yourself" Mama insisted.

After supper, with the dishes washed and the animals all fed, Mama and I were sitting on the couch in the den and Daddy was in his recliner near the TV. As we chatted during commercials, out of the blue Mama announced, "Jeannette, you're gonna be one of the winners tomorrow."

"Mama, you don't know any such thing."

"Listen to me, *you're gonna win!*"

The next afternoon, as everyone anxiously waited, the big wheel spun around with the names of interested employees posted to over three hundred positions. It wasn't long before three winners were chosen with only one more person to be selected. Mr. Jones, the president of the company rose from his seated position. "May I have the honor of spinning the 'Wheel of Fortune' this last time?" he asked.

The plant manager nodded his approval and Mr. Jones whirled the wooden peg-nailed wheel. Around and around it went. Nobody could hear the clicks because it was spinning so fast. Finally, the force of gravity slowed the wheel and anticipation peaked.

As I walked into the house that night, Mama called out to me, "Jeannette? I've washed your clothes that you'll be wearing on the trip, and what date did you say the Braves were playing?"

"Mama, how in the world did you know I'd win?"

"Shug, don't ask me how I knew. I just did. Just like I knew you'd get the cosmetic job. I can't explain it, Shug. I just knew."

Sharing popcorn with our two pet dogs Sam and Knottroot, Daddy looked at me with a twinkle in his eye and said, "Honey, your mother's special with her God given talents."

* * *

One morning near the end of February, Daddy noticed some blood in his stool. He recognized it as a hemorrhoid irritation, and the bleeding decreased somewhat in the following days. However, in the middle of the night during the first week of March, Daddy hemorrhaged terribly. He didn't want to go to the hospital, so Mama made him promise to go to the doctor first thing the next morning. Daddy insisted on Mama calling Dr. Ashley. In doing so, he firmly spoke of meeting them at Rex Hospital.

"Daddy, I've called work and told them not to expect me today."

"Honey, I'll be alright. No need for you to miss work. I can drive myself up and you can come after work and get your mother."

"Nonsense. I've already called and I'm driving, okay?" He didn't seem to mind. I guess he was just being Daddy.

Dr. Ashley had an orderly waiting for us when we arrived. He wheeled Daddy in with Mama right behind. After finding a handicapped parking place nearby, I rushed through the emergency area and entered the hospital. Walking hastily toward the waiting room, I saw Mama coming down the hallway toward me with Daddy's things. She quickly said the nurses had taken Daddy to x-ray and for us to go to the waiting room down near the information desk. It seemed like an eternity passed before we saw Dr. Ashley.

"Drusilla? It appears to be a little more than a simple hemorrhoid problem. However, I won't know for sure until all the tests come back, probably sometime tomorrow. We're going to admit John to the hospital . . ." Before he was able to say another word Mama said, "Dr. Ashley, go ahead and make reservations for me too. I'm staying right here with him."

"Yes, Drusilla, I know. Don't worry; there'll be an extra cot in the room for you too. This hospital is very much aware of your family, after Jeannette's little three-month stay in the mid-seventies and John's stay when he hemorrhaged from his nose, and had that stroke in his right ear in 1980. My, what a strenuous time that was."

"You remember that? I'll never forget it. John sat in his recliner for six whole weeks with both nostrils packed solid. How in the world he did it, God only knows. What a time! He had to not only sleep that way, but also to eat and swallow twelve pills daily. Then in November, his sister in Texas passed away, and we couldn't go to her funeral due to his health. Then in 1982 one of his brothers was shot at a grocery store near McGee's Crossroads and died in early 1983. I'm sorry, Dr. Ashley, I didn't mean to reminisce — it's just that so much has happened to us."

"That's perfectly alright, Drusilla. Your family has been dealt quite a lot in the last few years, not to mention your heart problems. Anyway, I'll be in to see John tonight, and maybe we'll know more then."

"Mama? Let's go get something to eat."

"Shug, let's wait and get your Daddy settled in his room, and then we'll talk about getting something to eat."

In about fifteen or twenty minutes, we saw Daddy being pulled out of the x-ray room. "How do my women like my new outfit?" he asked jokingly.

I was glad to see Daddy in such good spirits. Just as he promised, Dr. Ashley came by that night and said there was one more test he wanted to run. He placed Daddy on a liquid diet and began a regimen of antibiotics because of his heart condition. Dr. Ashley said he had scheduled a "cleaning process" first thing in the morning, and we all knew what he meant by that.

"John, the antibiotics are necessary for the special colonoscopy test scheduled for late tomorrow. Just as a precautionary measure."

"You know best, Dr. Ashley. I'll do whatever you say."

I'd just arrived from work around eight o'clock the next night when Dr. Ashley came in and pulled up a chair next to Daddy's bed. Mama had just come out of the bathroom and sat down at the foot of his bed.

"John? Looks like we've found your problem." He glanced over his wire-framed glasses with his big brown eyes. "We found some polyps in your colon and while we were in there, we removed several for a biopsy. John, I don't want to scare you, but the result came back cancerous. I've gone ahead and scheduled surgery for tomorrow morning at eleven o'clock. We're hoping that we've caught this in time to *not* do a colostomy."

"Is that the bag?" Daddy asked with much concern.

"Yes, John."

Just as Mama got up and headed toward Daddy, the telephone rang. Excusing herself as she passed in front of Dr. Ashley, I saw her reach in her pant pocket for a paper towel and wipe away tears. She blew her nose and cleared her throat before answering the phone. Dr. Ashley continued explaining the procedure and said he'd also leave instructions for a mild sedative should Daddy need one to rest during the night. Shaking Daddy's hand, he turned and smiled just before leaving the room.

"Well, honey," Daddy said to me with tears in his eyes, "Don't you worry none now, ya hear? The Good Lord has given me a good life, and this will work out too. He has been so good to me. I don't deserve all He has given. You and your mother are so good. I don't deserve either of you." Putting the receiver back on the phone, Mama and I both reached to take hold of Daddy's hands.

"Papa?" Mama spoke enthusiastically, "That was RoAnn who said she'd heard about your condition from tonight's Bible Study at church. She said the strangest feeling came over her to share with us about reading an article in the *National Enquirer* about a new treatment containing a three-minute non-surgical cure for rectal cancer. I told her about your scheduled operation tomorrow at eleven, and she said she had a copy of this week's paper and for us to come tonight and get it — that she'd wait up for us — no matter the time. C'mon Jeannette, time is of the essence."

"But Mama, can't we stop on the way home and pick one up? You can find 'em most everywhere."

"Do you know where to get one? I never read those kinds of maga-zines because of all the junk in 'em. But RoAnn declared this was on the up-and-up and that it laid on her heart so strong that she couldn't wait to get home and call, hoping we were still here."

"Mama, now don't you worry none either. I just told Jeannette that the Lord has been good to me, and I don't deserve you or her."

"Now, Papa. You stop talking like that. Everything's gonna turn out okay, just you wait and see. Jeannette and I are going to leave now, and we'll be back up here first thing in the morning. We've got a mission to do and if it's God's will, we'll get that paper and pray for His guidance for the rest. Now you lie back and rest and we'll call you as soon as we get home. Give us at least two hours 'cause it'll take a good thirty to forty minutes just to get home. We might end up over at RoAnn's if we can't find a copy. If we do, I'll ask her to call you so you won't worry, okay?"

"Mama, do be careful. It's dangerous out there, especially for women. I don't know what I'd do if something was to happen to you."

"Papa, we'll be fine. Now please, don't worry. We'll talk soon." We both leaned down. Mama kissed Daddy on the lips and I kissed him on the cheek and told him that we loved him.

Walking down the carpeted hallway, Mama shared with me her deepest heartfelt emotion. "Shug, your Daddy knows what's ahead of him and is very frightened about not being well enough to undergo surgery due to his lung condition. And I too, am . . ." Before finishing the state-ment her eyes filled with tears, ". . . looking forward to finding that National paper with that possible cure for colon cancer."

Standing inside the warm lobby while I went for the car wasn't to Mama's liking. She insisted on going with me while reaching into her coat pocket and pulling out a plastic rain cap, placing it over her head and tying it just under her chin. As we walked to the car, Mama removed a paper towel from her burgundy coat pocket and covered her nose so as not to let the cold March night air pierce her lungs. she was rying to ward off any possibility of having an Angina attack.

I just knew there'd be several of those magazines left at the gas station.

"Sold Out" read the sign in front.

"Not to fear, Mama, I'm sure the shopping center in Garner has at least two stands, one on each corner. Let's drop by there."

"Sold Out" read the signs in front.

"Hey Mama, I'm almost positive that the seafood restaurant on the way home has a stand. Let's stop and check it out. *Oh N-o-o-o.*"

"Shug, looks like we'll have to go to RoAnn's after all."

My car lights must have been a dead give-away as I hustled up their steep driveway. RoAnn was waiting at their back door in her nightie with the paper. Reaching for it, I gave her a hug and asked God to bless her. "We'll be praying this article will help John," she told Mama just before I shut the car door to head home.

The telephone was ringing when we entered the den. Putting away our pocket books, I overheard Mama exchanging her love with Daddy. While tears ran like a river down her cheeks, she gave thanks to Jesus for RoAnn's National paper and for her sharing the article with us.

"Papa, I know beyond a shadow that a miracle is taking place. Before you go to sleep tonight, ask the nurses to make a note on your chart that you want Dr. Ashley to come and see you as early as possible because you have something to show him before surgery. Papa, don't you let *nobody* touch you until Jeannette and I get there in the morning, okay?"

As soon as they finished talking, Mama informed me that we would get up at four o'clock, bathe, and head for the hospital. "Your Daddy just said the surgery has been moved up from eleven o'clock to nine o'clock, and they're gonna prep him at six-thirty so they could follow through with the cleaning procedures. Shug, you heard what I told him. That's why we need to be there before things get to happening. I know it's a miracle and that's all it can be. It was meant for RoAnn to call tonight. It was meant for this article to be in this type of paper. It was meant for us to get it — nothing shy of the Good Lord's work. Always pray and He will provide. Always expect the unexpected. God works in mysterious ways at times. We've just gotta be ready."

It seemed like I'd just laid down when the alarm clock was jumping off the head of the bed. To my surprise, Mama was already up, dressed and had her green cup full of black coffee. She set on the end of the couch reading that article with the Holy Bible her sister Louise had given her lying open across her lap. Mama didn't sleep at all the night before.

We arrived at the hospital around five-thirty. Papa was lying there wide awake. Once he saw Mama, a smile of joy appeared on his unshaven face, and tears began streaming down his cheeks. Just before six o'clock, Dr. Ashley came in wanting to know what was so urgent.

"Good morning, Dr. Ashley," Mama spoke up with an urgency of her own. "I'm the one that asked Papa to ask you to come by this morning, sir. Here, please take a look at this article."

Reaching for the National paper, he pulled up the chair, laid his coat at the foot of Daddy's bed, and proceeded to sit down while beginning to read the article. The room was silent as Dr. Ashley continued to read for several minutes.

"Drusilla, this is amazing."

"Dr. Ashley, there's even a telephone number listed. Would you consider calling and seeing if this doctor does exist and if this treatment is for real?"

Dr. Ashley rose quickly and was out the door like a whirlwind. Papa looked at Mama, Mama looked at Papa, and they both looked at me. They reached for each other's embrace. I went to Daddy's bathroom, pulled the door behind me. I sat, cried, prayed, and gave them time together.

About twenty-five minutes later — around the time Daddy was scheduled to be prepped for surgery — Dr. Ashley popped in, face beaming. "John, I've got some miraculous news. Drusilla, I've just spoken to Dr. Wynten about this three-minute, non-surgical rectal cancer treatment. He verified it's true! Said the *National* paper got wind of this new procedure through a former student. Dr. Wynten has used this technique on more than two hundred patients in the past nine years, with a cure rate over ninety-four percent, as good as the rate achieved with surgery. This endocavitary irradiation technique, using an instrument called a Phillips probe, is now available at major medical centers across the United States, and is used mainly on patients with early stages of rectal cancer. Before coming in here, John, I stopped by the nurses' station and cancelled your surgery. Dr. Wynten and I will get together very soon and schedule your first treatment with him in Rochester, New York. I am releasing you this morning and as soon as he and I talk, I'll call you.

"Drusilla, thank you for bringing this to my attention. You just saved John from surgery, and we all know with his emphysema and vascular condition how dangerous it was going to be. I also went ahead, knowing you didn't mind, and made a copy of this article. I might even contact the National paper and thank them for printing it." Laughing, he excused himself into the hallway.

"See Papa? I told you there was nothing to worry about. Jesus is taking care of you. He's taking care of us all as He promised. This whole episode's nothing shy of a miracle."

"Mama, you were right again."

As I came out of the bathroom, I saw both of Daddy's arms raised in the air. His fingers of his left hand were motioning for Mama and his fingers of his right hand were motioning for me as he pulled us close to his chest. We hugged and lifted praises toward Heaven.

* * *

Dr. Ashley called Daddy the first of the following week and said he'd arranged for an appointment with Dr. Wynten on Thursday. Mama decided at the last minute to fly up with him. I was surprised, knowing she didn't care at all for flying. She use to say that God didn't give her wings to fly or fins to swim. However, this was a different situation. So Mama put her personal feelings aside, held her head up high, and went with Daddy for his first treatment. Returning home around midnight, Mama was frozen and Daddy was laughing.

"I've *never, ever* been as cold in my *life!* That Phil-def-fia airport is the *coldest* in the world and *all that snow* in Rochester. I sure am glad we live in North Carolina."

"Honey, I don't think Mama will be going with me again."

"Daddy? How was it?"

"It wasn't too bad. A little uncomfortable, but not bad."

"Did it hurt or burn or sting?"

"Like I said, just a little uncomfortable. Dr. Wynten's a nice man. I'd say he's probably in his early sixties or so. Said they hadn't seen the ground since last October. He said too that I'd probably need three more treatments but could only schedule them about two weeks apart since the area needed a chance to heal some. With the scope, he was able to find three more polyps that looked questionable. He said he would decide as time went on as to the correct path to take.

"Mama? I've just checked the calendar for Daddy's next treatment, and it's scheduled the same day I'm to leave with the company employees for Cincinnati. I'll just tell them there's an emergency in the family and that I can't go."

"You'll do no such thing!"

"But Daddy, I'd be gone an entire two weeks and Mama will need me here."

"Shug? I'll be just fine. Besides, your daddy will only be gone for one day. He'll fly up that morning and be home before midnight."

"No, I won't hear of it. Don't you dare cancel your trip for me, ya hear?"

"But Daddy, I promised I'd go with you too. Your first visit I worked and the next two visits I'll be in Cincinnati and . . ."

"Honey, I'll be just fine, and so will your mother. Now, you go ahead and get your mind ready for a good trip, ya hear?"

When I returned from the company's trip, Daddy was eager to tell of visiting his childhood friend while in Rochester.

"How did you get in touch with SallyMarie, Daddy?" I asked with concerns.

"Well, I didn't. She called me the first of the week. Said she'd spoken to a relative and they told her of my situation. She insisted I allow time between flights to meet her and her husband. You know, her voice hadn't changed at all. First time in over thirty years I'd even spoken to her. SallyMarie said they lived only a few blocks from the hospital and she insisted on my having a meal with them."

"But, Daddy, how did she know you after all these years?" I asked.

"Well honey, it turns out her husband asked that same question and do you know what her answer was" he said, looking at me as if to receive an answer. I shook my head in the no position.

"John Ferrell, I told Frank I'd know you anywhere. Why, you'd have on your Sunday suit. White shirt, tie, and floor-shiny shoes. And, furthermore, you'd have your right hand in your right pant pocket. And sure enough, you did."

"Honey," spoke Daddy, "SallyMarie looks the same as I remember her looking. And, although she's lived there all these years, she hasn't forgotten how to cook 'southern style'. She served country ham, red-eyed gravy, homemade biscuits, cream potatoes, snap beans, and corn. Had tea for drinking and good ol' apple pie for dessert. Knowing I was a diabetic, she substituted a sugar ingredient with a home recipe using molasses that originated from her grandmother's generation. It was good to see her and meet her husband. They have a very lovely home and their neighbors are so friendly. Said that snow falls nearly every day."

It wasn't long before all of Daddy's treatments were administered and even his follow-ups with Dr. Ashley panned out just fine.

Yes, indeed, a miracle took place on that cool windy day back in March of '84. Daddy was definitely healed by a sheltering touch from Heaven. The cancer that tried to rage inside his body never did recur.

20

Quicksand

THINGS SEEMED TO be well-balanced at home in June of 1984. Daddy's Rochester trips turned out successful, Mama's angina attacks were finally brought under control with a higher dose of Cardizem, and my trip to Cincinnati was a life-long treasure. *Oh Jesus, what a wonderful time this is. How I do look forward to our family trips to the lake, the beach, and especially the upcoming trip to Florida to visit Henry George and Henrrietta and all their flock.*

I turned over, snuggling down under the top sheet and drifting back into a comfortable position. All of a sudden, a spiritual section from the Bible began to reveal itself. Coming into instant focus were bright golden letters that read, *Psalm One Hundred and Fifty.* I remember not wanting to rise at that particular moment. I began twirling it over and over as I tried very hard *not* to forget while in this relaxed slumber. *What is it Jesus? What are You . . .* Coming to my senses, I jumped out of bed and ran down the hallway toward the den. Mama was sitting in her little nook on the right side of the beige couch. Her feet were propped up as usual and she was still in her gown. She was enjoying her morning coffee, Coka-a-Cola and cigarette.

"You'll never guess what I just dreamed."

"Good morning to you, too. What, Shug?"

"Uh, I'm sorry, good morning. But, anyway, I dreamed I was to read *Psalm One Hundred and Fifty.* Mama, does Psalms even have one hundred and fifty chapters?"

"Chapters? Now Shug, where's your head this morning? You know good'n well that the book of Psalms represents songs — poetry composed for setting to music."

"Huh? I don't understand what you're saying, Mama."

"Well, let me put it this way. The book of Psalms was and is still used like devotion. I believe most of them were written by David and represent the true religious people in Israel. You know Shug, in essence, everyone touches upon every experience and hope of man and describes many phases of the Hebrew history and even of God's providence."

Gee, Lord, Mama really knows her Bible. As thoughts of amazement rushed through my mind, "Oh, Mom, you know what I mean. But, really now, are there one hundred and fifty Psalms?" She continued, looking over her plastic frames at me with those hazel green eyes. "Well, anyway, Mama, where's the Bible Aunt Louise gave you? Let's look it up and see."

"Gee, that dream must've been a humdinger for you to be interested in the Bible *this* early in the morning." I ignored her remarks, although aware she knew that I still hadn't been that involved in church in quite some time. She then lowered her feet to the floor, put her cigarette in the ashtray, reached down, and got the Bible from under the wooden coffee table in front of the couch.

"Here, Shug."

I fumbled to open the worn pages. Exhaling a draw of smoke, Mama spoke in a calm voice, "Here, let me have it. You're so nervous you might tear those thin pages and besides, you have no idea where to look." I looked up at her with puzzled concern.

"Once I find the Scriptures you mentioned, I'll give it to you so you can read it. Then we'll try and figure out what Jesus is saying to you."

"I've never dreamed about the Bible before, Mama . . . what do you think this means? I'm still going to church — well, not like I should be going, but I'm going just the same."

"Uh huh!" she murmured while fanning the worn pages with her right hand.

Sitting there anxiously waiting for Mama to find the verses, I didn't bother to make any more excuses. After all, Mama and Daddy had both read the Bible several times and knew more than I ever would.

Finally, she found the Scripture passage and handed it to me to read. As I began, I felt as though a thick wall was standing between His words and my mind.

"Shug? What does it say?"

"*Praise ye the Lord, Praise God in his sanctuary: praise him in the firmament of his power.*"

Mama heard God's words and began telling me that I was to praise Jesus in all that I did, really emphasizing the "*ALL*" part. It was only six short verses, but, though Mama and I were both hearing the word, I wasn't understanding His message.

"But, Mama, *I am* praising God. I'm saying my prayers, I'm saying God bless you when somebody sneezes, *I* say amen when Daddy says the blessings, I'm going to church when I'm not working — well, most of the time anyway. It ain't *my* fault my job requires me to work some on Sundays. At least its close to home and I can help you with Daddy and Tracey. And, of course, I feel like I need a day every now and then just to rest and enjoy life with you and Daddy. Those Sundays I have off (when I'm not in church) we're either visiting up home, going down to the lake, or at the beach in the spring and summer. The rest of the time I'm in church and doing what I can.

"Shug, you don't have to convince me of your activities; it's Jesus who is telling you to give Him more credit." I knew in my heart that Mama was right. The thing was, Mama was *always right. I*, seemingly, was always wrong.

In the following two years, the sign of the beast kept creeping up, becoming more and more evident. I knew, not only from that dreadful movie but also in my heart, that this was an evil sign. I would catch myself reminiscing about that movie I had watched, all alone, back in the late seventies. I actually saw those numbers as they were engraved in the crown of that child's head.

I began searching for ways to control its powers. I stumbled upon a cross sign. The inscription read, "Hold your first index fingers up so they will be between you and the sign of the beast. Make a cross and repeat this passage of Scripture, "*Get thee hence, Satan; for it is written. Thou shalt worship the Lord thy God, and him only shalt thou serve*," (Matthew 4:10).

At work, at home, and at the grocery store the sign would appear. Driving to work, the odometer would read this figure. When calculating checks, this number would appear. Every now and then, Mama would tell me that I would have a fit if my records would balance like hers and Daddy's with this number in print. But, for some odd reason, it didn't seem to bother them at all. I felt like a human magnet as the sign was constantly drawn in my direction.

Dear Lord, why is this happening? What can I do to stop it? Please, dear Jesus, help me to fight this sign of the beast. Show me what to do. Dear Lord, am I going crazy? Everywhere I went, every way I turned, that sign was always present.

I even got to the point that I dreaded going to work. I dealt with lots of figures daily, and it got to where that sign was literally everywhere. Change from the break room. Monthly tallying of the production of equipment. Serial numbers of the equipment. Weight measures of product line inventories. Even something as simple as registering the count for the monthly copy machine. This figure was taking over my life.

Once down at the lake I caught myself telling everyone I talked to about the sign of the beast. Some folks said they'd never heard of such a thing. Realizing the impact of this, I made a decision to have a Bible handy with each passage marked. I could then show these people where to go to find and study and ask God to protect them against the evil one.

It got so bad that Aunt Sally told me I was possessed.

"Me? Possessed? Maybe I am, but I'm just trying to warn you and anyone who will listen about that sign of the beast. That we all need to be careful and put on God's armor of protection anytime this sign is seen."

"Well, Jeannette, just give this a thought. You might be disturbing some folks, and they just don't know how to tell you to . . . to put it bluntly, bug off. What you are saying is true, but some folks just don't want it pushed down their throats, " Aunt Sally advised.

"Whaddya mean pushed down their throats? Hey, I bring the matter to their attention, and they're the ones who insist on my sharing more information with 'em."

"Yes, *you* do bring it up and *you* are the one and only one who brings it up."

"So?"

"So? As I just said, bug off."

"But . . ."

"Shug?" Mama was shaking her head. I quickly dropped the subject, then whispered to Jesus, "Please forgive Aunt Sally 'cause you and I both know she really doesn't understand the importance of my attitude." From then on, this subject was not mentioned. We would talk about the weather, the garden, happenings of their world or ours, but the sign of the beast was never mentioned around her again.

Although this subject wasn't a topic of conversation at the lake, it was still very prominent in my life. I even tried not to see the sign, and its presence did seem to subside somewhat at one point. However, another movie, the Exorcist, appeared on television and — wham! There it was in full force once again, penetrating my mind with doubts of my loved ones as I began to turn my ears back toward the co-workers.

Being responsible for thirty-eight percent of the paperwork in that department, I was beginning to be exposed to that sign again, fifteen to thirty-five times a day. At one point I counted one hundred and twenty-three times. Oh, I was really on a roll. I told directors, staff members, employees, everyone about the sign. I informed everyone who would listen. As my soul churned with deep urgency, I couldn't resist the need to tell all about this evil sign. The power it had on me was so strong. I lived it! Every waking moment my mind was engulfed with the sign of the beast, those numbers that were stamped in that child's head. I tried, but to no avail. I couldn't shake its strength of raging fingers surrounding my mind, as though a brown recluse spider was making a web of torment and draining my cells for his pleasure!

Mama and Daddy were very worried. I could tell they were getting nervous when I'd make just a simple comment about that sign. At work, some made a point of coming on their breaks to hear more about it and about the Scriptures where the sign of the beast could be found. After five months or so, I learned I had to be discreet about the subject. What began as only a dip in the road was becoming deeper than a grave. It was like quicksand. Only it got bigger and bigger. I even caught myself saying, "I just don't understand why that sign of the beast keeps following me around."

After several months, I began noticing that people were avoiding me. *Well Jesus, maybe I've been too critical in this matter. After all, I'm just delivering the message, it's really up to You to handle the rest. I think I'll put in for some time off. Besides, it's a good time to visit the mountains and some kinfolk and just have some family time. Maybe You can help me put this matter into a better perspective so I won't offend folks. Besides, Jesus, I once was a very shy person and now look at me. When I start talking about that passage in the Bible, folks listen. And, Jesus, it actually feels good to be noticed. Daddy doesn't say much, but Mama's all the time saying I'd better be careful. Yes, maybe it's time for some rest and relaxation, and just maybe You'll be able to get through this thick head of mine how to handle this sign of the beast so I can begin to understand things.*

* * *

"Oh, how much we enjoyed that vacation, Shug. Thank you for asking us to go with you."

"Mom? I didn't think I had to ask. We're family and families don't have to ask. I've just always assumed that we'd always do things together. In fact, I can't stand the thought of ever doing anything without you both. I love you."

"Shug, you're so sweet and kind-hearted. Your daddy and I pray every day for God to keep you safe and in His arms of love."

Thinking this vacation would help settle my attitude toward the workload proved to be unsuccessful. When I returned to work the following Wednesday, the situation had gotten even worse. Tempers were flying, work was behind, and everybody was near to just throwing up their hands and walking out. *Dear Lord? What in the world is happening around here?*

I stepped into Bill's office. "Jeannette, things have turned upside down since you've been on vacation. You couldn't have left at a better time. At least you weren't here when the news came about laying people off. Last Friday, twenty-one people arrived expecting to work. Instead they got a slip of paper saying they no longer had jobs."

"Twenty-one people? Just like that? How cruel. Sir, were any assigned from our department?"

"Fourteen of 'em. Here's a list. They're really gonna be missed."

"Whose gonna fill their positions?"

"Us!"

"*Huh?*"

"You're looking at 'em. Having to downsize is what the higher-ups are saying. I was informed about this a month ago but wasn't allowed to say anything. I know you have been working overtime a lot and I knew this was coming, 'cept I didn't know it would be this soon."

"But why didn't you contact me while I was gone, knowing you needed me to help in this chaotic situation?"

"You know why. I've seen your work, and I know your concerns about your parents' health. And, well, knowing we'll be working longer hours than before, I felt this would be a good time for you to recuperate. And I must've been right on target 'cause you look wonderful."

As I turned to leave his office, he added, "Jeannette, before you go, I haven't heard you mention the evil one. Has something changed?"

"Uh, well, no, sir. Not with my feelings anyway. While I was away, I had a down to earth conversation with myself and decided not to mention it unless someone sincerely asked. I believe I've gotten the word out everywhere, so I plan not to broadcast it anymore. That's something that is entirely up to the individual, and besides, that's what we have preachers for."

"Jeannette?"

"Yes?"

"Thank you."

"Well, vacation is over and time to get back down to some serious work. Looks like we're in for the long haul, right Bill?" We smiled, hugged, and left for our departments. Silently I prayed, *Jesus, thank*

*You for Bill and for all who have listened and maybe, one day, well . . .
You know . . .*

* * *

On September twenty-first in 1986, upon awakening I saw a Bible opened to the book of Isaiah, Chapter 10 in plain view. I remember thinking, *I need to remember this and tell Mama so she can help me to . . . or maybe not,* a tiny voice in the back of my mind whispered. *She'll just get after me about not attending church and with all the problems I have at work, I just don't feel I can take one more criticizing word. I'll get my Bible and read it in a minute and try to figure out what Jesus is telling me. Right now I've gotta get dressed and figure out what to do for Mama and Daddy's upcoming anniversary.*

That dream kept popping up throughout the day. At breakfast. While cutting grass. Even that night after supper. *Um, Jesus, You must really want me to read it with all these reminders everywhere. I'll read it before going to bed.*

"Daddy, you'd better wake up. You won't sleep a wink tonight," Mama hollered.

"Leave me alone. I was only resting my eyes."

"Sure Papa, we saw your head bobbing as you 'rested your eyes.'"

"Well, we've got inventory tomorrow, and I'll be leaving home around four-thirty in the morning. So I think I'll go and get ready for bed. I'll come back and say my goodnights before lying down." Exiting the den, I reached my hand around the corner of the kitchen and grabbed a biscuit left from supper.

"Jeannette? You better not've gotten the last one," Mama spoke sharply. "I was planning on eat'n one before going to bed too," Daddy chimed in.

"Don't you two worry, there's plenty left."

"I must say, Mama, you make some of the best."

"No, I don't either. Grandma Ferrell made the best I've ever eat'n."

"Well, Mama, I'll admit that one. Your vegetables and meats are cooked just like Grandma use to cook. But, your biscuits, well . . . they're soft and all but . . ."

"Watch it, Papa." Laughing, she continued, "I know you're right. I just can't get the lard, the flour, and the buttermilk just right as Grandma Ferrell could. Don't worry, you ain't hurt my feelings at all. Jeannette, leave him at least one, okay?"

"Mom, I only took one."

A short while later Daddy's voice blared like an alarm from the kitchen. "Jeannette!?"

"Uh, oh!" Hurriedly putting my pajamas on and grabbing a robe from the closet, I rushed down the hall to the den.

"I thought you said you just got one biscuit?"

"I did only get one. What's the matter?"

"There ain't none here."

"Papa? Are you sure?" Mama asked, getting up and coming toward us. "I know there were at least five left from supper. Where'd they go?"

I just happened to catch a glimpse of a snicker. "Daddy! What are you holding behind your back? Let me see *both* of your hands."

"Who, me? I don't know what you're talking about. Look. See for yourself. There's no biscuits left in the bowl. See?"

"John? Let us see *a-l-l* of your hands."

"Well, I ain't got but two, whaddya mean see all of 'em?" Though Daddy didn't usually have the breath to hustle, this once he found some extra breaths and flew back to the den, laughing as he went.

"*Joh-n?*" Mama called. Before Daddy could sit down, a biscuit fell on the carpet beside his chair.

"Ah, Mama, he's just pickin' with you and me."

"Papa? If five were left from supper and Jeannette only got one biscuit and you got three, then what happened to the other biscuit?"

"Other biscuit?" Daddy questioned as they both looked at me.

"*Uh, oh!*"

"Jeannette? Whaddya mean, 'uh, oh?'"

"Well, while y'all were watching those game shows, I just, uh, well . . . "

"Shug? You don't have to say a word. It's written all over your face."

Kneeling in prayer before lying down, *Jesus, what ever is going on with me, please bless Mama and Daddy with your hugs from above. And, Lord, thank You for this, our happy Christian home.*

21

The Mass

ON OUR RETURN from visiting friends in eastern Maryland, Mama said, "Papa, I'm still experiencing some discomforts in my lower stomach. I didn't say anything because I knew just how much you and Jeannette were looking forward to this trip."

"Mama, you know your health is much more important. We could've planned this trip another time. Maybe you ought to call in the morning and see if Dr. Burney can see you."

"Well, we'll see. If I'm still feeling the heaviness, I will."

Mama's morning routine helped make up her mind. However, she couldn't get an appointment until Tuesday at ten o'clock. Overhearing her confirm the appointment, I offered to take her.

"Thank you, Shug, but you go ahead and work, your daddy can take me."

"Well, I'll call you around one then, okay?" Work couldn't've been heavier that Tuesday morning. Before I knew it, one o'clock had arrived. Mama answered right away. "Shug? Go ahead and work all day. We'll discuss the findings when you get home."

"Discuss it? Whaddya ya mean discuss it when I get home? What's wrong mama?"

"I'm fine, Shug. Don't worry none. We'll talk about it tonight."

I rushed home. Sam and Knottroot greeted me at the car door with their tails just a wagging.

"Hi, honey."

"Hi, Dad."

"Mom? I've been worried sick since we talked. What did Dr. Burney tell you? Please, don't keep me in suspense any longer, please tell me."

"Well, Shug, after the examination, of course some blood was taken for testing. Then, he sent me over to the hospital for a lower body x-ray."

"What? Then something is wrong?"

"Let's don't count our chickens before they hatch just yet. They're just testing your mother's blood and taking a few x-rays. We won't know anything until tomorrow, honey. You go on to work and when we find out something, we'll call you."

"You promise?" They nodded.

The next day dragged. I might as well've taken the day off cause my mind surely wasn't on working. *Oh, Jesus. Please, let Mama be okay,* I prayed. Around three-thirty, the expected call came.

"Jeannette?"

"Hi, Dad."

"Uh, honey?"

"What is it, Daddy? Where's Mama? Is she alright?"

"Yes. Your mother is fine — but, well . . ."

"Daddy? What is it?"

"Honey?" There was a quiver in his sweetness. "Dr. Burney admitted Drusilla to the hospital today. She begged and begged to go back home to get her things, but he just wouldn't hear of it. Said that the hospital staff would have her a nice pretty gown just her size. Anyway, around one o'clock Dr. Burney met us here with the x-rays."

A big lump swelled up in my throat as Daddy coughed a time or two and cleared his throat. "The x-rays revealed a huge mass in the bottom part of your mother's stomach."

"Daddy! I'm leaving right now. I'll be there in thirty minutes."

"No. You go ahead and finish today's work. Tell your boss there's a family emergency, and ask for tomorrow off."

"Tomorrow?"

"Yes. Dr. Burney's already called a Dr. Presscault, a fine surgeon, and has scheduled the surgery for in the morning."

"S-u-r-g-e-r-y? Tomorrow morning? Why so quick?"

"Dr. Burney told us that if they didn't act immediately . . . Well, let's not talk about that right now."

"Don't worry about my work. I'll get Jacqueline to cover for me. When you and Mama are involved nothing else matters. Nothing and no one."

"Honey? Dr. Burney asked us to think it over and get back with him. But, with the urgency in his voice and the proof of the x-rays — we didn't mean to leave you out, but we went ahead and gave him our approval."

"Please don't feel bad, Daddy. Besides, Jesus is going to take care of Mama."

"Yes honey, we've already said a prayer and I feel in my heart that she's going to be just fine. Honey, we have such a wonderful daughter. We love you so much."

"I love you too, and tell Mama I'll see you both after work and, if she's up to it, maybe she'll feel like calling me after awhile."

That was another long day at the office. I didn't think closing time would ever arrive. I rushed home to gather some of Mama's bedclothes and Daddy's and her medicines. Answered a few calls, managing to get to the hospital just after visiting hours. As I entered Mama's room, I saw Daddy sitting in a cold, hard recliner, holding Mama's hand.

"Shish" she whispered, holding a finger up to her mouth as I walked in. She looked extremely pale against those white sheets. I saw her paleness but didn't see what *I* should've been seeing — reality *was not* a part of my world. I caught myself many times in a make-believe world where no one mattered but my parents . . . one in which there was no sickness, no heartache, no suffering, and no pain. Not in my make-believe world.

"Hi Shug," Mama said in a low whisper so as not to wake Daddy. I leaned over and gave her a light kiss on the cheek.

"Mama?"

"Shug? Don't you worry none, ya hear?" She whispered with eyes full of tears.

"But Mama. The trip."

"Shish. I'm gonna be just fine. Trust in Jesus, Shug. Just put your trust in Jesus."

"I hear y'all talking. I'm not asleep. I'm just resting my eyes," Daddy mumbled.

"Mom? I'm staying the night. Daddy can go home and get a good night's sleep. He's been here with you all day and I know he needs some rest, but I'm staying."

"What about work?"

"I've got that covered. I only have one more day this week. Jacqueline's working for me tomorrow so I won't miss any pay."

"Oh Shug, we have such a wonderful daughter."

"Well you both needn't worry. Dr. Burney said he'd leave word at the desk for the both of you to stay with me as long as I need. He said it'd be nice if all families were close like ours. Shug, I'll admit that trip over the weekend was kind of painful. I knew something wasn't quite right, but I just didn't know the seriousness of it."

"Drusilla?" Dr. Burney popped in the doorway. "For sure, the weekend trip didn't do you any good. But, it could've just saved your life."

"Whaddya mean?" Daddy asked.

"It could've been months before this thing would've come to a head and by then it probably would've been too late. However, we're still not out of the woods. I've seen masses before, but not quite like this one and that's why I went ahead and acted on it so quickly," he said while holding a metal clipboard that had Mama's medical papers attached to it. He got up from the chair and said, "Unless you have any more questions or comments, I'll see you bright and early. We'll all go with you to the operating room." He assured Mama, patting her on the hand. "I'll leave word for the nurse to give you a mild sedative to help you rest. Now don't worry, ya hear? Everything's gonna be just fine." Daddy rose, shook Dr. Burney's hand and thanked him for coming. I got some blankets and a cot for Daddy to lie down on and took that hard, cold recliner for myself.

"Daddy, do you have enough medicine with you?"

"Yes, honey, Mama made sure of that before we left home."

"You didn't by any chance have a premonition about this, did you Mama? Getting Daddy's medicines?"

"And I've got mine too," She said back. "Why, I ain't paying the pharmacy here, when they charge three dollars for just coated aspirin!"

"That explains it."

"Whaddya mean, Shug?"

"I stopped by the house before coming. By the way, here are two gowns for you when you're able to put 'em on, and here's your mouthwash and toothpaste, too. I also brought your comb and hairbrush, but I couldn't find all of your medicine. Daddy's either. I didn't know if I should get some refilled or not."

"Heaven's no. Like I just said, we have a mighty fine daughter. You're all the time thinking of others instead of yourself."

"I love you and Daddy so much. You're all I have, and I'd go to the ends of the world for you."

"We know you would. We love you too — and honey?"

"Hmm?"

"Thank you for coming and for caring."

"Hush ya fussing now before I start messing up my face too." We hugged and began to settle down for the night.

I'd reached a point in time when I actually couldn't express any emotions. The divorce; my mind believing I didn't fit in; everywhere the sign of the beast — it all played a number on me. I'd already begun pulling away from just a simple touch. Every now and then Mama would ask if I was too good to be touched. The truth was, I didn't feel worthy. I had broken God's word by destroying a marriage. I felt looked down on and disgraced when I was around anybody other than my parents. I felt ashamed I couldn't warn people about that sign of the beast without causing a riot amongst my aunts and uncles. I began sliding into a self-contained mind-boggling supernatural state, pretending no one in the world mattered except Mama, Daddy and me. Taking care of them was all that really mattered. I felt like such a failure to all except them and yet I couldn't be touched, even by the ones I loved the most in the world. I wasn't good enough to be touched or loved.

Daddy and I got as much sleep as anyone could that night. Bright and early, as the sun was peeping over the trees, the anesthesiologist came and gave Mama a stronger sedative. About twenty minutes later, the nurses came in to prep her and looked toward Daddy and said they thought it'd be good for us to go and freshen up a bit. Just as we returned, Dr. Burney popped in.

"You ready to get this show on the road, Drusilla?"

Mama's eyelids popped up and down as she tried to focus. "Well, whatever you say, I guess I'm as ready as . . ." Just then two orderlies arrived. One walked around to the head of the bed and the other placed himself at the foot of Mama's bed and they literally rolled her, bed and all, out of her room and down the hall to the elevators. Dr. Burney met us near the operating room. Grinning from ear to ear, the hall lights flickering upon his shiny red hair, he said, "John, don't you and Jeannette worry none about Drusilla's heart condition. We've got the finest cardiologist on hand, and she's gonna be just fine once that mass is removed. It won't be no time till she's up telling you what to do."

Daddy leaned down and whispered softly to Mama, "I love you, Sweetie. Don't worry none now, ya hear? Jesus is going to take care of my Doll Baby, and I'll see you after while."

"Papa, I love you to and if it's God's will . . ." Mama returned in a sluggish whisper.

"Sugar? Shish! Don't talk that way. Everything's going to be just fine, just like Dr. Burney said, and I'll see you soon."

"You bet your life I'm gonna be just fine, Papa. The Lord ain't through with me yet. He wants me to stick around to make sure you behave yourself," she retorted as tears welled in Mama's eyes.

Daddy's unshaven face beamed with love. "That's my girl. I'm a handful, and I need you to keep me straight."

"C'mon, Drusilla. Let's get that thing out of you so you can get back to keep'n us all straight."

Mama looked at me as straight as she could with her drowsy hazel eyes. "Shug, you take care of your daddy. Don't let him drink too many caffeinated drinks, okay?"

"Okay. We'll be right here waiting for your return, Mama." I mustered as much energy as I could as it was so hard to show any emotion, "Mom? I love you." I bent down, gently lying upon Mama's chest for a moment, then raised up and kissed her on her cheek.

Then the orderly pulled her bed into the huge operating room. As the doors began to close, Daddy and I heard Mama's fading voice: "I'll see you both after a while!"

We looked at the clock every five or ten minutes. An hour passed, then two. Finally, the surgery was over and Mama was in recovery. In another hour we could see her. I overheard Daddy pray, "Thank you for bringing Drusilla back to us, Jesus, and for your gracious love."

Why is he praying this way? Of course Mama's gonna be okay. He must've thought she wasn't gonna make it or something. Even I know better than that. Then, this inner voice spoke saying, "All you need is me and your parents." My mind raced. *"Jesus, is that You?"*

"Mr. Ferrell? You and your daughter may go in, just for a few minutes, to see your wife." Oh, the tubes that were coming out of Mama seemed like what you would see on a movie! She was so fragile looking and groggy. Her words were so sluggish they were hard to understand. Then, when she realized it was Daddy and me, Mama broke into a smile.

"Is it over?"

"Yes honey, it's all over and you're gonna be just fine. The good Lord looked after you, and Dr. Burney said all looked really good. He said it'd be a couple of days before we'd know for sure, but he didn't think it was cancerous." Mama began thanking Jesus as she and Daddy shed a few embracing tears. When I sensed the evil one not looking, I reached down and squeezed Mama's left hand. To my amazement, she squeezed back.

Still letting myself listen to some co-workers who kept insisting I should be on my own and not living at home, I began to get confused. Some ugly thoughts slowly filtered my mind. It seemed that each time my co-workers and I were together, they would make it a point to continue delivering penetrating resentful remarks. Well, it didn't take long until I again began thinking that they could be right. I'd noticed on several occasions that whenever Mama and I began a conversation, we'd almost always end up in a argument. *Dear Lord*, I'd pray silently. *Is Mama really my enemy? But, Lord Jesus, I love her so much how can this be? They are wrong, aren't they, Jesus?*

A few days later, with a spring in his step, Dr. Burney popped around the corner of Mama's hospital room, "Drusilla? Are you ready to go home?"

"Home?"

"Yes, John. All tests came back with negative results, and I'm happy to give Drusilla a clean bill of health. However," he said, looking at Mama with his bright blue eyes, "Call Monday and set up an appointment. I want to see you in two weeks."

We all hugged and praised God! I excused myself and left the lovebirds alone for a while, finding myself at a place that hadn't been familiar for quite some time — the hospital's chapel. I kneeled and prayed and thanked Him for Mama's good news. *And, Jesus? Help me not to be ashamed to touch. And, Lord? Why did I insist on taking this trip?* I asked as the blinders brought guilt and shame to the surface from deep within my soul

22

Longing for Adventure

*G*RANDDADDY FERRELL'S FAMILY hadn't met for a reunion since the mid seventies. Like a lot of families, we'd promised to get together. Then one day Mama happened to mention how often her family met and wondered why the Ferrell family didn't get together more often. "Papa, you all live within ten miles of each other. Wouldn't it be great to have a reunion?"

"Daddy, I don't even remember attending those park reunions over in Raleigh. My only memory is through the black and white photographs I found in Grandma Ferrell's shoeboxes. Please, Daddy, let's get everybody together, just once more. Whaddya say?"

The next day I invited Cousin Leslie and her parents over for a family discussion. My, how Daddy did favor Uncle Thomas even though there was a twelve-year difference in their ages. Anyway, it didn't take long before excitement was in the air as our parents left most of the decision making up to Leslie and me.

"Aunt Drusilla, if I may ask, what are we going to eat and where are we going to have it?"

The community clubhouse was suggested, then Daddy spoke up. "What's wrong with having it right here? What better place to have a reunion than near the place where we all grew up, and this is as close to the original home place as we can get."

I suggested that we do BBQ chicken with homemade potato salad and baked beans. Leslie countered with the idea of having the food catered.

"Leslie, I like that catering idea. It's simple and easy. When we call the families and ask 'em to come, we'll tell 'em to pay for their own part. Do you have any idea of the cost? Have you ever done this before?"

"Uh, no Aunt Drusilla. But where I used to work they had things like this every once in a while. Tell you what, I'll check with them and we'll go from there."

"Sounds good to me."

"Leslie? Don't wait too long. It's only three and a half weeks till June, and although we may have the food catered, there's still lots of work to be done."

"Ok, Uncle John, I'll get a move on it right away."

Sure enough, Monday night Leslie and Aunt Molly came over with the cost of full catering service. During the discussion Leslie suggested, "We can save a lot of money if we let the caterers put the food in throw-away containers and also by picking it up ourselves."

What an exciting time it was turning out to be. I just knew, down deep in my soul, this was gonna be the best ever. Mama and I scurried around cleaning the house from top to bottom. We went upstairs and brought all extra lawn chairs down, cleaning them and even waxing the side porch tile. Daddy's job was to make sure the grass was cut and all the shrubbery was properly trimmed.

"I sure hope it don't rain."

"Daddy, don't you dare even as much as think such a thing. You'll put a jinx on it just as sure as heck."

"There isn't no such thing as jinxes, Jeannette. You know better than that."

"By the way, before I closed the shop, Thomas called and offered to bring over some of his hand-made wooden tables. Said that we could use 'em to put the food on, and he'd also bring some of their lawn chairs too."

"Dad? Are we using your horse benches?"

"Yes. And, thank you for reminding me. I need to sweep the shelvings off of 'em, too."

As Daddy headed toward the shop, Mama went back into the house to check the beans on the stove. Leslie helped Aunt Molly into the car, turned, and continued talking to me. "Jeannette, after speaking to BettiLou on the phone, I found out that she's planning on visiting Vegas after the reunion. What do you think about us driving her out there?"

"Do what? Did I hear you correctly? You want us to drive her to Las Vegas, Nevada? Are you serious?"

"It'll be fun, Jeannette. That is, if you want to go, and if it's okay with Uncle John and Aunt Drusilla."

"But Leslie, what about your parents? Uncle Thomas and Aunt Molly aren't in the best of health either."

"You're right. I'll just be sure that Daddy has all his medicine up to date and that Mother will be able to take care of him while I'm gone. Besides, Rufus will be there at night if they need an extra hand. Didn't you say you had some extra time coming from work?"

"Leslie, I know you need a rest after taking care of your parents and all. But, to go cross-country to get it? You know the farthest I've ever been was to Nashville with Charles and the children between Christmas and New Year's."

"See, Jeannette? C'mon, it'll be fun — the three of us traveling across country together. Well, if you don't want to go . . ."

"Don't want to go? Are you out of your mind? Of course I want to go, it's just . . ."

"Yeah, I know. You don't want to leave Uncle John and Aunt Drusilla, right? It'll do you all good to be away from each other for a few days."

"Fourteen days isn't just a few. I'll have to think about it and talk it over with Mama and Daddy. We'll see. I'll talk to you later. Thanks for coming over and helping us today."

"Yes, you're welcome. My, look at the time. I've gotta get going. George and Sandra are coming in tonight, and I'd better be there when they arrive."

"Don't forget now."

"Don't worry, I won't forget." After supper, I mentioned Leslie's idea to Mama and Daddy.

"Shug. I think that would be wonderful."

"Huh?"

"Yes. Me too, honey. You'll enjoy that a lot."

"But, Daddy. I was planning on us going out together one day. It'll be so different without you and Mama. I don't know about this."

"Shug, call Leslie right now and accept. You'll have a wonderful time."

That wasn't at all what I'd expected. *Dear Lord, Mama, and Dad seem to be happy about this trip for me and Leslie and BettiLou. I didn't expect to hear them approve, and so quickly, too.*

Before I knew it, I was dialing Leslie's number. The cross-country trip was on — what an exciting and scary time. This would be the *first time* I'd ever been away from home on a vacation without my parents. *Oh Dear Lord, it's gonna be so different. But then again, Lord, this is my opportunity for doing things I've never done before and seeing things I've only read about. Jesus, please be with us as we travel such a long distance away from home.*

Finally, the big day for the reunion arrived. We had low humidity with a few soft, white clouds overhead gracefully floating just beneath the deep blue Carolina skies. The entire Ferrell clan enjoyed themselves immensely. They continually commented on feeling our loved one's presence and how pretty Daddy had landscaped the grounds of the charming old home place.

The next day or two, I drove BettiLou and her brother Reddrick (Red) up country to visit some of their family near Rolesville.

Later that evening, they said they could hardly believe all the changes that had taken place in a span of thirty years, and how nice the couple was to let them go inside of their former home. The old high school they had attended was now being used for senior citizen apartments, and the library had been torn down to make room for a shopping center and parking lot.

My, how quickly this week did fly. It was time for our cross-country trip, and Leslie was in the driveway waiting for BettiLou and me at six A.M. We were up, but we weren't moving too swiftly.

23

Hanging Loose

O THIS VERY day, I don't know how Leslie got that humongous suitcase of BettiLou's in the back seat of her car. The trunk was full of our suitcases and small bags of snacks. The back seat was three-fourths full with BettiLou's suitcase. The back floorboard was full of video cameras tapes and a small cooler of ice and drinks. If that wasn't enough, we had Leslie's two cats to contend with for about two hundred miles. Leslie was taking Crystal and Rosemarie down to Columbia, South Carolina where George and Sandra lived.

Not knowing any shortcuts, we drove all the way up to Asheville, North Carolina, to get back onto Interstate 40. Arriving around three-thirty, we filled the car with gas. Pulling away from the tanks BettiLou popped up, saying, "Go West, young girls. Go West."

Almost five hours later we were just east of Nashville, Tennessee.

I'd picked up some drinks before leaving home, to help cut expenses. Thought I got a deal at eighty-nine cents for a two-liter soft drink. However, once we stopped and got settled in our hotel room, we decided to go shopping across the way. BettiLou had spotted the Wal-Mart as we drove into the parking lot. To my surprise, the drinks there were selling for fifty-nine cents with a limit of four. BettiLou and Leslie had a good laugh at my expense.

"Ah, don't feel so bad, Jeannette, we didn't know it either," BettiLou said about the incredible bargain.

After browsing a little, we headed back to the hotel. Once settled in and just before going to bed, I decided to call home. "What about you two? Are y'all calling home tonight?"

"Not me. I told Mother I wouldn't call until we got to Vegas."

"Nah, me either. My kids know when I'm headed for Vegas they won't hear from me until I get home — to show 'em what all I won," BettiLou said laughingly as she headed for the shower.

"Well, I promised I'd call every night, but Daddy told me not to promise cause I might not be able to get to a phone."

"Uncle John's a wise man, Jeannette. He's been off before and knows what he's talking about. Since you told 'em you'd call, better go ahead and do it before it gets any later."

I was happy to call. I missed Mama and Daddy. I was scared, but didn't want my cousins to know it.

* * *

R-I-N-G! R-I-N-G! R-I-N-G!

"Git up! Git up! Git up! Time to head toward Vegas," Leslie said with a spring in her voice.

I just wanted to slump down, pull the covers up over my head, and continue snoozing. But, BettiLou pulled all the covers off of me while Leslie dashed a few sprinkles of water in my face. I quickly got up.

"Hey! Y'all just wait . . . Payback is . . . I ain't gonna say it. 'll just catch ya when you're not looking."

We were on the road by seven. Friday morning. The scenery was breathtaking. Tennessee is much like home, with rolling hills, oak, birch, and even pine trees. When we crossed the Mississippi River, the landscape really began to flatten.

"I hope we'll get to see the cattle farm that Rufus and I saw a few years back."

"You've been cross country before, Leslie?"

"Yes. Couple, three years ago. I also hope you'll get to see how they irrigate crops in the mid-central states. The farmers have these long bars that seem to go on for miles, and they have these wheels attached to them that resemble an old wagon wheel except each of 'em have some kinda round wire contraptions. Through tiny holes in these metal strips, water spurts out and the entire contraption rotates while thousands of gallons of water spreads over the land. The best I remember, there were also these funny-looking windmills somewhere between Tennessee and Nevada. There were five or six of 'em, with huge white blades that projected from this really tall pole. They were pointed like a woman's peaked toe shoe and looked like some kind a airplane propeller.

"Jeannette? Whaddya think about this highway?" BettiLou asked.

"I never seen so many eighteen wheelers in my life. I thought back home had a lot of B.J. Hunt trucks, but this has even got that beat. Why, they're everywhere. Bet if you get lost, all you gotta do is pull into a truck stop and ask a B.J. Hunt driver, and they'll get you back on the right road."

"You're very observant."

"Observant ain't got nothing to do with it. All you gotta do is open your eyes. It beats all I've ever seen. Reminds me of the yellow brick road."

"That isn't exactly what I was asking you but you're right about the truckers. Anything else you've noticed?"

"Yes. The countryside is so different from home. Look. You can see for miles and miles — lots of flat land, just like Daddy said it was when he and Mama went to South Dakota a few years back to visit some friends who used to rent from them."

"Jeannette, the best way to view the countryside is to get off the main road and drive through the back roads and farm lands."

"Yes. You're right, BettiLou." The prettiest sight Rufus and I saw was traveling in the heartland of the country. Why, one time we even had to stop in the middle of the road for cattle crossing. It was hot and dusty and we just happened to have some extra water bottles with us. We waited nearly an hour for all those cows to cross. Then we fell in behind a farmer pulling a load of hay. I believe that took us another forty minutes — seems like it anyway — before he turned off down some God-forsaken pig path."

"You know Leslie, I'm really surprised your husband agreed about your taking this trip," spoke BettiLou while reaching for another sip of water.

"Yes Leslie, Rufus almost seemed happy you were going." I spoke with amazement.

"Well," spoke Leslie, "Guess I need to let you girls in on something. You see the company Rufus works with has him traveling a lot. And, knowing our reunion was in the making, he and I talked about it and, whoopla. His traveling and our trip's timing worked out to both our advantages."

Glancing around, here I was scrunched in the back seat, knees up under my chin, camcorder on my right shoulder filming everything in sight to show Mama and Daddy and make copies for the families, too. To my left was BettiLou's huge suitcase, under it was Leslie's sloshing ice chest and under my feet were our pocketbooks, two bags of blank video tapes, and four extra battery backups.

"Aren't y'all hungry yet? I'm crammed in here like sardines in a can. Speaking of which, I'll even eat that — and I don't like sardines — except the way Daddy fixes 'em. He'll open the can, sprinkle some vinegar over 'em, get some saltine crackers, and eat 'em right out of the can. Anything would be good along about now. C'mon, ain't y'all hungry yet?"

They both looked at the clock, then checked their watches and, about the same time, spoke what turned out to be our famous trip sentence: "We left s-o-o-o early that we forgot to eat.

It's nearly two in the afternoon. Let's start looking for a place that has lots of cars. We'll know by that if it's worth stopping. Thanks for reminding us, Jeannette. We've picked up an extra hour. That's why it doesn't look like middle of the afternoon. Let's turn the radio on and check for the correct time."

Finally, we found a place to stop and refresh. Then we rode on till we reached another time zone in the outskirts of Texas near New Mexico. We stopped and spent the second night. I rushed to call Mama and Daddy while my cousins unpacked their things and raced down the sidewalk to find some ice for a cold soda.

Daddy answered. "Honey? Where are you now?"

"Dad, we're about half way cross New Mexico."

"Honey, you're where? Who's driving?"

"Leslie. Why, is something wrong, Dad?"

"Well, let's just put it this way. She ain't loosing no ground. There sure ain't no grass growing under her. Honey? Y'all be careful."

Whispering as low as I could, I said, "Dad, I ain't got nothing to do with it. I'm in the back seat, video'n. BettiLou's in the front seat with her. They're just a talking and driving, and I'm just a riding and filming. Daddy, you wouldn't believe the scenery here. It's absolutely beautiful."

"Hey, Shug. Your daddy has a U.S. map and is following you across country. It's as if we're right there with you."

"I hope one day we all can visit this part of the country together, Mama. I'd love for you to see it, too. Mom, it's so beautiful. Well, it's been a long day and we're bushed."

"I bet you are Shug," Mama said.

"I love you both and I'll talk to you tomorrow sometime. Goodnight."

"Goodnight honey. We love you too and do have fun and be careful, you hear?" I hardly remember lying down on the bed when all of a sudden . . .

R-I-N-G! R-I-N-G! R-I-N-G!

It was still dark when Leslie said we needed to get up, get dressed, and get on the road. "If we wanna get to Vegas by tonight we'd better get a move on."

Slow to rise out of bed, I showered and dressed before BettiLou even turned over. Hearing a snore coming from that area, I grabbed a sock and crammed it in her mouth. That's all it took. She immediately jumped up and screamed at me.

"Why'd'ya think it was me? It's time to rise and shine. You might be pulling that one-armed bandit before the day's over."

"I don't care about that *@%#." Instantly it all came racing back that she was not a morning person. She splashed cold water on her face, brushed her teeth, and gathered her belongings while Leslie and I filled the chest with more ice, refreshed its contents with drinks and emptied the trash bags. Then off we went, into the stillness of the night. After about an hour or so of driving, I noticed a huge light gradually approaching from behind the car. I turned around to see what it possibly could be and . . . "Hey!"

"What is it, Jeannette?"

"Oh! That's the sun coming up."

"N-o-o. You know it's not."

"Yes it is. We didn't stop till twelve, took showers, went to bed at one, and we've been on the road in total darkness for at least two hours or more. That means we only got about two hours of sleep. My body won't ever be the same again."

Our adrenaline was flying high. We laughed and carried on and had a wonderful time as cousins. *Thank You, Jesus, for letting this trip be possible and for the wonderful Ferrell reunion,* I silently prayed. Sitting back and enjoying time itself, BettiLou told about her family and shared some childhood memories, peppering in some funny stories along the way.

Every now and then Leslie would cite a tale about her work and some stunts that different people had pulled over the years. "What about you, Jeannette. Got anything funny to tell?"

"No. Except the time Henry and Katie were involved in the Junebug flight and when Henry put a big, juicy wiggle worm in his pants pocket and . . . " Just then I noticed they weren't paying me any attention and had gone back to their own conversations of the past.

While we drove through this area I'd never seen before, I let my mind drift.

Thank You, Jesus, for their letting me tag along and for helping me to grow in my spirit. Maybe this trip will help my mind to the point where I can do more for Mama and Daddy when I return. Thank You for providing this time away.

I just don't understand. All that workload I'm under with the layoffs, and some of my co-workers still not understanding my being comfortable living with my parents. Then I get home and feel loved, and yet — feel empty too, but I don't know why. Sometimes I don't even want to go home after work 'cause, Lord, I don't know why. Dear Jesus, help me to understand, please. I'm sure it's my fault. Mama's always right and I'm always wrong. It's just that I feel like I'm being smothered at times. Lord, why do I feel this way?

Then there's Daddy, Jesus. He's so wise, and yet, he too is on my case at times. Oh Lord, please, I don't mean to sound like I'm complaining. I love them so much. Please, don't let nothing happen to them for a long, long time. Lord? It'd be nice if You would take us all home together. I don't think I could survive without 'em, Lord. Life wouldn't be worth living. I love 'em so much.

Jesus? I don't know why I'll sit in the car at work thinking I should be at home. Then, I'll sit in the car crying and asking You why I don't want to go home. But when I get there, I find their outreached arms of love. Lord, what's wrong with me?

My thoughts began to fade when the most glorious sunset I have ever seen appeared across the horizon. It'd been raining nearly since we left Albuquerque. Needing to fill up before crossing the mountain, we decided to go ahead and stop for gas in Flagstaff and grab a bite to eat. While there, the heavy rain clouds began to roll away, leaving nothing but a pure ray of golden heavenly lights dancing against the clay hills. The distant clouds were a dark gray underneath with a touch of royal blue in their midst, followed by a hint of soft breezes as the brilliance graced gently across everything in its pathway.

As we were continuing on down the road, Leslie said, "Quick. Roll down your windows."

"Huh?"

"We're climbing and it'll be better on the engine if we slow to forty-five or fifty with the windows rolled down. I'm cutting off the air conditioning, too."

The four-lane road became two-lanes. For miles, it seemed, all we saw were taillights from tractor trailers, campers, vans and motor homes, along with all the fumes that hovered close to the ground on this dark night. As we slowly approached Hoover Dam, we realized that these were the same vehicles we'd passed an hour or so before we'd stopped to fill-up and eat.

"Did'ja hear that?" Leslie asked.

"Hear what?" I said.

"That noise."

"What noise? All I hear is screeching of brakes, all I see is taillights, and all I smell is diesel fuel from the truckers."

"Shish. Listen!"

About that time we were sitting completely still. Numerous green and blue lights flashed all around and then, we heard what sounded like thunder.

"What was that? Are we gonna fall or something?" I said with a fright.

"No. That's the sound of the dam," BettiLou said. "They say you can only hear it at certain times of the month. We're in luck. Perfect timing. The flashing of the lights is the signal of its mighty performance that will last about an hour or so. With the narrowness of the road, there isn't anywhere to park and view this magical wonder. They say only a chosen few have ever had the experience of witnessing it."

"Can't they make a parking lot?"

"Yes, and they are in the process of building it — someday. Jeannette, you just wait till we come through here in the daytime. You'll see just how treacherous this area really is. Then it'll help you to understand the mighty forces of the riverbanks and its jagged rocks."

After passing through the Dam, we came upon a place called Boulder City. It reminded me of South of the Border back home, 'cause the closer we got, the more signs we saw advertising all sorts of things: *Try your luck at the Palace. Just ahead bronco is a table wait'n for you with nothing but lady luck hands — wheeling and dealing just you in mind.*

Then, not more than thirty minutes later, we topped a big hill to witness the most brilliant sight I have ever seen. Miles and miles of nothing but lights flickering in the stillness of the night air. Just like the magazine pictures I'd seen. Here was this mirage of golden, picturesque lights. In the far distance I saw a ridge of mountain ranges — yes, even at night. The lights were so radiant from the valley below that they emanated a shine that seemed boundless.

Arriving in Las Vegas at eleven-thirty that night, we stopped for something to eat. BettiLou's experience landed us a wonderful steak place. This was the first time in my life I had used a toilet that flushed automatically.

I excused myself quickly and tried to be as discreet as possible. I waited for the cousins to go and see if they noticed anything different. They didn't speak, and neither did I. I just went on pretending all was just fine, although I was simply amazed by this first-time experience. I couldn't wait to get to a phone and tell Mom, knowing she'd get a kick out of the fact that I had encounted a newfangled bathroom.

After the meal we decided it was time to find a place to settle in for a couple of days. Driving along, there were casinos right up against each other and some were far apart. The Pink Flamingo, and Circus Circus, and the Holiday Showboat, and down a little ways we could actually see Sands Hotel/Casino.

We passed the famous Caesars Palace. I never thought I'd ever see this amazing place. Why, the magazine pictures I'd seen hadn't even come close to showing its real beauty. "Reckon we can walk through that while we're here? I'd love to take some pictures to carry back home." I asked.

"Sure we can, Jeannette. You just hang on back there, ya hear?"

"BettiLou? Where do you suggest we stay?"

"Well, I like the Mirage myself. It's a little ritzier, but it's worth it. After all, we're only coming this way once, and why not? That's what we're all working for, isn't it? To enjoy some of the good life?"

"C'mon, Jeannette. Live a little. Be your own boss. Aunt Drusilla and Uncle John aren't here. So, just let loose and enjoy life some."

That sounded awfully familiar, just like back at work. "Well, alright. I'll try and, as you say, let loose a little." *Oh my, Jesus, there's the sign of the beast again, and now I'm twenty-five hundred miles from home!*

I let loose all right, galloping faster and digging deeper in the wrong direction. It was fun, for a while. But then I realized I was falling into an area that was all new to me. I'd never been by myself like this anyway. Always before when I was alone, I had instant contact with friends and family. But here, the only ones I knew were my cousins. I really didn't know what they were talking about, letting loose and letting my hair down and having fun and go and do my thing. The only fun I'd ever encountered was with Mama's family. Now that was fun — visiting and joking around and playing Rook and some Rummy and Aunt Sally trying to play the piano and all of us trying to see who could out sing the others. Then came time for the sisters to weigh themselves to see who was the heaviest. Aunt Marie was always in front, and they'd better let her win, cause if she didn't, she'd ride you to death by saying, "take your shoes off or take your sweater off" or "No, let's turn the scales around — that'll sure make the difference." Now look at me, in a strange place and among strangers. Over twenty-five hundred miles from home. And they want me to hang loose?

Leslie parked beside the volcano display in the Mirage parking lot. BettiLou jumped out and went to see if there were any vacancies. All of a sudden, the volcano exploded, scaring us half to death. Water splashed over the wall and headed our way. We hustled to raise the windows just in the nick of time.

"Jeannette? Can you reach the cooler?"

"I think so. Why?"

"I've heard that water splash since before we went through Hoover Dam. If I hear it slush one more time I think I'll be turning into a Hoover Dam."

Laughing, I opened the car door, pulled the ice chest up over the run board and opened the side flap, draining the water onto the shiny driveway beneath.

"I hope we don't get a ticket for this."

"Jeannette! With as much water as there is from that volcano that just exploded, I don't think they'll be able to determine where it came from."

BettiLou was running toward waving some paper in her hands. "Hey girls. I got us two rooms for two nights. That okay?"

"How much?"

"Not bad. Not for this town."

"How much?"

"Staying here at the Mirage and it being a central location?"

"How much?"

Finally, BettiLou told us the price, and I nearly swallowed my tongue. "Do you know how long it'll take me to work to pay for that?"

"Jeannette. Don't worry. Like I said, what are we living for? Lighten up and live a little." Oh, well. What could I possibly do anyway? So far away from home. Away from Mama and Daddy, away from Sam, all alone except for these cousins of mine. I'd never paid that much money before for a place to stay, and it'd take me months to pay for it. *Oh Jesus, what have I got myself into?*

BettiLou got a room to herself, while Leslie and I shared a room. After our baths, I don't think Leslie knew she was even in the world. Rising early on this Sunday morning, I reached for the small Bible I'd bought at K-Mart when I was a teenager and read a few scriptures. Just as I was getting into a solemn state of prayer, a knock came at the door. It was BettiLou raring to go eat. Seeing Leslie sound asleep, she and I spent a few moments enjoying the scenery and pretending we were really somebodies. We ate breakfast at the Mirage but out on a terrace with all its finery. Afterward, we tried our luck at gambling, and getting on toward dinner time I told her I'd eaten so much breakfast that I wasn't hungry. She stayed with the machines, but I decided to go up and check on Leslie.

I told her of BettiLou's and my morning and she was raring to go eat and try her luck, too. She told me to stay there and rest a little while she caught up with BettiLou and likely ended up over at the Holiday. She said that after I'd rested some and refreshed to come on over and join them. Trying to be brave and not show any fear, I agreed. *After all, I'm a grown woman, aren't I Jesus? I've been told so many times that I can do what ever I want to do. Isn't that right, Jesus'?* After putting away my clothes and straightening the suitcases, I looked out the window. All I saw was wall to wall people. The sidewalk was full and the streets were jammed with cars. *Oh dear Lord, please help me to be brave and to find BettiLou and Leslie.*

I stepped outside the room and into the hallway where many strangers were scurrying around doing their thing. When I reached the lobby, people were everywhere. Not just Americans, but all sorts of people. I found myself clutching my pocketbook and walking in amazement of the magnificently decorated Mirage. From the outside, no one would ever know how huge the space was just inside its walls.

Jesus? Please be with me as I attempt to cross this busy street and please, please help me find Leslie and BettiLou. Thank You, Lord. Taking a deep breath, walking, and trying to attract *as little* attention as possible, I finally reached the other side. *Thank You Jesus, there they are.* I began to smile with the excitement of finding them so quickly, expecting to be greeted as if I had just performed a great task. Instead, Leslie said, "Jeannette, go get the camera and let's take some pictures."

"But I just got here. Have you won anything yet?"

"Go on now. Look at that sun and that blue sky. I'd surely like a shot of that before it goes down today."

"Well, okay." Fear crept in my soul. I swallowed hoarsely, *Jesus, please help me find my way back to the room safely and let Mama and Daddy somehow know that I love 'em and wish they were here.*

24

The Security Blanket

PROUDLY APPROACHED LESLIE and BettiLou a second time.

"Jeannette! What in the world! I only wanted the small snapshot camera, not the camcorder. And here you not only have your camcorder but you have mine, too. Why did you bring all of that?"

I felt myself turning several shades of red.

"You said you wanted to take a shot of the sun setting. Waiting several minutes to cross that busy street, I hurried just in time to catch the elevator going up. Then I realized the room key was no where to be found. I panicked. I had to ride the elevator back down, and then I went to the front desk and asked for another key.

"Well, to say the least Leslie, I was given the third degree and they even called my bank back home to verify I was who I said and who my license card said I was. After about twenty-five minutes, they finally gave me another room key."

"Why would they investigate you this way?"

"I don't know. Ask 'em when we get back. Maybe they'll tell you."

"I just might do that."

"Good! Well, anyway, after all that interrogation, I forgot our conversation and decided to bring it all. This way, I won't have to go back to fetch anything else, okay? I wanted to spend as much time with you all as possible. I do enough fetching of things when I'm at home, and I didn't know I've been elected to do it here too!"

I guess all our nerves were on edge with Leslie driving all that way and not even letting BettiLou or me drive while she took a break. She wouldn't hear of such a thing, so we had to let her have it her way. Now she was totally worn out. Before we knew it, the three-day stay in Las Vegas was over — but not before they took me through Caesars Palace.

"Leslie? Where are we gonna put our souvenirs?"

I looked at her, she looked at BettiLou and back to me. Then we busted out laughing until we cried. The car was packed to the gills — and then some.

"While we're here, wanna go to California?"

"Can we? Do we have time?"

"We're only fifty miles from the border. We can drive up, get out, and touch the soil — just to be able to say we did it. That will last us a lifetime. Whaddya say, wanna do it?"

"Why not. We've done most everything else on this trip. We might as well go there, too."

When we returned to Hoover Dam, I realized what BettiLou had been talking about just a few days earlier. The terrain was very rough and rocky. While slowly driving through, I noticed some men high up on heavy-duty coil ropes, appearing to be hanging in mid-air. They were attaching some steel beams to another side of the rocky mountain edge. There was a posted sign advising that a parking facility would be constructed in the next few years for more visitors to view the breathtaking scene.

"BettiLou? Isn't that what you were telling us?"

"Yes, that's right, Jeannette. You see, it's much different in the daytime than at night, isn't it?"

"Yes ma'am."

"What have I told you about saying ma'am to me?"

"Uh, I'm sorry."

"BettiLou? Jeannette's a whole lot like me. We were brought up to have respect of others — no matter whether young or old. And, this *is* her first time ever away from home and I think she's done very well, don't you?"

"Jeannette? This is your very first time — ever?"

"Yes!"

"Well, how does it feel to be away from your parents some?"

"Different!"

On the way back to BettiLou's home in Texas, we talked about a possible visit with an astrologer. I shared with them about visiting a palm reader once. "Did what she tell you come true Jeannette?"

"Well, it wasn't so much about what would happen as what had happened. Seemed like she knew an awful lot about my past. I haven't yet figured that one out. But, she did tell me I'd get married and have three children — and, come to think of it, I did marry, but there were only two children. There would've been a third, but I had a miscarriage three weeks into the pregnancy. I never went to the doctor, and I never told my parents."

"Jeannette, you never even told Uncle John or Aunt Drusilla? How about Charles?"

"Yes, Charles knew . . ." *Oh dear Lord, I pray I don't have to explain.*

Listening to their chitchats, all of a sudden that memory began to haunt me again. It was during the time those phone calls had kept coming and coming, during a time when Charles kept telling me what I was feeling was all in my head. My uneasiness over those calls was driving me crazy. *Why Charles wasn't home was beyond me. Dear Lord, am I truly loosing it?* Thoughts of being out of control had raced through my mind. It got so bad that one night, one unbelievable night while the children were in the living room playing, I grabbed Henry's BB gun and held it up to my head. The children screamed, Charles came running, and grabbed the gun away from me as I slid down the wall near the dining room entrance while tears and chills of terror encased me.

Oh, dear Jesus. I thought I'd put that far behind me. Why did You let it resurface. Dear Lord, I'm two thousand miles away from home, and now You've let this raw, ugly, uncontrollable memory reappear. Why?

Horns began to blow as a vehicle tried to pull in front of Leslie, bringing me back to reality. She and BettiLou were still discussing the astrologer.

"How about you, Leslie? Ever been or had dealings with one?"

"Well, now that you've mentioned it, some school friends and I went to a fortune teller at the state fair one year. But I just wasted my money. I think she got me tangled up with one of my friends cause she kept talking about my parents' separation, and that was Suzie's parents, not mine."

"Interesting. How about you, Jeannette?"

"Why, yes, BettiLou. I've even dabbled into some of those telephone fortune tellers. Talk about costing you money. They ask you questions, and then they just tell you what you want to hear. The money comes in during the waiting period. They transfer you here, then to another and finally, after about twelve minutes or so, you're connected to someone who says they're in California, Nebraska or some far-away state. So, my question is, what's the difference between them and this lady you're talking about?"

"Jeannette, wasn't there something you could do about it?"

"Well, no and yes! *No*, because it was a 900 number, and I didn't want to tell Mama or Daddy 'cause I knew they'd scold me for doing it. And *Yes* because after having to pay nearly one hundred dollars for a thirty-minute call that came to just over three dollars a minute — *I* never called back."

"This lady can read your palm, your zodiac sign using the stars or, if you like, she's an excellent reader of the cards. C'mon girls. It'll be fun. I believe all you'll need is your birthday, your parent's birthdays, and the place where you were born. I've been to her on many occasions, and that's how I know when to come to Vegas. She's only been off base two times, and that could've very well been my fault. Won't you both consider it? How about you Leslie?"

"Umm, I don't know. Aren't they expensive? Isn't it considered a type of witchcraft?

"Well, I guess if you get right down to it."

"I don't know. I've got a funny feeling about this. I'm not so sure I ought to go. How about you, Jeannette, what are your feelings?"

I hesitated, yet a part of me was jumping with excitement, knowing very well I should totally avoid the subject. With what I'd gone through in the past several years with the sign of the beast, the human side of me was saying yes, yes, and yes — let's go. "Well, we're on a once-in-a-life-time vacation, and we'll never be together like this again. So, Leslie, why not? Daddy, being so practical would advise me against it. He'd say be careful who you associate with, but Mama would say, go for it. But then, Mama is a very strong Christian and can see right through things, and with God's protection she's able to cast it off her shoulders."

"Yes. Uncle John is a very wise man, Jeannette, and Leslie and I both know he would never tell you something wrong. You have a mighty fine daddy. Now, Aunt Drusilla is somewhat different. She's so much fun to be with. Jeannette, I bet you really enjoy your mother."

Oh, if only they knew the truth! *Dear Jesus, what am I to do? I'm torn. Mama's all the time telling me she doesn't understand why I don't under-stand. Jesus, I wish I did. Maybe then I'd not be so tormented inside. Between work and the pressure of my coworkers' remarks and indications about Mama being my enemy, and home life, and making room for cousin Tracey's needs — oh, Dear Sweet Jesus, do You really want me to go and see this astrologer? If it isn't Your will, please put a stumbling block in our path.*

For three days, I did not talk to Mama or Daddy. I was "hanging loose." I was doing as Jeannette wanted to do, and that included not talk-ing to my parents. That included not being respectful when I didn't want to be. That was not eating at designated times. I didn't have to take any pills, so why did I have to eat at nine o'clock, twelve o'clock, and five o'clock like they did? Besides, this trip had my body all messed up any-way. I didn't know when it was nine o'clock, twelve o'clock, or even five o'clock. We'd been through four time zones in less than four days and my entire system was out of whack.

Finally, we arrived at BettiLou's home. I was sleeping in the next morning when her telephone began to ring and ring. Cracking the small bedroom door, BettiLou asked, "Jeannette, it's Aunt Drusilla. Wanna talk to her?"

"No."

"Are you sure? She seems mighty anxious to speak to you. She seems kind of angry. I think you'd better talk to her, *now.*"

My mind filtered back to home, and the memories of Mama began all over again: "If those coworkers are bothering you, tell 'em to bug off. Tell them that you like your life just the way it is. Have you talked to Henrrietta lately? If only you'd go to church more often and get involved." *Lord, I guess the worst problem in my life is Mama. It's just that, well Jesus, the more she talks about this church thing the more I ignore it. I, for the life of me, don't understand what's so important about going to church anyway. As long as I read my Bible and listen to gospel music, I don't see what all the fuss is about. I'm getting the Word. Why should I, as she says, get involved? They'll just talk behind my back and I'm not going to subject myself to that humiliation ever again.* I hesitated talking to Mama.

I managed to crawl out of the comfortable bed and mosey down the hallway into BettiLou's room. Sitting down on the stool beside the night-stand, I picked up the receiver. "Hello?"

"Is that all you can say after we haven't heard from you in three days. Hello? Shug, what is going on with you? Are you all right?"

"Yes Mom, I'm okay."

"Jeannette, something is wrong. You don't sound like yourself. What is it, Shug? Are you running a fever?"

"A fever? Heck fire no, Mama. What makes ya say that?"

"Hey, honey? How's my little girl this morning?"

"Hey, Daddy. I'm just worn out from all the traveling. When I get home, I'll tell you all about it, okay?"

"NO! I want to know this instant what is going on with you! Are you sure you're not sick? This isn't like you, Jeannette. This isn't like you at all, not calling us. We've been worried sick, and we've been praying for your safety and for God to bring you home to us in one piece. Shug, we love you and miss you something awful. Every time we mention your name, Samantha runs to the back door looking for you. I even got down to her level yesterday and told her that you were on a long journey and wouldn't be home for five more days. She just turned her little head, laid it in my arms, and nudged up against my body as if to let me know she understood."

"Mama? I didn't mean to worry you. I was just hanging loose."

"*Hanging L-o-o-s-e?* What in the world is hanging loose?"

"Now don't go and read anything into that. I'll explain it all to you when I get home. It's so good to hear your voices. I've missed you so much. (Just hearing 'em began clearing the muddy waters that were beginning to fill my unsettled mind.) Maybe one day we all can go cross-country together. It's not the same without you. I love you, and thank you so much for calling."

"You trying to git rid of us?"

"No ma'am. I just know it's costing you and . . . "

"Costing? It don't matter how much it costs; just hearing your voice has made our day. Do you know that BettiLou put me on hold?"

"On hold?" I chuckled to myself.

"Yes! On Hold! Twice! I waited for fifteen minutes to get to talk to our daughter. Why, I was fixin' to hang up and call the operator and tell her it was an emergency."

"You wouldn't've, would you, Mama?"

"You bet your sweet life I would've! That's why we thought you might be sick or something, and BettiLou and Leslie didn't know how to tell us that you were in the hospital."

"*Hospital?* Now Mama! You know good'n well I wasn't in any hospital."

"We knew nothing' of the kind. Thank God, Shug, you're all right."

"Honey, don't you worry about the cost of this phone bill. Your mother and I'll let you pay it when you get back home."

"Ah, gee, thanks, Dad." Their sweet voices were music to my ears. Three days was a long time to be without their love and support. All kinds of things can go wrong, and as long as I was under their security blanket I was protected from the outside world.

Before I left BettiLou's home, she was able to make an appointment with an astrologer. She asked the usual questions just like BettiLou said she would. The lady went back several years, describing things that had happened in each of our lives that no one could possibly have known about. Then, getting our full attention, she pulled out some charts and even asked if we cared if she read some cards.

"Ma'am? I really don't believe in that and, personally, I'd rather you wouldn't."

"That's no problem. The cards just give a detailed description of any information I might be instructed to share with you. Turning her head, she asked, "How about you BettiLou and Leslie? Do you have any objections to my using the cards?"

"No, we don't object." The session began. Very interesting information at first, followed by the present status of our lives. Then, with approval for using the cards from my two cousins, she began to describe, in graphic detail, each of their futures. When my turn rolled around, the lady didn't provide a graphic description of the future, but only a vague profile.

When the session was finished, BettiLou thanked the lady for seeing us on such short notice and we respectfully turned to walk out. As I approached the door to step out on the front porch, I felt a vibrant sensation when the lady laid her hand on my right shoulder. In a flash she whispered, "You will find yourself in fragile times, standing on the threshold of deceiving the basic morals you were raised on and in your family's love for Christ. However, after a tribulation period, you will shine, once again, in God's grace."

Stunned by her remark, and yet knowing the struggles I was silently encountering, I felt an urgency to hurry to the car, find a piece of paper and write it down for future reference should she be right.

* * *

Early the next morning, Leslie and I pulled out of BettiLou's driveway, throwing kisses and waving our good-byes.

"Oh Leslie, what a wonderful vacation this has been."

"Yes, I've enjoyed it tremendously. This was a perfect idea."

"And, Jesus has been with us all the way. But I'm looking forward to getting back home and settling down again. I don't think I could do this every day. Cross-country riding in a truck twice in a week? My hind parts feel like I've sat in a basket of thorns, and my shoulders are worn out from holding this camcorder the entire trip, not to mention carrying the regular camera everywhere else for those still shots."

"I know what ya mean — yep! I know perfectly well what ya mean." Laughing, we looked at each other and let out a huge sigh.

I finally got to ride in the front seat and, with directions in hand, we arrived at Red and Joan's place in Louisiana around four-thirty. They insisted we stay for some rest and relaxation.

For supper, Joan and their daughter KathyLou prepared some down-home Cajun food, Louisiana style at its finest. I'd never eaten much hot stuff, but this was too hard to resist. I looked over at Leslie once and she was digging in, sauce not only smeared across her face but was even running down her arms. "Umm. This is right up my alley, Joan. You and KathyLou's gotta share the recipe with me."

After that delicious meal, I reached to help clear the supper table.

"Jeannette, we don't do dishes here," Joan answered.

"Whaddya mean you don't do dishes. You don't throw 'em away, do ya?"

"Jeannette. Thought you just came from Vegas. And I know BettiLou has one."

"C'mon, Jeannette, you know" piped in Leslie.

"I do?" rolling my eyes upward and repeating, "Oh, yes, now I remember," though I didn't have the vaguest what they were talking about.

"The dishwasher will take care of it."

"Leslie, Joan and I have to go in to work early, and KathyLou is staying over at a friend's house later tonight, so you girls can sleep in as long as you wish. Just be sure the door is locked behind you when you leave."

"Red, then let us thank you now for your wonderful hospitality. Your accepting us into your home for the night is more kind than words can express."

"Us accepting you into our home? Don't be ridiculous. What about you and Uncle John and Aunt Drusilla accepting BettiLou and me into your home for over a week? Oh, how much we enjoyed that reunion. Joan and I were just saying a few days ago that that might be the last time we would all get together, and you know, even so, you can bet your bottom dollar we had a super good time. Well, it's time to hit the old sack. Thank you for coming, and always remember that we love you."

* * *

Around seven, Leslie and I were up re-packing the car for our journey homeward. Around nine, I said, "Aint'cha hungry yet?" She looked
at me and started laughing. "Jeannette, seems like I remember not too
many days ago you asking that same question."

"Yes. I only had two hours sleep and had gone nearly eight hours
without any food. I think you were trying to tell me something. After all
that, I feel like I've lost ten pounds."

"My body will never get used to North Carolina's time again."

"Don't do that, Leslie," I said holding my stomach.

"Don't do what?"

"You know very well. If I start laughing I'll have to stop and if I've
learned one thing on this trip, it's that you don't like to stop once you
get started."

"Yep! That's right. We had a lot of miles to cover in a short time and
if you didn't grab something to eat and use the facilities when I stopped
to fill'er up, why, you were just outta luck."

Moving on down the highway, and listening to some country tapes,
Leslie said, "Jeannette, I'm planning on going by Sandra's."

"Sandra's? Outside of Columbia. Today? Aren't we gonna stop and
spend the night somewhere and go there tomorrow?"

"Nope! I've checked my watch, and I believe we can make it."

Once Leslie made her mind up to do something, I learned to consider it done. Sure enough, a little after eight o'clock, we pulled into
Sandra's driveway. You should've seen Sandra's face when she answered
the door and saw her Mama standing there. In the course of getting the
puppies, their food and their chains, I overheard Leslie saying we were
heading home.

"Leslie? Are you sure? Aren't you tired? You've been driving since
seven this morning. Don't you want me to drive?" I asked.

"Nope! Get in the car. We're homeward bound."

And home we went with camcorders, suitcases, dogs, and all.

As we pulled in the driveway at midnight, the carport and the
porch lights were all on. I jumped out of the car, cats and all, and here

they came. Mama and Daddy's arms outreached, as the four of us embraced. Crystal, Rosemarie and Samantha, too, were jumping with joy. Sam's ears were laid back and her amber eyes were even squinted with smiles. Her light, furry body was just twisting with her tail nearly wagging off. Our hearts were so overwhelmed with happiness and love that I couldn't help but shed a tear or two.

"It's so good to be home," I said as I smiled and hugged 'em again.

"Daddy? How did you and Mama know we were coming home tonight?"

"Ask your mother. I told her this morning that Leslie wasn't losing any time and we'd soon be together again."

"Shug? He's tell'n you the truth. He started turning the lights on even before the sun went down. He said he wanted to make sure none were burned out, and he even had me to wash the window panes in the yard light so they'd give off the brightest light possible. It's so good to have you home. Thank God you both made it safe and sound," Mama said as tears welled in her eyes.

I gathered my suitcases, camcorder, and tapes while Leslie gathered her puppies and put them back in the car. We hugged and I thanked God for her safe driving, then we said our good-byes. "Leslie? I'll talk to you late tomorrow." Laughing, she got into the car and headed toward her home just over the hill.

As I prepared for bed that first night back, Mama popped around the corner of my bedroom. "Can I help you unpack, Shug?"

"Thanks, but I think I'm just gonna wait until tomorrow."

It wasn't long till Sam came jumping on the bed, snuggled up close and lay her head on my hip, seeming to understand every word Mama and I was saying.

"Honey? It's so good to see your light on in this room. It's been dark in here far too long. We ain't never gonna let you go off without us again." I hugged 'em both. Daddy went to get a handful of peanuts while Mama refreshed her snuff.

A little later, Daddy passed, heading toward their bedroom. "Honey? Thank dear sweet Jesus above you're back home. You sleep good, and if it's the Lord's will, I'll see you in the morning. I love you."

"Daddy, it's s-o-o-o good to be back in my bed. I love you too. Goodnight."

A minute later, here came Mama down the hall. "Shug? I am so thankful you're back home — where you belong." Mama had a way of putting in her two-cent's worth. "I love you Shug." Laughing as usual, she asked, "if you need me, call Papa. Goodnight."

"Goodnight, Mama. I love you, too."

25

An Outward Journey

*I*N THE EARLY hours of a cold November morning, a gentle gust of wind brushed against my body. It called my attention to a beautiful bronze centerpiece where pages of a Bible were flipping softly, one by one, until they rested peacefully at the beginning of the book of Proverbs. Startled, yet filled with a great warmth, I asked, *What is it Lord? What are You trying to tell me?* I searched throughout this mysterious place for some kind of an answer when suddenly a brilliant flashing light appeared with the words *four through twelve.*

Lord? Whaddya mean? Is it verses four through twelve? Is it chapters four through twelve? Or could it be a certain chapter with verses four through twelve? I pondered this message from above so long that time nearly got away from me. Hustling toward the kitchen, there sat Daddy drinking his morning coffee and reading the local newspaper. He asked how I had slept.

"Daddy, tell Mama when she gets up that I dreamed about the Bible again last night."

"You did?"

"Yes. Something about Proverbs four through twelve."

"Honey, we've been trying to get you to go to church, but you keep resisting."

"Now Daddy, don't start! I haven't time this morning to talk, okay?" Trying to avoid his comments, I hurriedly ate cereal, swallowed some vitamins, and grabbed my coat — but not without bending down and giving Sam a hug as she hustled beside me toward the back door.

Throughout the day I found myself wondering not only about last night's dream but about the other dreams I'd received from the spiritual world. I had kept a list of them in the back of my Bible giving the time, date, and other notes I thought might be of interest should it happen again. *But, I can't do anything about that now. I'll check it out when I get home.*

The fall storm we were having slacked up just enough for me to run from the car to the house without being drenched. As soon as I entered the den, Mama called. "Jeannette, Papa said you had another dream last night. Would you like to talk about it?"

"After supper I'm gonna do some studying and then we'll talk, okay?"

"'Bout time. We've been trying to get you to go to church. 'Bout time you took an interest in the Bible. It's a shame though that the only way Jesus could get your attention was through a dream."

"Mama, don't start. I've been going to church some and you know it." I was already beginning to feel very uncomfortable when the word "church" was mentioned. It didn't matter who I was around. I felt so humiliated when anyone spoke the "church" word, and especially when Mama and Daddy kept nagging me to be more involved. The more they pursued the matter, the more determined I was to avoid it. The less I had to deal with this church thing, the better off I was. My desire grew stronger and stronger to be in another world where there was no one to contradict everything I said and everything I did, or put me down every time I turned around. I tried so hard to act the way my coworkers had said I should act.

I reached into the drawer and picked up the Bible the church had given me when I graduated from high school. I sat down on the blue bedspread Mama'd helped me get from a mail order catalog, dusted off the top cover and gently opened the fragile pages. I decided to look for the dated material of years back. Sure enough, there it was, written in black ink on the backside of the last reading of the book of Revelation. As my eyes anxiously grazed the writings, I discovered the first dream was Psalm one hundred and fifty. *That's the one Mama helped me with. It begins with "Praise ye the Lord . . ."*

And then the second dream was Isaiah Ten. That chapter began with, "*Woe unto them that decree un-grievousness*" . . . whatever that meant. The head notes refer to it as judgments for pride, etc. *Oh well, I'm not having any trouble with that. I'm very appreciative of all the blessings You've given me, Lord. You know that I pray and give thanks to You daily. And as far as the Psalms go, well . . . After supper, Mama headed for the keyboard, Daddy started patting his foot and I tried to pluck some on the guitar Aunt Ruth sold to us back in the fifties. Oh, how we love singing and lifting praises to You, Jesus, in some good old gospel favorites. But I don't understand why You sent these two Bible readings to me in the first place. Though I do thank You for thinking of me.*

Recognizing this was a third dream from the spiritual world, I searched through my pocket book and found the paper I'd written on that morning. Hum, Proverbs four through twelve. It took awhile to find the passage in the Bible 'cause I didn't know exactly the location of Proverbs.

The notes at the top of the pages said, "Keep the heart." *Jesus, I'm keeping my heart open to You, so, I don't understand what You're telling me here. "Mischiefs of whoredom?" Now what in the world am I to make of that? I'm in no such way of that. After my marriage dismantled, I came back home, and I haven't been unfaithful to You or myself because I know I have a living spouse. Oh dear Jesus, I make enough mistakes without being an adulteress, too. I really don't understand that one.*

Okay, I thought, *that covers chapters four, five, and part of six, seven and part of eight reads, "True and false wisdom? I might have to ask* Mama and Daddy to help me here. *After all, they are much wiser than I'll ever be, and Mama's instincts are top notch. I'll just have to grin and bear this church thing with them. Oh Jesus, here I go again, avoiding Your Holy* ground, and yet I don't have to attend church to be saved and walk with You. Even I know that.

"*Wisdom's eternity, She keepeth open house.*" "Yes! Daddy is fluent in wisdom, and Mama does keep an open house to all. They are thrilled to have anyone who will come and visit. *Thank You, Jesus, for letting me at least understand this one.* Oh, that carries over into chapter nine as well.

Chapter ten, "*Proverbs of Solomon.*" *Now You're talking about Solomon's days here on earth. What does that have to do with me?*

Here I go again, not understanding. Jesus? All I know is You've really got me to not understanding a thing, and though You could open anyone's eyes any-time You wanted to and help 'em see Your Light. You've surely got me puzzled on this one, and You know I ain't good at putting puzzles together. What in this world is "*Sundry proverbs?*" That's what it reads, right there on the top of the page. *Jesus, You think I can understand this? Like I said, I ain't good at solving puzzles. You should know 'cause You made me.*

I finally reached the end of this seeming nightmare, feeling very confused. *Lord, what in the world are You saying here? Chapters eleven and twelve, "Moral virtues?" You know good'n well I'm an honest person and have the highest regard for righteousness and justice. Although I must admit I don't like being on a jury and having to sentence a person — especially when there's a murder trial. Your Word says not to kill, and I have strong reservations about being a part of that, although I know, too, that we've gotta have some sort of law and order. Without it, this world would be a total disaster. I didn't get everything I wanted growing up, and I sure as heck didn't get by without some punishment either. I got my bottom spanked many a time, mostly for talking back. And You know, I deserved every spanking I got and then some. Not having a brother or a sister, I didn't have anyone to blame things on. I was the only one and almost always got caught. I was stubborn, for sure. Nobody could tell me anything. I was fourteen and extremely hard-headed.*

Lord? Mama and Daddy is all the time telling me that they've lived in the world and I haven't the experience they've had. Well Jesus, how can I get experience if they're all the time shielding me?

I thought about how it makes me so mad and I get so frustrated that

I can't stand myself. I get angry then I'd just as soon be by myself. Even at work, I'm much better off alone than with a crowd. I've often wondered what it would have been like if my twin had lived. Many times I've wished for its presence so I could be a normal person. *Its hard being an "only" Lord, it's so hard.* I get scolded at work because of it. It gets broadcasted at reunions by relatives saying, "Well, you don't know, Drusilla, cause you only had one child." How many times have I seen Mama cry over that statement, knowing she had no control over the miscarriages that took place? One was lost and one was saved. *I can't help it You didn't like me enough to let it live. Why did You take my twin away? Why did You let my beautiful marriage be destroyed? Why did You . . .* suddenly a tap came on my bedroom door.

"Shug? Are you all right in there?" I moved some papers around in an attempt to cover the sound of my sniffles while quickly drying my eyes and clearing my throat. "Yes, ma'am. I'm fine. What time is it?"

"Going on eleven o'clock."

"Oh, I'm sorry. Time got away from me. I'll be in there in a minute." Gathering the Bible and notes and motioning for Sam, I headed toward the den.

Approaching the entrance, Daddy asked, "Honey? What did you find out about your dream?"

"Some of the head notes are kind of disturbing, Daddy, and well, I don't understand what Jesus wanted me to read. Chapters four through twelve or chapter one verses four through twelve."

Mama suggested I talk to Reverend Rogers at the church and see if he might have some insights into why I might be having these dreams in the first place.

"Now really, Mama! I only attend church on occasion, and the preacher really doesn't know me well. You really want me to go and talk to him about this personal matter? I don't think so. Besides, he'll think I'm crazy and that I'm mixed up with some kind of cult or something."

"There you go again. It's all in your mind, Jeannette. He'll think no such thing. Matthew is a man of God, and he speaks the Word of God. You ought to give him a chance."

Once Mama had said this, calmness flooded my soul and for a split second I caught a sliver of some radiant, everlasting love. The clock began striking the half-hour, and the calmness vanished. "I need to get to bed," I said. "Let's discuss this later, okay?"

"Yes, look at the time, we all need to get to bed. Mine and your daddy's doctor's appointments begin at nine tomorrow. Will you call us when you get up at six-thirty?"

"Sure. They're just regular routine checkups, right?"

Passing by the doorway, Daddy called, "Honey, you sleep good tonight, and if it's the good Lord's will I'll see you in the morning. I love you."

"I love you too, Daddy. Goodnight."

"Shug, thank you for sharing your dream with us. Think about talking to Matthew, okay? I love you, and if you need me, call Papa."

"Goodnight, Mama, I love you, too."

* * *

Perhaps it was the harassment by my co-workers that caused me to wrestle with my soul. Not knowing how to say no brought about much conflict. I really wanted to please them and yet, living at home like I did, I knew my main goal was to please my parents. *Jesus, I can't go on like this. I'm tormented on which way to go. Please, can't You help me?*

After many prayers along with a few church visits, Jesus came to me a fourth time, on January fifteenth of '92. In the stillness of this night, I remember looking into a total darkness that surrounded me. A blonde painter's easel came into focus sitting all by itself and surrounded by a brilliant glow. On the easel's ledge was what appeared to be a thirty-six inch high by eighteen-inch wide piece of tan canvas. Somehow, the canvas was sitting slanted on the easel's ledge without any support to its back. Then, Christ appeared. The image of his face began to bulge through from the back of the sackcloth canvas. I began to slowly walk by.

Amazed, I noticed His eyes piercing my soul and His lips beginning to move. Slowing to a crawl, I was able to read them as they formed the words, *I love you, I love you, I love you.* The glowing light that surrounded this beautiful easel soon vanished back into the darkness of the dream.

I awakened to find myself trembling, sitting straight up in bed in the middle of this night. Looking into the dresser mirror at the foot of the bed, I silently whispered, *I love you too, Jesus.*

With Christ not appearing between February and September, I was beginning to think that maybe Mama was right after all, and my mind was only playing tricks on me. However, with Jesus not appearing, the sign of the beast was on the rampage, appearing everywhere — on books, sales receipts, records at work, gas purchases, bank accounts, commercials on television, telephone numbers and even vehicle tags. Those three consecutive numbers were ever-present in my mind's eye. They were everywhere. Why hadn't I ever noticed it before?

I've wished a thousand times that I'd never gone to see that movie called *The Omen.* Why was I so gullible as to fall to those co-workers constant harassment? It was the excitement of a totally different world than the one in which I was raised. The grass seemed much greener on their side. *Lord, if I've asked You once, I've asked You thousands of times to help me get rid of this thing that continues nagging at my soul.*

Lo and behold, a fifth dream was revealed during the later part of September. It was as though the Lord and I had passed each other on a road. There He was in a radiant, glowing white garment, and I can still see the darkness that began to encase my entire body. For some reason I turned, and about the same time He was looking over His right shoulder saying, *I love you, I love you, I love you.* Not taking a second, I instantly replied, *I love you too, Jesus.*

I prayed and gave thanks for His appearing that night. I knew it was an answer to my dilemma. I had it all figured out that Jesus was taking care of my troubles with the sign of the beast and that I didn't have to do it. He was doing it by placing a protective shield around my household. But I wasn't prepared for the next chapters in my life as they began to unfold.

* * *

I'm being bombarded by spiritual dreams. *Jesus, I thought Your telling me You loved me would be sufficient.* But, now, on February first. of '93, a year later almost to the day, the sixth spiritual dream appeared.

Awakening enough to pull up the extra quilt from the foot of the bed over my chilled body, I snuggled back under the covers on this cold winter morning. It didn't take long until flying scriptures were coming from the sky. I reached up to grasp one or two and here came, in a flash of a golden arch, the book of Jeremiah.

Later that morning, I wrestled with memories of the dream. Mama was still in bed, and Daddy was already out in his shop. I grabbed my Bible and headed to the kitchen to fix some coffee.

Through the window, I saw the shop smokestack boiling with its gray colors assuring me that Daddy was warm. I grabbed the Bible and headed to turn up the heat and start the gas logs in the den only to discover that Daddy'd already done it.

Jesus, I don't understand why You keep letting me have these dreams from Your world. Guess I've just gotta keep searching and praying and hoping some day, some way, I'll understand Your ways.

Back in the kitchen, I pulled out a chair, opened the Bible, and began reading the head notes at the top of the page, "Man's unkindness," and "Judah worse than Israel." Now what in this world does that mean for me? *Oh Lordy, Jesus, You know good'n well I ain't good at parables.* And look here — "Israel's confession of sins and Judah called to repentance?" *Lord, I'm not sinning. I'm not like those people. I've never done nothing like they have. Jesus, I don't understand why You're trying to scare me.* I didn't know if I wanted to continue reading or not.

I took a break for some cereal and toast, then continued reading those head notes. A distinctive volcano began building within me. Chapter five and six's notes read, "The prophet lamenteth — God's judgments on the Jews." *Whew! There for a moment, I thought You were really fixin' to judge me.*

Chapters seven and eight read, "Vain confidence of the disobedient." *I'm not that way.* But doubts did begin to filter into my conscience. Glancing over to chapters nine and ten: "Impenitency of the people and Trust in God." *Lord, You know I trust in You. I talk to You nearly every moment of every day. And, what in the world does impenitency mean? Please, please won't You help me to understand?*

The head notes of chapter eleven read, "Jeremiah proclaimeth anew." *A new what?* Maybe one day I will understand, but right now . . . I've gotta get this Bible back to my room before Mama wakes up and Daddy comes in from the shop. It won't do for them to catch me reading. Why, they'd be all over me in no time, and I'm just not in the mood for their criticizing comments about my not going to church. I can just hear them saying if I went then I'd understand what the Lord is telling me and if I'd only go and talk to Reverend Rogers I'd understand even more. Nope! I am not up to that this day.

26

Mrs. Cottler

THAT EVIL ONE was sticking to me like sap on a pine tree. Calling out to Jesus with nearly every breath I had was like talking to a brick wall. I got no response at all. The evil one continued making sure those blinders fit snugly as his urgency for control overpowered my soul. I was being drawn deeper into the evil one's web of destruction. Instead of looking away and avoiding this issue, I actually began to look forward to seeing that beastly sign and wasn't content unless I encountered at least one sighting daily.

Then one day in the cafeteria, I just happened to overhear a conversation between some co-workers discussing removal of jinxes. For days, their comments roared in my head. As hard as I tried, I could not shake their remarks. Then, one evening after supper, I asked my parents, "Reckon that movie I saw caused the evil one to place a jinx on me?"

"Shug, I've heard of folks being that way. I wouldn't think it'd happen to you, although your Daddy and I have been trying for years to get you to attend church on a regular basis."

"Okay Mama, don't start up with that church thing."

"Well, you asked and I gave you my opinion."

"Your mother's right, honey. But I sort of doubt your not going to church has anything to do with being jinxed — although every now and then you happen to mention about seeing that sign. I think it's bothering you more than you're letting on."

A month or so later my car's battery had run down when Richard, a short man with reddish blonde hair and eyes of coal, had parked beside me that morning and just happened to have a set of jumper cables. While he prepared the jumpstart, I inquired about a conversation he and the others had a few weeks back concerning jinxes.

"Jeannette, you're bothered lots about 'the sign of the beast' aren't you? There's some folks around here that just wouldn't mind their own business, kept nagging at you until you gave in and went to see that movie. You went alone too, didn't you?"

"Yes! Yes I did. I don't understand why they smothered me so about a movie I really didn't want to see to start with."

"They're just so — and please excuse me for saying this, but it's the truth — darn jealous of you that they could hardly stand for you to be happy. You've been raised in a good home, a Christian home — much better than some that you work with. And you being an 'only' hasn't helped the situation any either."

"But, Richard, I can't help it. It's just the way the Lord wanted it. Why are they so cold-hearted and jealous? Besides, I've tried to share love with them. I've tried and tried and yet something is missing. For some reason, I just don't fit in. I thought if I went to see that movie it'd show 'em how brave and strong I was. But instead, it just began to bring me down."

"You're right, Jeannette. However, it not only brought you down, it brought you down to their level."

"Their level? I'm not in competition with them. We're all created equals in the sight of God."

"Yes, we are, but you being different and they knowing it made it difficult for them. Some were brought up hard and some didn't have much at all, and here you came in all prim and proper — well."

"I'm sorry, I had no idea I was that much different. All I wanted was to fit in. Everywhere I go, I'm different — here at work, at home, and even at church. I don't fit in anywhere. All I want is to fit in somewhere, and I've even messed this up. What am I going to do? How can I fix it?"

"You can't do it alone, Jeannette. You need some help."

"I've been having some dreams over the years from the spiritual world, and I've been praying real hard for Jesus to help me, but no answer has come."

"Jeannette? I might be able to help. I don't know, maybe Mrs. Cottler can help."

"Mrs. Cottler? Who is this lady?"

"Don't know about the lady part, but I do know the kind of work she's in. Mrs. Cottler has a special way of removing jinxes."

"JINXES?"

"Shish! Don't let anyone hear you say that word around here. I'll be fired for sure. Be quiet."

"Huh?"

"Jeannette. With what all you've been saying about the sign of the beast following you around, seems to me like you've been jinxed — probably by that movie you saw a few years back."

"Oh c'mon. You don't really think that, do you?" *Dear Jesus, just a few days ago I happened to mention this same thing to my parents.*

"It ain't noth'n to joke about, Jeannette. Sometimes certain things have a way of penetrating people's minds without them even knowing it. A movie like the one you went to see is a *prime example*. I wish you'd never listened to 'em."

"Me too! My life has turned upside down since that movie. I've done things and said things I'd never have done or said before."

"That's why I really feel that Mrs. Cottler will be able to help you with your situation. I know you've been struggling to suppress the mark, but I also know that avoiding it will only hurt you in the long run."

"You're very observant, Richard. I've tried desperately to avoid telling anyone about the sign of the beast. I made a promise to myself on vacation not to mention it anymore."

"And you haven't. But it's written all over your face. I can see the frustrating unbalance in your behavior. Like I just said, I strongly feel that you really need this therapy. Here." He handed me a folded piece of paper. "Mrs. Cottler's telephone number. You call her — the sooner the better, ya hear?"

"Do you really think she can remove evil spirits from people? What is she, some sort of witchcraft person?"

"Heck no. A witchcraft person puts spells on people. This is a 'good' person. She has a special talent. One that can actually remove the evil spirits."

"Oh. I guess it's like my Uncle Thomas. He has a special skill of removing warts. I can't tell you the number of people who've gone to see him."

"How'd he do it?"

"Some in the family says he'll silently quote a Bible verse or two. I had a wart on the inside of my left hand. And although I really had doubts about it, I decided to ask 'im to remove it. After dinner one day, Mama and I went over for a visit, and I showed it to him. Uncle Thomas said for me to go on about my business and not think about it. Just erase it from my mind. Arriving home, I told Daddy about it and he said, 'Well, Thomas is right. You need to forget ever going over there and before you know it — it'll be gone.'"

The car started. "I really do appreciate your willingness to help me out, Richard. Must've been God's will, your being available and all. I might not've gotten this lady's name and number if my battery hadn't run down."

"Wait! Wait, Jeannette, please. Did the wart leave?"

"The wart hasn't been seen since."

"Now c'mon, Jeannette. Did your uncle really remove those warts or did you get something from the doctor to shrink 'em?"

"No. I'm telling you the truth. Uncle Thomas not only removed my wart, but he also removed a strawberry wart from Mama's face."

"A strawberry wart?"

"Gotta go Richard, but yes. Mama had a wart in the shape of a strawberry on her right cheek. Grandpa Boyles said she was marked due to her mother craving 'em so just before she was born."

* * *

Not wanting to go to bed with yet another argument about that church thing, I decided not to mention my conversation with Richard to my parents. The next day an opportune time happened. Daddy was out at the shop working on some cabinets, and I somehow knew Mama would understand better.

"Uh Mama, yesterday while Richard jumped started my car our conversations led to his sharing with me about a woman who has the ability to remove evil spirits."

"Really? What's her name?"

"I can't believe my ears. You seem almost delighted."

"Shug, I've not only heard, but I've also read of folks like you're talking about."

"Well goodness, Mama! Knowing my struggles, why hadn't you already said something?"

"Mainly because *you* are the one who should mention it, not me. You see, you can't be helped unless you are willing to be helped. That goes with everything in life. As with church."

"Uh, oh! Here it comes."

"No, don't misunderstand me now. What I'm saying is, unless you want to change, no one can help you, not even Jesus. You've got to be willing to do your part, and the rest will fall in place."

"Mama, *I don't understand*," I said while reaching for the remote control to turn to our favorite soap. "Anyway, reckon Daddy will go with me to see this woman?"

"Shish now, let's see what old Ricktor's up to today."

That evening I mustered enough courage to mention Mrs. Cottler to Daddy. "I was wondering if you and Mama would mind going with me to see her?"

He looked at Mama.

"I just told her unless she wanted to change, no one could help her, not even Jesus. Papa, I can't see that it'd hurt anything, as long as we're with her."

"Well, since your mother feels this strongly. Maybe, just maybe this could be your answer. But we need to check around and see just how legit this woman really is."

"Yes sir."

"Now, honey, don't go and get your hopes up. After all, she might turn out to be a scammer. I'll ask Franklin if he'll run her name through the courthouse records. What did you say the telephone number was?"

"It's in my bedroom, I'll be back in a jiff."

"In a jiff? What kind of statement is that?"

"Oh, Daddy! I'll be back in a minute."

"Mama. This younger generation. What is gonna happen to the language?"

"Here's the number and the address of Mrs. MaryAnn Cottler."

"Now, like I said, don't get your hopes up, but I'll have it checked out in the next day or so. In the meantime, let's pray about this. As your mother always says, dear Lord above knows if you're gonna need some extra attention, and if its His will, it'll work out to your advantage. And, if not, it won't."

"Daddy?"

"Yes, honey?"

"Thank you!" I reached down and kissed him on the cheek.

Saying my prayers that night, I thanked Jesus for two of the most wonderful parents in the world and for Richard, too. How good it felt to be up front and honest with them, as though a change was already taking place.

* * *

About two weeks later Daddy and I were out at the shop when Mama hollered from the house saying there was a call for Daddy.

After the call he sat back in his recliner and stared out the window in thought. "Well, seems like Mrs. Cottler is legit after all. Franklin said she has successfully removed thousands of curses and jinxes over a period of sixty some years. And talking out evil spirits seems to be her specialty. Said that she is only known through word of mouth. So honey, I guess it's okay for you to set up an appointment. I just told Franklin it was a matter of concern for someone we knew and I was just passing along a favor. He said if it were someone else beside me, he wouldn't have checked as thoroughly."

"Mama? What did you do with that telephone number?"

"Me?!"

"Yes. I saw Daddy give it to you the other night after supper."

"Oh, gee. Let me see. If Papa gave it to me — no telling where I put it." She hurried into the kitchen and shuffled through several pieces of paper. "Here it is! Right where I laid it."

"I'll call tomorrow. It's after four-thirty, probably too late now."

"Why don't you try, Shug? Who knows? She might just be there and she might be able to see you this week."

"You're as anxious as I am, aren't you, Mama?"

"Yep!"

It's taking me a while to learn Mama's ways. *Why Lord, why haven't I picked up on her inside abilities before now? Have I been so blinded to not have seen?*

After three rings someone answered, "Mrs. MaryAnn Cottler." Pausing to clear my throat, I told her my name and how I had come to receive her name and number. She asked for a brief description of my dilemma, then suggested I come down as soon as possible. Right over the phone she spoke of detecting a negative spirit and said that if it continued much longer, I might not be able to escape. That scared the daylights out of me!

My hands were shaking as I hung up. Noticing my nervousness, Mama began her questions. I explained and said I had an appointment for that upcoming Thursday at nine-thirty in the morning.

"Well. I've been telling you that all along. It's as though you're carrying a frightening attitude around. It hasn't just happened, it's been gradually coming on ever since you went to see that scary movie. Isn't that right, Papa?" He nodded in agreement.

* * *

We all were up early Thursday morning, getting ready for the long trip. Helping each other with necessary medicines to take along, we were driving on Interstate 95 by seven-thirty. It wasn't long before Daddy spoke of eating, and we really did need to stop and stretch our legs, as it was still quite a drive to Bellmount. I was too excited to eat. "Papa, bet she'll be hungry when we head back home," Mama remarked. "I've never known Jeannette to turn down food before!" They both chuckled.

There were several cars already lined up in front of Mrs. Cottler's small frame house. Some were old jalopies, some were fancy vehicles with sunroofs, and even an extra antenna attached to the back windows. Because of Daddy's breathing problems, we found a parking place up close and walked together to the front of the home. The sign on the outside read, "Don't knock. Make yourself at home and c'mon in."

Chairs lined the tiny room we entered and the walls were oddly papered. Some were newspapers of long ago mixed with sheets of bright yellow flowers. The room's hardwood flooring showed signs of wear. A tiny television in one corner had a set of clothesline wire being used for rabbit ears. We greeted the five men and four women already seated and found three empty seats together behind the front door. After only a short while, a tall, slender man came from another room. Looking into my eyes, as if he'd known me my whole life he said, "You're Jeannette, aren't you?"

I looked at Mama. Mama looked at Daddy. Daddy stood up and looked this man straight in the eye. "How did you know my daughter's name?"

"Sir? I didn't mean to frighten you. My mahda sent me out here to see if that was Jeannette who just came into our home."

"Sir? Your mother, Mrs. Cottler, is it? Did she see us arrive?"

"No, sah. You see, sah, Mahda's blind. She's been giv'n this talent, and it is so amazin' to how she can tell, just by da sounds a person makes. Anyways, she asked me to tell Jeannette that she would see'r in fifteen minutes. She also told me to ask if y'all'd like to have somethin' tah drink. Mrs. Ferrell? Mahda said to tell ya she has yer Coca-a-cola drinks in the 'frig. The small one's yer favorite, i'n it right? And, Mr. Ferrell? Mahda says yer peanuts on the table an' for ya to help yerselves." Then he turned and walked back through the doorway and closed the glass door behind him.

"Papa? This is spooky. How'd they know what kind of drinks I liked and about your peanuts? Oh well, must be the Lord's will for us to be here. Shug, you want us to go with you in there to see this woman?"

"No. Like you said, I need to want help in order to begin improving.

I'll be all right. Besides, I'll just be on the other side of that wall. Don't worry. I'll be just fine."

Sure enough, fifteen minutes passed and I was called. Standing, trying to generate a sense of self-dignity, I followed the young man through the glass doors. Just as I approached the doorway, Mama said, "Shug, would you like for me to hold your things while you're in there?" "Sure, Mama," I handed her my jacket and a book I'd been reading. Then the man who had greeted us led me down a narrow hallway and suddenly stopped, pointing to a small room on the right.

No words can explain the peace that engulfed me as I entered this room. As I looked at the woman sitting behind an old wooden desk, I saw a radiant bronze glow surrounding her entire being. I couldn't help but stop and stare.

"Jeannette, please have a seat. I'm glad you came when you did." I sat down. There was a single bed in the corner of this small room with a beautiful patchwork quilt and what appeared to be the kitchen area was just off to my left. A wonderful aroma of freshly baked bread wafted past me.

"As you can see, I'm not wearing any sunglasses. I have no need of them. I rarely go outside and when I do, I am totally blind, seeing nothing but darkness inside. But I feel with my heart, and God has given me a talent to help others."

"Mrs. Cottler? After your sharing with me about my not being able to escape, I felt an urgent need to come quickly. I'm glad you were able to see me on such short notice. I am a Christian, and I've never been in any trouble."

"Jeannette. Please, don't speak another word. The spirits are very angry. Every word you say is being used against you. They do not like it, your being here seeking help."

"Ma'am?"

"As I said. *Be quiet.*"

Sitting behind this dark brown wooden desk, she wore a pale grayish blouse with black buttons down the front. Her skin showed signs of wear like an old western saddle, and her hair appeared more like pepper than salt. Although Mrs. Cottler's eyes were black in color, as she spoke

I noticed a golden amber light glistening like a candle flame deep within her pupils. The radiance of the bronze rays was ever so prominent around her and even the desk tablet, on which she was resting her elbows, appeared to move on one occasion. Yes! I did sit quietly, and I *did not say another word* until she told me it was okay.

"Jeannette? First, you are an only child. You were born in the fall of the year, (sharing with me not only the exact date, but also the exact time and the hardship Mama had in delivering). Second, you graduated in the mid-sixties (again, the exact date and the current events of that time). Third, you married a nice Christian man and adopted two children that were your husband's from a previous marriage. Fourth, he wasn't faithful to you (she told of the exact reason) and fifth, you are living with your parents who love you so much that they are willing to go to the ends of the earth for your welfare."

I was amazed, but kept quiet.

She continued, "I can't urge you strongly enough to accept this medicine." Reaching under the desk, she pulled out this half-gallon jar of some muddy looking liquid that appeared to have several kinds of food particles floating in it.

"I want you to take seven tablespoonfuls of the medicine seven times a day until it is all gone. Do you have a dollar piece on you? Ah, you may answer my questions only."

"No ma'am."

"You see? Your manners are so precious. I can tell you are a very dedicated child. Not only to your parents, but to Jesus as well. It's a shame that the evil one is trying to overtake you." While Mrs. Cottler talked, I noticed her making some type of pouch.

"Jeannette? Do you happen to have four quarters on you?"

"I don't know. We stopped and ate on the way down this morning and they did give me some change. Let me see."

"Jeannette? Just answer, 'yes', 'no' or 'maybe.'"

"Yes ma'am. Maybe." Not saying another word, I fumbled through my pocketbook until I found the quarters and handed them to her. Taking the four pieces of money, she asked me to silently pray the Lord's prayer along with her as she finished sewing. Then Mrs. Cottler began speaking in a foreign language. I don't know to this very day what she said. It was in a language I'd never heard before and haven't heard since. I guess it was okay, 'cause I felt an electrical vibration that left me tingly all over.

"Jeannette? Women have a way of wearing things on their persons. I'm asking you to wear this seven weeks, never taking it off — even during bathing. After which time, keep it in your belongings until . . . (She disclosed the amount of time and asked me not to reveal it to anyone. To this very day, I haven't).

"Jeannette? Should you ever need to speak to me again — and chances are you might — I'm just a telephone call away, day or night. I can tell the spirits aren't as strong as they were when you first arrived. I've also prayed for your parents' safety. Go in peace. Remember: seven tablespoonfuls, seven times a day, and wear that pouch the appropriate given time I specified."

She rose and, feeling the desk as she walked, she grabbed both my shoulders with her frail hands, as I slowly stood up. Pulling me close to her, she gave me a hug and said, "God go with you, go in peace, you are His blessed child." I turned, gave her a gentle kiss on the cheek, then walked out of the room with pocketbook, pouch, and jar in hand.

Back into the sitting room, Mama and Daddy were ready to go and eager to hear about this most unusual episode. Although not as much as I'd thought. Mama mentioned that she knew I wasn't able to share everything but asked me to share some of the highlights. I pondered over this during the drive back home. I guess Mama had just had another one of her intuitions.

Driving along on the expressway, we weren't two miles off the ramp when we noticed a logjam of vehicles — both lanes, bumper to bumper. Mama turned on our CB radio just in time to hear, "Anybody listening to our voices out there in the airways? Listen up good. If you can turn around and go back to another exit, do so! There's a tractor-trailer up ahead that has jackknifed and three vehicles are involved. Several people are injured, and it looks like we might be here for several hours."

"Did you hear that?"

"Sure did."

"Good thing I turned it on when I did — you see? It was the Lord's will." We smiled and thanked Jesus again for His protection. "Shug, do you have the Statler Brothers cassettes in this car?"

"Yes ma'am. Wanna hear 'em?" Mama nodded as Daddy instructed me to not have too much bass so he could hear the clear tones of Jimmy and Harold.

* * *

A couple of weeks later, things at work were still aggravating and disturbing at times. I tried so hard to have a good attitude, and yet I could still feel the presence of an uneasy spirit. It seemed like this oddness was ever so present in the worst of times. *Lord, I'm wearing that pouch and I'm still taking the medicine as Mrs. Cottler instructed. I just don't understand why these spirits are still around. I thought my visit to her would be the end of it.*

Then, like a light bulb bursting, I realized, "I forgot to read that Bible Scripture that I promised God I'd do last month! What was it? Hmm. Ah! Isaiah Chapter Ten." I scrambled around my pocketbook and found the small Bible I had started carrying around with me back in the summer.

"Oh No! Where's Isaiah? It's not here. Where'd it go?"

"Ah, here's the book listings. 'The New Testament. Let me look in the index for the book of Isaiah. Not here? Oh, now I remember. There are two parts to the Bible. One is the Old Testament, and one is the New Testament. Isaiah must be in the Old Testament — which I don't have with me. Jesus? I promise, I'll read it when I get home tonight."

Sam was at the door to greet me. She was so faithful. I could talk to her when I couldn't talk to anyone else. She always seemed to know exactly what was in my heart. Then she'd rub her little head up against my body and give me lots of loving.

"How was your day, Shug? Before you say anything, I'm stewing your favorite. Thought of you at work having to do all that extra due to some more being laid off, and besides, your Daddy and me ate the leftovers from last night."

"Mama? You mean you peeled and sliced these just for me? Thanks, Mama. While they're cooling, I'm going to get my Bible and look up a Scripture I dreamed."

"You've had another dream about the Bible?"

"Uh, yes ma'am."

"What was it?"

"Isaiah Chapter ten. I dreamed it last month and completely forgot to read it."

Gee, Lord, I hope Mama doesn't read much into this. I don't need her breathing down my back right now too. Please, Jesus, please protect me from Mama's urgencies. When I returned with the Bible, to my surprise, Mama didn't inquire much at all.

Umm, Jesus, You surely work quickly — sometimes. Thanks.

"I didn't fix you a drink not knowing what you wanted."

"That's OK, Mom." I reached and got a glass of water.

"Water? I'd never've guessed you'd get water," Mama commented, shrugging her shoulders with a laugh. I sat down to the table, and Mama also pulled out a chair and sat down with me. We talked about our day, and Mama said Daddy had gone over to a neighbor's house to help them with some house plans. *Oh Jesus, this feels so good. Just Mama and me.*

"Have your feet been swelling much lately, Mama? I've noticed you propping 'em up a lot."

"Oh, Shug. You always did notice things like that. Not to worry, I'm just fine. How's those carrots?"

Mama never did like talking about herself and didn't want anyone bothering over her either. She always seemed to change the subject whenever I brought it up and I'd let her. The dream of the Bible only came up once. She just said that I should pray about the matter and that maybe Jesus would reveal to me a clearer understanding.

Umm, maybe Mama really does know what I'm going through —although, dear Jesus, I can't talk to her about it 'cause I really don't know myself what all is taking place. After our mother-daughter togetherness, which I always treasured, we cleaned up the kitchen and then enjoyed each other's company in the den while waiting for Daddy's return.

Before lying down for the night, I got the Bible and read the Scriptures. "Woe unto them that decree un-grievousness which they have prescribed." *Umm, I'll just pray about it. I know You'll show me as I read the rest of the thirty-four verses — that is if it's Your will for me to know.*

I vaguely remember asking in a semi-conscious state of drowsiness just before falling to sleep. *Jesus, am I experiencing the world? Is this part of Your answer to that question I asked when I was operated on back in the Seventies?*

27

Once in a Lifetime

*L*ESLIE AND RUFUS invited us over for supper one evening. She said she was having some country ham, homemade biscuits, and molasses for sopping. This was right down Daddy's alley, so Mama jumped on it before Leslie changed her mind.

After helping with the dishes we settled down to enjoy each other's company. We laughed about our trip out West, especially about us just plain old country gals using those fancy toilets that automatically flushed.

Before we left, Leslie asked if I'd like to ride with her to visit her daughter down in South Carolina that coming weekend. After checking my schedule, I agreed.

"This'll be a good time for me to visit 'em too. I haven't really talked to them since the reunion — just briefly, when we stopped by there to pick up your puppies on the way home from that trip."

We left early Friday morning and arrived around dinnertime. Not finding anyone home, we drove back up to town and found a fast food restaurant. When we returned, we were greeted by their pets, which reminded me of Sam as they jumped for joy.

On Saturday, Sandra and Randy said they had a special evening planned. "Okay, Sandra," Leslie said, "I'm your mother and I don't like this 'special' bit. I've learned over the years that whenever you start with that, something is up with you. Now out with it."

"Well, Randy and I have found this really neat restaurant. On Saturday nights they have a live band that plays country music. What's awesome is it's a clean atmosphere — lots of families attend with their children."

"Sandra, that sounds a whole lot like Shadracks up near Grandfather Mountain."

"That's exactly right, Jeannette. I knew I'd been to a similar place before, I just couldn't remember. Randy and I went there when we visited the Highland games last summer. Anyway, the food is good and the price really isn't all that bad for all the entertainment you get.

"Umm, I haven't been dancing in a long time. Don't know if I even remember how," I murmured. "Charles was a good dancer, but not me. I seemed to have two left feet."

"Jeannette, we'll make it easy for you, we'll teach you line dancing."

"Line dancing? I've never heard of it"

"Where have you been, Jeannette? Even *I* know what line dancing is!" Leslie exclaimed.

"I thought you knew about line dancing, Mama, but I wasn't sure if Jeannette did, so I stopped by the video store and rented these instructional tapes. I need to feed the animals and do a load of clothes for Monday morning. While I'm doing all of that, you two watch the tape and practice for tonight, okay?"

"I knew I taught you well, Sandra. Good thinking," Leslie said.

Arriving right on time, we found a table spread with food that'd feed an army. We found a perfect spot to see the stage, just as down-home country music began playing. "Oh, Leslie, if only our parents were able to join us. I know Mama would have a ball. Although she and Daddy wouldn't be able to dance, we all would have a great time with 'em."

"Yeah, I know what you mean, Jeannette."

After we finished eating, I said to Leslie, "We can't do any worse than they're doing, right? So, let's give it a try, whaddya say?"

The band got caught up in the action, but the music kept right on going. Folks on the sidelines started laughing, and even the workers stopped to watch all of us on the floor trying to keep up with the music, the line, and ending up bumping into each other. So, what do you do? You just jump in, hang on, and have a down-home good time.

The Sunday morning sunrise peeped through the blinds in the small bedroom. We showered, gathered our suitcases, and reminisced about the total enjoyment of the past few days. We stayed as long as we could to still get back home by sunset, knowing our parents would be uneasy if we arrived after dark.

After we drove about two hours, Leslie asked, "Jeannette, I'm getting hungry, aren't you?"

"I was just doing great until you mentioned that four-letter word."

"Wouldn't you know it? Restaurants are just like policemen — when you want 'em, you can't find 'em. Hey, look, there's a sign, 'Home Cooking at the next third exit. Look, there it is again. Did you see it Jeannette?'" Leslie asked with enthusiasm.

"Yes ma'am, boy, does it ever sound good. It's only fifteen miles ahead. What time is it getting to be? Let's see, it's five-thirty now, and after we stop and eat that should put us home just before nine or so, right?"

Exiting the ramp, we crossed the east-west road and drove down a side road. We drove into the unpaved lot and got an excellent parking place. We walked from the dirt lot onto weathered plank boards that reminded me of a western-style saloon entrance.

Instantly entering the small restaurant, I was amazed of the atmosphere. Smiles were immediately seen upon not only the customers but the workers as well. Everyone seemed to know each other. There were men in jeans and some even with suspenders clipped to their pants. Most of the women wore skirts and blouses with long top aprons. Leslie and I thought their outfits looked like Grandma Ferrell's. The tables were all wooden with red and white checkerboard tablecloths. The chairs were wooden and straight back. Sort of like a barbecue place.

"Jeannette, do you see what I am seeing on this menu?"

"Yes ma'am, can you believe all this food for such a little price?" As the friendly waitress came over to take our order, the folks eating were turning around in their chairs to greet us, as though, they had known us all our lives.

"Jeannette, I feel just like I'm at home."

"I agree. I know this sounds strange, but Leslie, it seems like we belong here. I feel so comfortable and at peace."

"Yes, I know what you're saying. I feel the same way. Why, those two couples that just left made me feel like I ought to know them, and look how they spoke to you, as if they'd known you all your life."

Ah, the *food*. The biscuits were made from scratch. "Leslie, these remind me of Great-grandma Simmons', Mama's mother's mama. Sort of light golden brown on the bottom and with big and cloud-like softness inside. Why look, I can even pinch some small pieces and roll them like Grandma Ferrell used to do."

"I'm gonna put some butter on mine, what about you?" Leslie asked.

"Just watch!" I reached for a jar sitting on the table that read, "Homemade Molasses." Next, I added some butter and stirred it all up. Then I commenced to sopping.

"Umm, that looks good. I think I'll do the same," Leslie said.

"Daddy taught me to do this. He said that when he was growing up, sometimes all they had for supper were biscuits and gravy. Even on rare occasions they would have biscuits and molasses. Said that Granddaddy Ferrell had a sugar cane crop. That Granddaddy's favorite mule, old Rhody spent many hours going round in circles hitched up to that winch."

"I didn't know that," Leslie spoke with amazement.

"Me either until the reunion. Uncle Thomas told me about it." As old Rhody went around the circle, the weight on the winch would press the sorghum (Papa called it sugar cane) so tight that the juice was expelled. After a certain amount was squeezed, Papa would put the container over an open fire and cooked it down until it thickened. After Mama prepared it in different size mason jars; pints, quarts, half gallons and gallons depending on the size of the family, Papa would sell it at the store for ten cents a quart and twenty-five cents a gallon.

And, Jeannette, almost all the farmers in the area had their own cane crop and I believe there were only two winches in the area and Papa had one of them. Neighbor's all around would harvest their canes at the appropriate time and bring them, as they'd say, for Mr. Willie to process. Poor old Rhody, why I don't think she knew of a straight path except for the circled ones. It's a wonder she didn't walk herself to death. It was a lot of hard work and took a long time to process from planting to harvesting to processing — but, it was well worth it. You just don't find that kind of good nourishing nutritional product these days. So you see, Jeannette, that's how molasses was made, from God's recipe."

"These chicken and dumplings are out of this world. Jeannette, this reminds me of the way Grandma Howard use to make 'em, mixing flour and lard and rolling the dough using a rolling pin with sprinkles of water every now and then. Even some of the dough isn't completely done, just the way I remember liking it best, when it sticks to the upper part of your mouth and you've gotta push it off with yer finger because it's so gooey, and all. Now you ain't telling me nothing — that's down-home eating."

"That's exactly right, ma'am. We believe in the old fashioned way around here," the waitress said as she refilled our tea glasses.

"Oh, Leslie, if only I could take this home to Mama and Daddy – how they would enjoy it. Why, I'm right back to being a kid again."

"How's your roast and vegetables, Jeannette?"

"Simply delicious. Why, I do believe the snap beans and the corn are stewed just like Mama cooks 'em. Daddy's all the time saying she cooks like Grandma Ferrell."

"Leslie, I hate to finish. I don't want it to end."

"My sentiments exactly, Jeannette. My sentiments exactly."

We just couldn't get over how at home we both felt. The atmosphere was perfect. While we were eating as slowly as we possibly could, the kind waitress came over and gave us a list of all their homemade desserts and she added that they were actually made the old timey way, from scratch. Key lime, chocolate, huckleberry and pumpkin pies along with apple dumplings. We have carrot, german, five layered chocolate, and dried apple cakes plus five different kinds of ice cream. Suggesting we think it over a bit, the waitress turned to wait on some else who just entered the restaurant.

"Well, Jeannette, you were very informative on the making of molasses do you have any idea how they made the dried apple cake?" Leslie asked.

"Oh, yes. Uncle Ben told about he and his brothers spreading the sliced apples on a white sheet and lying it on a screen on top of their shed's tin roof. One of us would go out there at least once a day and ruffle the sheet causing the apples to shuffle. This would help get the air under them so they wouldn't rot. And if a shower of rain came, we younguns had to rush and jump up on the roof and gather the sheet with the apples and move them under the roof so as not to get wet. Oh I guess it'd take about a week or more, wouldn't it John?" As I turned to see Daddy's head bobbing yes, Uncle Ben continued, "For those apples to dry. But, you talk about good eat'n. I don't know anywhere these days where you can get a homemade dried apple cake made the old fashioned way."

"Ma'am," Leslie motioned for the waitress, "We would like a small slice of dried apple cake, huckleberry and key lime pies and some vanilla ice cream on the side." They each tasted exactly like the ones we remembered from our past.

We got home as planned around nine o'clock. Sam was just bubbling over. I thought she was gonna twist her tail plum off, licking and jumping, she stayed right beside me the rest of the night. I could hardly wait to tell Mama and Daddy about the trip. The shopping, the dancing, and especially about the restaurant and how it brought back so many wonderful memories of Grandma Simmons and Grandma Ferrell's downhome country cooking.

* * *

Vacation was soon approaching and we'd already made plans to visit those dear folks in Florida. As the excitement built, I could hardly wait to share that restaurant with my parents.

I remembered it being near the South Carolina line, and as we approached, I searched every road sign in sight. I even turned around in the back seat to read the ones facing the northbound side, but I didn't see a single advertisement for it.

"Mama. I know we weren't dreaming. I have it written down, the exact exit we got off at. I don't understand. It doesn't even appear to've ever been. Daddy, stop at this next station and let me go in and ask about it?"

"Sir? I'm from out of town and on a visit about four months ago I had a great pleasure of eating at a down-home country restaurant around here. Could you please tell me where it moved to?"

"I'm sorry ma'am, there's not a restaurant of that kind in these parts."

"Sir, are you sure?"

"Ma'am, I've been living here all my life, and I'd be nice to have one like you just described. Why, even I'd like to go back in time for some of my grandma's cooking. I'm sorry, but I haven't heard of one anywhere around."

I know Mama saw the disappointment on my face as I reentered the car. Out of the blue she said to me, "Shug, Papa and I prayed for your and Leslie's safety as you traveled. He answered by placing a restaurant right when you needed it the most, and you may never find it again."

"You may be right, Mama. I remember what the waitress said to us, 'We are always here for you when you need us.'"

"Uh huh." She and Daddy's eyes met with that special look.

To this very day, neither Leslie nor I have been able to find that once-in-a-lifetime restaurant.

28

A Spiraling Mile

IN THE LATER part of September, to celebrate Mom and Dad's forty-ninth anniversary, Clara Smith and Rachel Stine were asked to join us as we toured the Dutch country. Our plans included lots of sight-seeing along the mountainous terrain of Virginia, Maryland and on into Pennsylvania. On a crisp Thursday autumn morning, a welcome relief from all the heavy humidity earlier that month, we managed to get on the road around nine o'clock. Making our way toward Virginia, Mama spoke of hearing about their lottery. It wasn't long until she had our adrenaline running sky high.

I'd never seen this part of the country. Daddy said he and Clara's husband had come up this way once to check on some horses.

"How about you, Clara? You ever been in these parts?"

"No, Drusilla, can't say that I have. Rachel?"

"No, not me either. Sure is pretty through here, isn't it?"

"Yes. You're right about that. I can hardly wait to see the town where the Statler's grew up. Wonder what kind of museum they have?"

"Daddy? Help me get through these mountains, okay? I need some advice on gearing. I never did learn when to use second or third. Hey look. There's a sign saying something about a natural bridge and waterfall."

"I only caught a glimpse of it as we passed by. Jeannette, you were driving too fast to catch it all. Better slow down in this mountain range, okay?" Daddy spoke.

"Look. There it is again. Y'all ready to stop for a snack? I could use something to drink." I asked as Rachel's head bobbed with agreement that seemed to cause a chain reaction from the other three.

The store where I stopped had signs everywhere announcing, "Virginia lottery tickets sold here."

"Jeannette? Here, buy me three dollar's worth of tickets," Mama said.

"Here, wait a minute. I may as well get two myself. Here's mine," spoke up Daddy.

Bringing back the five tickets, I fanned out ten. I was hoggish. I bought five dollars worth for myself. I wasn't stingy like Mama and Daddy. Mama chose three tickets, and Daddy chose two from the ten, leaving me with the rest.

"Jeannette? Let me buy one from you. Here's my dollar," spoke up Rachel

"Ok, here."

"Jeannette, I'm not buying nothing. I don't do it at home, and I ain't doing it here either," Clara announced.

Except for Clara, we each began tearing into the tickets. Mama lit up like a Christmas tree. You could read her expression a mile away.

"What is it, Drusilla, did you win something?" Rachel asked.

"I got myself five dollars. Here Jeannette, I ain't gambl'n no more. Take this ticket in there and bring me back my five dollars."

"Me too. I won two dollars. Jeannette, go back in there with your mother's and my tickets and bring back our money. Besides, we need to get back on the road. I don't want to be stuck in these mountains if we can help it. Okay?"

"Rachel, did you have a winner?"

"Yes. Fifty cents — making me win half of what I lost — right, John?"

With three of our five riders winning some money, we were having a delightful time. We took our time, trying to catch each sight and grasp each moment as though it would be our last. My hoggish behavior caused me not to win any of the prizes offered. Not understanding the significance of the incident, I just thanked Jesus for our wonderful time together while pulling back onto the two-lane curvy road. After crossing over a mountain or two we saw a huge billboard announcing the natural bridge and waterfall again.

"Gee. I'd surely like to see that, wouldn't you, Papa?"

"Okay with me, Mama, if I don't have to walk too far."

The attraction was about twenty minutes away. We found a handicap parking space and walked into the center just in time to hear the announcement: "The departure time for walking down to see the waterfall will be in twelve minutes. The walk will take approximately thirty minutes. Be sure you have enough film in your cameras, and for those who need assistance, wheelchairs are available for a small fee."

Well, that took care of that. All of our travelers were handicapped except for me, and I surely wasn't gonna leave 'em sitting there for an hour and a half while I went down just to take a picture of a waterfall.

"Jeannette, you go ahead, we'll wait for you," Mama said with insistence.

"No way. There're other sights to see, and we can see them together. I ain't leaving you."

Smiling and putting his arm around my shoulder, Daddy pulled me close and said, "Thank you honey. We're mighty lucky to have you as our daughter." Then Mama reached for my hand as we were walking out of the center and gave me a gentle squeeze.

"Would anyone like a drink of Hill Top water?" I asked while reaching for a nice cold bottled water from the cooler

"Just imagine our own personal waterfall," Mama said while opening the trunk, "sure feels good going down, don't it?"

Moseying on toward our destination, taking our time and enjoying the scenery of the Shenandoah Valley, we decided to stop and visit some of the Virginia caverns.

I took the tour while the rest of our group inspected the visitor's center.

A little over an hour later, before I even reached the car, I heard laughter and giggles from within. "Shug, you sure missed a good show," Mama said.

"You surely did," Rachel chimed in.

I tried to tell them of the oyster-looking rock and the formation like an ice cream cone when Daddy popped up to say, "You know, I just learned about a part of a car I never knew before. Why, they even had (as he called the foreign part) that made it easier to fix the motors way back then. It probably cost a pretty penny, and I could hardly afford to feed Mama, Drusilla, and me after Papa passed . . . just was getting by. You remember those times, don't you, Clara and Rachel?"

"We sure do, John. All too well, I'm afraid."

The first night we stopped near Stanten. The next morning we visited the Statler Brothers museum. At the gift shop, we signed up for the mailing list for their schedule of roadside shows and special events. After a couple more pictures of us standing beside their photographs, we were on our way to a motor lodge located in Gettysburg, in the southern tip of Pennsylvania.

After a while Clara said, "Look! Betcha that's a good place to eat. Look at all the cars."

I had my doubts. The place looked old. The windows needed caulking and painting. The roof had patches of odd colored shingles. The outside advertisement showed signs of weathering and even the folks coming out of the restaurant looked like they'd had hard lives. But, seeing as all the others were agreeing with Clara, I started slowing to a crawl just as a spot came available. I swerved Dad's Lincoln right in, silently giving praises to Jesus for His help right when we needed it so they wouldn't have to walk too far.

The place reminded Mama of Stanley's, a restaurant that used to be in Stanleyville. This one was a two-story rock building with white wooden windows and a big, heavy white wooden door. The steps that led up to the entrance were also made of stone, and attached to the steps was an iron rod used for a guardrail. Inside were antique wooden booths that had old-timey jukeboxes in each section. We all got a kick out of it. And to think I hadn't wanted to stop. Once again I was reminded not to judge a book by its cover.

It wasn't long before the sun began to set. Around eight o'clock, I asked Daddy to check the map to make sure we were on the right track. Riding and talking, around ten thirty — we all were getting antsy. Finally finding a nice looking station where we could freshen up a bit, I decided to call the lodge. We were only about fifteen minutes away.

After registering and driving around this one story building, we pulled into a garage enclosure and to our surprise, parked only three feet from our rooms. Daddy was so amazed by this structure that he left us to unpack while he went to ask for information from the management.

He found out that the lodge had been built for the elderly and that made it mighty convenient for many travelers. Not only the travelers but their vehicles, too, were safe from all kinds of weather. When it came time to remodel, they decided to enhance the original building and make it more comfortable instead of tearing down and rebuilding with modern technology.

"I'm hungry."

"Me, too."

"Dru, what y'all got to eat?"

Chuckling, Daddy said, "We got some peanuts — want some?"

"Papa, you always got peanuts. Didn't you bring anything else?" Mama asked with a stern voice yet laughing all the whole time.

In no time we women were settling down to a good old fashioned game of Rook while Papa enjoyed his peanuts and tinkered with the remote control.

"Papa, you mean you came all this way to mess with the remote? Not me, I ain't watching no TV. The girls got a mighty good Rook game going in here. You ought'a come and join in."

Guess we all were getting some of the crazy giggles after driving since sun up. Mama's adrenaline had been running overboard since she won that five dollars yesterday and she was still on a high. Clara and I won the Rook game and Mama and Rachel went into the hole. They demanded a re-match. We gave in and then the tables turned. It was Clara and me going set big time. Although the difference was only by a few points they didn't stop there; they kept rubbing it in that they had won by a long shot.

* * *

The next morning we discovered we were just a hop, skip and a jump from a Big Boy Restaurant. Since four of the five of us were handicapped, we decided to drive. After parking we learned why we had to park near the back. The front was nothing but flowers, grass, a sidewalk and Main Street.

Mama, Clara, and Rachel hurried ahead of Daddy and me and entered the restaurant's side door. I turned to Daddy and asked him to look at the pretty flowers. They formed the United States flag flowing beautifully onto a slight hillside.

Daddy turned his head to the right and looked. All of a sudden his shoes seemed to stick to the walkway. He suddenly sat down on the pavement. I rushed to his side, knelt down and called for Mama.

"Papa, what happened?"

Noticing two couples heading our way, Mama jumped up and frantically asked them to come and help carry Daddy inside. The two men grabbed Daddy under his arms, even grabbing the back of his navy blue pant loop to help steady his balance. Throughout our entry into the restaurant, Daddy spoke of not having any control of his right foot and leg. The men gently sat him on the inside bench and made sure he was okay before they left to join their wives. The restaurant workers were also very helpful. Mama asked Daddy if he had taken his sugar pill that morning, and he assured her he had.

"Papa, we gotta get you to a doctor, but how, and where is one?" Mama started biting her lip and popping her fingernails in her upset. The restaurant manager told of a hospital just down the street, about a block from there. Daddy kept saying he'd be all right in a minute or so and for us to go ahead and order something to eat.

"Sir, would you like for me to call the rescue squad for you?" The restaurant manager asked

"No. I'll be all right. Just, if I may, sit here for a little while and gather myself."

"Yes, Sir, that'll be just fine. If I can help, please have your wife to come and get me."

"Mama, my right leg keeps flopping around like a bowl of jelly."

"Sir, would you mind helping get my husband to our car? It's parked beside the building in the handicap space."

Soon the front manager and four big strong workers gently raised him, two on either side, one in back and one in front to clear the pathway to our parked car. They gently lowered Daddy into the front seat, making sure he was as comfortable as possible before closing the door. Daddy insisted that we go back to the lodge and load up the car before going to the hospital. "You don't know how long we will be there, and we need to be prepared for whatever happens."

"Guess you're right, Papa. Are you in any pain?"

He nodded no, and we went back to the lodge and loaded up. About fifteen minutes later we found the hospital. Two emergency staff employees were waiting for us as I pulled up under the shelter. They immediately took Daddy back to be examined while Mama and I handled the paperwork. By the time we'd finished getting the insurance and paperwork completed, the on-duty doctor came in smiling.

"Well, Mrs. Ferrell, we can rule out a stroke for your husband. We can rule out a sudden increase or decrease in his sugar level and we can rule out any type of heart problems. x-rays are showing your husband's right hip is broken."

"His hip is broken?"

"Yes ma'am, and he wants to see you. Please come this way."

Finally, in what seemed like hours, Mama came to the waiting room and told us what the doctor had said.

"A *broken hip*? How in the world did Papa's hip break?"

"Calm down, Shug. Papa keeps insisting on going home. He keeps saying that Dr. Ashley's the only one who knows his health condition."

"He's right, you know," Clara said.

"Yes, Clara, I know. This young doctor told us there were two alternatives. The hospital could take Papa to the airport, which is about an hour away, but they didn't know just how long he'd have to wait for a flight to Raleigh. On the other hand, the hospital could arrange for him to be transported to Rex by way of an ambulance. However, John's main concern is how you and Rachel will get home should he take this route."

"You tell John not to worry about us, Drusilla. We'll get home even if we have to ride a bus. That's no problem."

"And then there's Jeannette. She doesn't drive alone. She's never had to, and we know she'd never leave us no matter the circumstances with her job. She'd quit before leaving us alone."

"Yes. We know exactly what you mean. She loves you both so much."

"Anyway, that's another story. Right now, the doctor said that since we were driving a Lincoln Town car, and this particular year's passenger seat was adjustable to several different positions, that this was the better way to travel."

"*The Lincoln?*" Clara asked.

After visiting with Daddy, I shared with Mama that he was in a jolly mood and that we'd make it home just fine. I told her that Jesus was with us. She reached up, patted my shoulder, and then turned and headed back to be with him. I didn't want to be rude and leave Clara and Rachel alone in this hospital, but the need to call our preacher and inform him of our misfortune was so strong that I excused myself and headed toward the car.

"Jeannette, want me to go with you?" Rachel asked.

"No. I'm fine — no really, Rachel — I'm okay."

It wasn't long until I got a motion from the emergency room entrance to bring the car around. Then an ambulance arrived, and I was unable to achieve the mission at hand, so I pulled back to my original parking space as a few of the staff members began rolling Daddy to the car. Behind him Mama was carrying his shoes. Clara and Rachel raced ahead to open the car door, while I began adjusting the front passenger's seat.

The emergency staff carefully placed Daddy in the car, making sure he was in the best position possible to avoid damage to tissues surrounding his hip.

"Mr. Ferrell," Dr. Erikson said, "We gave you a mild sedative just as you arrived, and here's three more. This should be enough to help you with the pain until you get back to Raleigh. One thing's for sure, the good

Lord's guidance is truly with you all. I've never met nicer folks. I'll call ahead and have the medical staff attendees at Rex be ready for your arrival."

As the kind doctor continued speaking to Daddy, the medical staff made sure they had braced his hip and leg securely with pillows and a rolled up blanket or two.

"Thank you, Dr. Erikson, for all your kindness, and please extend our appreciation to your medical staff as well."

"Oh mercy me, we've gotta get in touch with Roger and the family and . . . "

"Mama, don't worry. It's all been taken care of."

"Huh? Whaddya mean it's been taken care of?"

I took it upon myself and asked Jesus to help me remember the telephone numbers of all I needed to call — *and* He did."

"You mean everyone's already been contacted? Roger? Sally and Anita and . . . "

"Yes, Mama, everybody I could think of."

"Honey, what in the world would we do without you? You are such a wonderful daughter."

This made me feel so good and happy. Both parents approving of my help was so gratifying. I silently prayed from my heart, *Jesus, now comes yet another obstacle, the drive home that You've entrusted me with. I sincerely pray for protection as I drive back to Raleigh with Daddy, and help him with his broken hip.*

It started to rain. The farther we went, the heavier the rain poured. I began slowing down on the interstate and several folks were pulling off due to the gusting wind. I kept going. I'd rather have pulled over, but with such precious cargo, and knowing the severity of the situation, I kept crawling along looking through the side mirrors and the rear-view mirror. I was the only one still on the road. Finally, a few breaks were seen in the clouds. The rain began to let up, and the wind began to slow somewhat.

The rain slowed to just spouts of showers. I slowed the wipers. The blades were gracefully flowing smoothly until the rain dwindled to only a few sprinkles, just enough to run the blades at the lowest speed, which caused them to squeak.

"Honey? I can't stand that noise, please. Shut 'em off until we have to use 'em, if you don't mind."

"Sure Daddy. No problem. But, Papa, why are you jumping every few minutes?"

"I don't know. Unless it's my leg hitting the side of the door rest."

"Jeannette, when you get a chance, pull off the road and let me in the trunk," Mama said. "Maybe putting an extra pillow between papa's leg and the door will help the jarring."

I found a place to pull off. It was on a downhill slope. Since it was raining, I decided it was the best I could do before the bottom fell out again. Mama rolled out of the back seat as I popped the trunk lid. Cars flew by as Mama hurriedly got the pillow and opened daddy's door.

I turned deathly white after hearing the excruciating sound that came from him. Mama had opened the door without thinking about Daddy's broken hip, and his leg simply flopped down and landed on the car's running board. There was no blood whatsoever in Mama's face either. She stood like a zombie.

Recovering, she reached and, as gently as possible, picked up Daddy's leg and helped him secure the pillow while shutting the car door. Crawling back into the back seat, Daddy gently placed his knee against the closed door until it came to a complete rest. We sat there on the downward slope for a few minutes, still in shock over what had just happened. It took a while for all of us to come to our senses.

We rode several miles in complete silence. Mama was astonished at what she'd done. This was the first time in my life I've ever known her to be speechless. Then suddenly she broke the silence.

"Well, there were four of you in the car. You all saw what I was fix'in to do. Why in the world didn't you stop me from doing it?"

Every one of us knew exactly what Mama was saying, and the sad part about it was *she was right*. Why didn't we have enough foresight —

just a little bit — to prevent this dramatic pain to Daddy's already ailing body.

"Drusilla, it was just a matter of a simple reflex."

"Reflex? Hmm." Mama slipped further into the corner of the tiny seat.

"I'm sorry Papa, I'm s-o-o-o sorry. I didn't mean for that to happen." We all heard the crackling in her voice as tears started flowing down her face. "I'm so sorry."

Somewhere from within, love began to peep through as I witnessed Mama's sincerest apology. I've never seen her so devastated over something so innocently done.

"Papa, I'd never in a million years have had that happen."

"Don't worry, Mama, no harm was done," Daddy said reassuredly.

"No, lots of harm was done. Your leg is already broken, and I tried to break it again."

"Drusilla, don't be so hard on yourself. Accidents happen, and we know you'd never do that intentionally. We know you better than that. Like Rachel said, it was just a pure streak of reflexes. I'd probably have done the same thing if I were sitting on the outside. Who knows?"

"No, Clara, you'd have had better sense than to do what I just did."

Well, after that ordeal, Daddy asked in a whisper so Mama couldn't hear him, if I would stop at the nearest station so he could take another pain pill. It wasn't long until a service station appeared on the horizon. "How's the gas gauge, Jeannette," Daddy asked. "Might as well fill up while we're here, right?" As we stretched and got a drink and some chips, I said a silent prayer thanking Jesus for holding off the rain while we freshened up before heading back through the mountains.

"Jeannette? Are you going back the way you came?" Mama asked.

"Yes ma'am. I know of no other way, do any of you?"

"All I can say is you're a mighty good driver. I've never ridden with anyone as cautious as you are," Rachel said.

"It ain't me doing the driving, Rachel. It's Jesus."

The drizzling continued until we reached the mountains.

Oh dear Jesus up above, please don't let it rain while we drive through these mountains. Please don't let it be foggy and messy. Please, dear Lord I ask this only if it's your will. To this day I don't believe any of them realized just how in control Jesus really was from the time we left Gettysburg's hospital until we arrived at Rex Hospital in Raleigh.

* * *

The staff members were eagerly waiting our arrival and had everything set up and ready to operate, *except . . .*

Dad's doctor was out of town for the weekend, and another physician was on call. Not knowing the severity of Daddy's medical condition, it wasn't until Sunday night around eleven o'clock and after Daddy went into cardiac arrest that this doctor gave his permission to operate. Mama and I stayed until Dr. Frate came and talked to us.

"Mrs. Ferrell? Your husband came through the operation, and we've moved him to CICU. Do you have any idea why he wasn't operated on when you all arrived Friday night?"

"Yes Sir. This on-call doctor wouldn't sign the release papers. Said John would be all right until Monday when his doctor would be back in town. So, my not knowing what else to do, John just had to suffer all that while. Dr. Frate, he'd even jump nearly off the bed at times. Do you have any idea what was causing him to do that?"

"I'm afraid so, Mrs. Ferrell. I'm afraid so. You see your husband was having muscle spasms. When he'd try and move his right leg, the nerve endings were so badly damaged that the least amount of movement would cause a reflex — like being burnt by grease popping out of a frying pan."

"I know about reflexes," Mama said as she dropped her shoulders in a slumbered position. "Dr. Frate, is John going to be alright?"

"Your husband's in the loving arms of our Lord. It's really up to Him. We've done everything humanly possible. We've repaired his hip with a steel ball for flexibility; we've kept his heart steady, and his blood pressure is stable. As far as I can tell, your husband has a very strong heart. He has to have, to have ridden for nine hours on a broken hip, all the way from Gettysburg, Pennsylvania, and then to go through what he went through after arriving here. Dr. Frate turned to me, "Why don't you take your mother home and get a good night's sleep? If there's any change, we'll call you."

I grabbed Mama's tiny warm hand and together we walked down the hallway toward the outside entrance. Mama seemed frail, so unlike her usual way of being, *so strong and self-willed and always having a word to say.* This time, Mama was *silent.*

* * *

The drive home in the wee hours of this Monday morning was a quiet one. Noticing Mama wanted to be alone, I went ahead and unloaded the car, putting our suitcases in their proper places, but not taking time to unpack. Rest was much more important for us now. I put on my gown and crawled into bed, giving Mama all the time she needed — just her and God.

Bam ah lam ah lam! The crash sounded like the living room had fallen in! Startled, I jumped out of bed. By the time I got to the hallway, Mama was coming with broom in hand. Holding it upside down, she grabbed hold of my gown and began pushing me in front of her. We headed slowly toward the living room door. I immediately jumped behind and began slowly pushing as her hand-held broom caused the door to open.

"Where in tha hell is a light when you need one," she muttered. Once inside this darkened room, I ran to turn on the overhead light. To our surprise, there near the fireplace hearth was the Guardian Angel picture Daddy'd picked out and given me for my birthday the year before, lying face down on the carpeted floor.

"Shug, I'm sorry I said that 'h' word."

"Don't worry, Mama. We're so tired and worried about Daddy, we didn't need for this to happen to — unless . . . Look. There's not a single broken piece. The picture is intact, and the china cup and saucer that was sitting in front of the mantel isn't even chipped."

"Watch your steps, Shug, there could be some glass around. After all, you're barefooted, and I just can't deal with another family injury."

"Mama? You don't have to worry anymore about Daddy. He's gonna be just fine. This is an omen." The expression on her face was worth a million dollars. She smiled and then said, "Why did you jump behind me in the hallway and push, causing me to be the first one in here? You were scared weren't ya? It's just amazing that nothing was broken and that particular picture just up and fell off the wall and for us to 'av heard it. Just like you said, it was just meant to be. And I agree, Papa's going to be okay. Well, let's pick up the things that fell, put the picture back on the wall and go settle down a little."

Mama gave me a hug, "Shug, I've already brushed my teeth, and I'm going to lay down now. I hope you sleep good, and I'm really proud of the way you drove us home last Friday night. I know . . . " I felt her hazel eyes penetrating my very soul . . . "I know Jesus was with you — I saw Him in your face. I love you and if you need me, call me around seven, okay?"

"Thank you, Mama. I love you too."

* * *

During Daddy's ten-day hospitalization, he appeared alert and vigorous after being upgraded up from critical to stable. Happy wasn't the word for his radiant behavior. I can't remember when I'd witnessed him feeling so good and being so jolly. He wasn't just picking with us, he'd even joke with the nursing staff and the doctor and all the wonderful visitors that took time out of their busy lives to come. Emphasizing that he wasn't going anyplace, he insisted on us staying home and running those errands that needed tending to.

We were on our way back to Rex, not five miles from home when all of a sudden Mama began crying. A strange feeling came over me as I sensed Mama's tears were coming from the depths of her soul.

"Mom, what's the matter?" Although I felt as if a block wall was between us, I continued asking, "Have I done something? Have I said something?" Before she answered, deep within my soul, I knew I was fixin' to hear something *I didn't want to hear*; and yet, I *knew* I had to hear it.

There was no response — only severe crying as she wiped her eyes and blew her nose a time or two. The tears kept coming. Finally she got a hold of herself and yet her emotional pain was evident. I checked the traffic and found a place to pull over.

"Shug, just listen to me for a minute. You need to hear this, so please don't interrupt until I'm finished." She was very somber in her speech, very serious.

"Shug? What I'm about to tell you I know you won't understand." Tears continued streaming down Mama's soft white cheeks as she paused to catch her breath, hesitantly speaking the words that seemed difficult to form. "I've asked Jesus to take me before He takes your Daddy. I can't bear the thought of living without him. I love you, Shug, but I'm just not a strong person. With Christ's help, John and I have fought and conquered many battles together. I know this is an awful lot for you to take in honey, and not my usual talk. You're my only daughter, and I know I don't express my love to you like I should at times. It's just that, honey, your daddy is the strong one. He's has always been and always will be. I love him more than life itself . . ."

The sun peeped through the overhead Carolina cloud as Mama continued to talk. It was as if this dark time of reality wasn't happening as we sat along side this country road in southern Wake County. While tears and humility generated from Mama's being, a volcano began to erupt within my soul. I was feeling wretched, astounded at Mama's remarks. And yet, *I knew* way down deep that she meant every solitary word.

It took every bit of strength I had left to reach over and put my arm around her, trying the best I knew how to console her. As the cars whipped by, my main concern was to get to the hospital and see how Daddy was doing.

I knew that putting Mama on a pedestal and worshipping the

ground she walked on was wrong of me, but I loved her so much that I'd have done anything for her — at least until that movie, those co-workers and the other side of the green grass filtered in. Satan was working overtime in my mind as I tried to embed our togetherness. Mama was so full of life, and everyone loved her. Life wasn't any fun without her. Folks would come from miles around just to hear her talk, just to receive a hug, just to be around her and Daddy. She was my best friend and yet at the weakest point in my life. Satan had overpowered my mind, causing me to push away from my best friend. Our family was so tightly knit that I didn't think anyone could come between us, but I had been proven wrong.

Pulling under the carport later that week, Mama and I were talking about the stars. "Shug, I don't understand why everyone, including you, seems to think there's a man in the moon. I've always seen a woman in the moon with long wavy hair draped over her right eye and lying gently on her right shoulder. And, by the way, when does the Little Dipper appear?"

This was Mama's way of telling me about the vision she'd had. Instantly, my heart fell to my stomach, and I was speechless. Trying not to let on that I knew what she was talking about, I motioned for her to follow me and look up in the evening sky. Pointing to the Big Dipper and explaining the best I knew how of its origin, I know to this day that Christ was speaking through me, 'cause I never was good at science in school.

Mama just let out an unusual sigh and hung her head when I spoke of the Little Dipper appearing from late April to early June. In the pit of my stomach, I had the strangest feeling that mama's request of the week before *would* come true, and yet, I could do *nothing* to stop fate. I could do *nothing* to stop the evil one from using me to destroy my tightly knit family. He had a hold of me and wouldn't let go, no matter how much I prayed to Jesus above, no matter how many good deeds I did for the public's eye, no matter how hard I tried to break away, I was always an arm's length away from Christ.

29

Stones of Destruction

ABOUT A WEEK before Christmas, as the family gathered for their annual event, Greg Deafer, a friend of a cousin, spoke excitedly to me about a newly formed telemarketing business. As he paused to grab a mouthful of food, I urged him to continue, my mind racing ahead to thoughts of striking it rich. The cosmetic job I had wasn't anything compared to the promises Greg was offering. This was music to my ears. The more he talked, the more I soaked up the vital information — especially the part about making a huge amount of money once reaching a certain plateau.

"Oh, Jeannette, you've gotta get on board. This business is really hot!"

On the way home I brought up the subject. Mama was eager. Daddy — as always — had his reservations. "Honey, remember our health situations. Although this sounds good, it's probably too good to be true. There's gonna be an awful lot of leg work, and you already said you really didn't want to do a door-to-door type business. Am I right?"

"Yes, you're right. But instead of walking, I'll be calling. Only after someone agrees will I make an appointment for the final contract signing."

"See? See what I mean? You'll still be knocking on doors. It may not be in the same manner as now, but you'll be selling just the same. I don't know about this, honey. Don't sound too good to me, " Daddy said.

"Shug? We know how quick you are to jump on anything that comes along. Papa and I are here to advise, but one day we won't be. Papa, maybe this would be good for her. Even if it doesn't work out, we'll be here to help when the fall comes."

"Mama, you don't have to say another word. I'm reading you loud and clear."

I hadn't a clue what they were talking about. I was very much aware that Daddy was recovering from hip surgery and Mama's health was declining somewhat, but the idea of owning my own business continued to infest my mind — especially with Greg calling two to three times a week.

* * *

"Jeannette? You're not thinking seriously about joining this, are you?"

"Well, I have considered it, Daddy."

"I sure hope not. You have enough to do as it is, taking care of your mother and me."

"Shug? What seems so right could be very wrong."

"There you go again, not letting me do anything I want to do."

"I give up, John. She won't listen to me."

"Jeannette, your days off of work are already filled with your mother — carrying her to get groceries, to the drugstore for our medicines and whatever we need do for Tracey. Then there's the cleaning and upkeep of the house and your helping me with the yard work at the tenant houses and . . ."

"But Daddy, with your help and Mama's, I don't expect to have any problems taking care of this. Besides, I'll only be working part-time."

"When are you to give Greg an answer?"

"Well, he said he'd call me Thursday."

"Uh, oh. Hasn't been even three weeks since Christmas, he's sure moving fast. How much is this gonna cost you?"

"Two hundred to join, and Greg said that they were getting stocks before the summer was out. Oh, Daddy, you're gonna be so happy to see me succeed! You and Mama's have always told me I could do anything I put my mind to."

"Honey? Please keep in mind our needs as you make the right decision."

"But Dad . . ."

"That's enough. Your mother and I have nothing else to say about the matter."

I blocked out everything they were saying, lost in my own thoughts. *Why don't they want me to do this? What's the big deal anyway? I thought they wanted the best for me and would be proud of me for doing something on my own. I just don't understand.*

Knowing all along what my answer would be when Greg called, I still wrestled with my inner spirit as Daddy's words rang out loud and clear.

Near sunset on that Thursday, I dreaded having to make my final decision. *Maybe Greg has forgotten to call. Oh, Jesus, I hope so — so I won't have to tell him!* Then the phone rang.

"Jeannette, can you answer it? I've got biscuit dough up to my elbows," Mama said.

Running down the hall, I grabbed the receiver. "Uh, hello?"

"Hello, Jeannette. This is Greg. Hope you had a good day."

"I did Greg. Thank you for asking."

"I'm calling to see if you're still interested in joining the telemarketing team. We're gonna be involved in lots of new promotions in the next few months, and this it the time to get on board. How about it, Jeannette, what's your answer?"

"Uh, Greg? Uh, I don't know about this."

"Ah, c'mon, Jeannette. But, I can't answer for you. This is totally up to you. I'd like nothing better than to have you on my team, but if you don't want to join, then . . ."

"Uh, well, maybe."

"Maybe? No Jeannette. It's either yes or no. Come on, we'll have lots of fun growing as a team, not just making money for ourselves but saving our customers money, too. It's a win-win situation. Nobody loses in this business. Whaddya say?"

No longer could I hesitate. No longer could I stall him. The time had come for an answer.

"Okay. Yes, Greg. Yes. I'll join you — but, only part time," I mumbled.

"I'm sorry, Jeannette, what did you say?"

"I said yes, Greg. I'd . . . I'd love to join," I said pushing my parents' feelings to one side and stepping out to do something I thought was best for me. I wanted nothing else but to get on board and have some fun. I was tired of the same old humdrum life I was living. Nothing but sickness all around. With Mama and Daddy involved, I figured this would help bring us closer together. And besides, a new adventure might even help them have some fun, too.

"Oh, Jeannette. This is wonderful! Let me see. I'll be down in the Raleigh area the first of next week. Will Monday be all right with you? I'll have that day off from my regular job, and my wife Rebecca will be delighted to come down with me."

"Monday? Yes! That'll be fine."

"You just wait, Jeannette. We're gonna have lots of fun doing this together. With the experience you've had with the cosmetic line, you can't help but be one of our top representatives. You're so outgoing, and with Aunt Drusilla's personality, why, there's no reason you can't be on top of the ladder in no time. You go ahead and start recruiting customers, even today. Before you know it, you'll have a solid base. Before long, you'll even have your own ladder started. You know, this is an opportunity of a lifetime, and you don't know which of your customers will want to join you in this rewarding field. Remember, the more customers you have and the more reps you help get started, the more money you'll receive in commissions. Jeannette, I can't express to you how good you've made me feel."

"Thank you for calling, Greg."

"No, Jeannette, thank you for saying yes. Okay, we'll see you around five-thirty Monday evening, okay?"

Oh Jesus, how am I going to tell Daddy? I had in my head to say the 'n'

263

word and yet, the 'y' word is what came out of my mouth.

My heart pounded as I turned and walked slowly toward the den. I'd tell them straight and to the point, I decided, while pronouncing every syllable in a clear and understandable tone!

"Jeannette? What did you tell Greg?"

Oh boy, the moment of truth. But Lord, I don't understand why I am feeling so lousy?

"Jeannette? Answer me."

"Uh, Dad?"

"Oh no. You told him yes, didn't you? After I told you not to. Why? Well, you just call him back and tell him you've changed your mind." Daddy's disappointment in me was extremely obvious.

"No John. She's gotta learn. And you know it'll be better for her to learn it with us both than without either of us."

As soon as Mama said this, I started thinking, *Jesus, what's Mama talking about? What does she mean it's better to learn with 'em than without either? I don't understand.*

"Well, Shug, I'll do what I can to help you."

"You don't have to, Mama. After all, I'm just starting out part-time. It won't be until next year sometime till I'm up in ranks."

"Yeah, you can believe that if you want to. Best believe Greg is looking after Greg and not you," Daddy said sharply.

"John, this might take the best of me, but let's help Jeannette. She'll soon learn the real truth behind our reservations, and it'll be better if we're behind her with our love instead of against her."

"I reckon you're right, Mama, it's just that…"

"I know, Papa, I know."

As I washed up the supper dishes, my thoughts were lifted to Him. *Jesus, what did Mama mean when she said it might take the best of her? What's she talking about? Why is Daddy s-o-o-o against my having own business? Why can't I do anything right around them anymore? They never agree with me on anything. I don't understand, Lord.*

* * *

Before long the business began to show some headway, and Mama jumped right in working the phone lines and making appointments. I soon had a very nice clientele, just as Greg had predicted, and I was really having fun. We were so busy that the first four months seemed to fly.

In May, lots of new horizons were in focus for the representatives. Working side by side, Mom and I were getting closer and closer. Every now and then I'd lift up thanks to Jesus for our time together. *It feels good, Lord, to be close to Mama again. Getting to know the happiness and peace she has for You. Maybe, just maybe some of it will rub off on me."*

On Friday, the tenth of May, Mama and I were on our way to visit with a telemarketing friend and his wife. Just before arriving, I noticed something was different about the car. After about an hour or so of visiting, I happened to mention it to Grover. It turned out he needed a lift to town to pick up his truck, and he thought his mechanic would be able to see about my problem.

However, because Sunday was Mother's Day, only the shop manager and a part-timer were available to check on my problem. The owner of the dealership came out just as they discovered I had a bad alternator. Luck was on my side that day because they just happened to have the exact part that was needed. Soon it was repaired and I thanked everyone for their kindness on such short notice, soon Mama and I were back on the road headed homeward.

In the dead heat of the five o'clock evening traffic, I cried out, "Not again!"

"What is it Shug, what's the matter?"

"Mama, the steering has gone, and I can't steer the car!" I managed to manually maneuver the car over into the right lane that led to an exit toward a less traveled road at the intersection. Cars were coming and going in all directions as I glanced over at Mama, who to my amazement, was as white a snow.

"Mama, don't worry, we're gonna be just fine, ya hear? Don't worry."

"Shug, we're gonna be hit. This is a bad intersection, oh Lord, I know we're gonna be hit." Then the car knocked off, came to a snail's crawl over by the right hand curb of the exit ramp, and stopped dead in its tracks. It would not move another inch.

As I got out and reached to open the passenger door, a kind soul pulled in right behind and offered a push. "Get in," he said, "and my wife and I will push you to safety. Others also stopped and offered to help. I began almost immediately telling them I didn't understand what was happening because we'd just left the dealership where they said it was fixed.

"Ma'am, I see you have a car phone. Do you happen to know the number of the dealership? Maybe they haven't left yet. It's only about two miles." Fumbling through my pocketbook and finding the business card Mr. Matthews had just handed me, I called. Moments later he told me he'd have a tow truck come and get the car. Just as I pressed the "end" button, another young man had stopped to check out my dilemma. "Jeannette, is it?" he asked. "I found your problem."

"You did?"

"Yes. The cable that attaches to the alternator doesn't seem to've been put back on properly. I've got some tools in my truck, and it won't take more than a jiffy to fix it. I'll be right back."

Thanks to Jesus, within no more than a minute this young fella brought the car to life again. Mama and I lifted silent praises and gave each other hugs of joy as we thanked everyone who had stopped to help us on this busy weekend. None of them would take any money. Mama and I stood there on the corner of Purfoy and Main Street, hugged and praised God for sending His angels to our aide. On the way home, Mama said most of them had told her that if their own moms were ever stranded along the side of the road, they hoped someone would take the time to stop and help her too.

Just as we were passing through Five Points and before traveling under the railroad overpass, Mama said, "Shug, you are a very strong person, and God will take care of you as he has taken care of your dad and me . . ."

Driving with my left hand, I lifted my right arm from my lap, flexed a muscle or two, and agreed with Mama's statement. But my stubborn nature caused a most uneasy feeling to emerge from deep within. Shame and guilt fueled my deep feelings as I began, once again, to wrestle between Satan and Jesus. I tried to push Satan down to open an avenue for Jesus to answer a question, *Lord, what was Mama really trying to tell me? Dare I ask? I dare not ask as I really don't want to know the answer, although I have a gut feeling I know what's lying ahead.*

As the novelty of my telemarketing business began to wear off, I learned Greg wasn't always available. I'd call him mornings, during different times of the day, and at all hours of the night but get no response. Remembering his comments about our having fun in the business together. I learned a hard lesson was in progress. It was one that I'd never had to handle before. He was right about one thing though: this was my business. Eventually I came to realize he was only interested in my doing all the hard work and making just enough to keep my head above water while he laid back and enjoyed a richer life.

I answered the kitchen phone one weekend as Daddy was enjoying one of Mama's salmon cakes. It was Greg. He asked me to attend a business extravaganza in Myrtle Beach, South Carolina. Because of Daddy's health, I finally got courage enough to tell him I would have to talk it over with my parents first before I gave him an answer. His reply sent chills up my spine. "Ah, c'mon, Jeannette. Ask Aunt Drusilla to get someone to stay with Uncle John so you can attend."

"Greg, we don't work like that. Either we all go or none of us go."

"Well, anyway, it was only a suggestion."

"Thank you, Greg, for calling and asking. I'll see what I can work out, and I'll get back with you. Bye."

"Honey, what was all of that about?"

"Dad, Greg wants me to attend a rally down in Myrtle Beach on Thursday night, May sixteenth."

"Well, do you think attending would help your business?"

"I don't know. All I'm going on is Greg's opinion that this is the chance of a lifetime. He said that many dignitaries were speaking, and there would be some breaking news of great importance and that everybody from this area was attending.

"Well? Everybody's not attending. If they were, he'd be going too, right? Anyway, there's not a place big enough to hold everybody. Besides, this breaking news will be in the next magazine issue won't it?"

"Dad? What are you saying?"

"You know good'n well what I'm saying. We didn't raise no dummy. I'm still having some strong reservations, I guess. Well, if your mother's up to it then I guess we can go with you."

"Didn't I hear you talking to Ruthann on Monday?" Mama asked.

"Yes. She seemed interested and was thinking about signing up. Said she'd been looking for some part-time work, and this might be just the thing."

"So, that means we'll be visiting her as well. That'll be great. I'll get to visit my niece, and we'll talk her into going with us to the rally. Oh, we'll have lots of fun," Mama said.

"Wait a minute! Wait just a minute. Where am I going to be while you girls are out gallivanting? I'm not able to be running with you. Don't forget I'm still mending from a broken hip."

"How could we forget, Papa? You remind us every hour of every day," Mama said.

"Now, Mama . . ."

"Well, it's the truth and you know it."

"Anyway, breathing at the coast is a little easier on me, but I'm still slow getting around."

"Daddy. Don't worry. I'm sure it'll be okay for you to stay at Ruthann's."

"I don't know. You'd better call her tonight and make sure. We don't want to get down there and run into any surprises."

Hi, Ruthann, "I'm calling to see if you might be free tomorrow night. There's a telemarketing rally being held down at Myrtle, and Mom and I would love for you to attend it with us. However, we'd also like to know if it would be okay for Daddy to stay at your place."

"Of course it's okay, Jeannette. What are cousins for? You know good 'n well I'd have it no other way. I'd love for Papa to stay here. And, yes, I'd be more than happy to attend the rally with you all. Now, there's two places you can stay. Either where Dennis stays, at the Holiday Inn about three miles from here, or a motel in town just around the corner from me."

"Since we're just staying overnight, I guess the motel will be best for us. This way, you can come over, and we'll be able to be together longer. Well, I'd better let you go so you can go to bed. I've kept you up long enough. Bye."

"Bye, Jeannette. Five o'clock comes mighty early. Being you all are coming down tomorrow, I'll just go in to work early. Don't forget: give me a call. If I'm not home, leave a message, and I'll get back to you. Goodnight."

* * *

Oh, the excitement Mama had for this business of mine. She was definitely a people person and so full of life. She never met a stranger and could talk to anyone, anywhere, about any subject. Once you met Mama, you knew instantly who she was and what she stood for. Daddy was a little different. He was more practical and down to earth, although his sweet nature would cause you to grasp at his every word, which he spoke with a great wisdom that everyone knew came only from above.

The blinders on me were placed exactly where the evil one wanted them. Between work and Avon and this telemarketing business, I was in a tizzy as I rushed to get things lined up for our upcoming Thursdays trip. I shrugged off Daddy's comments about Mama not feeling up to par and about my involvement with the business, and I didn't pay any attention to his warning remarks. I was so happy. What could possibly go wrong? My life seemed as perfect as it could be. My relationship with Mama was finally back on course and, with Daddy's approval of my home-based business, I was even going to church a little more often now. *Thank You, Jesus. Thank You for my wonderful parents and our fantastic relationship.*

This Thursday morning was so pretty. However, before we got to South Carolina, I noticed an orange light flickering in the dashboard. It would flash and then quit for a spell, and then it would start up again. It continued to flash off and on for several miles. The motor sounded ok and the steering wheel seemed within normal range. I didn't recognize any unusual sounds, and the tires seemed to be balanced too.

I wondered about that light as we conversed between gospel songs on the cassette. I also wondered why Mama was riding in the back seat. Why had she insisted on Daddy riding in the front? She had said something about Daddy being more comfortable in the front and that he'd be able to adjust the seat better. Still, with her claustrophobia, I was surprised that she kept insisting. *Jesus, will be the first trip in my entire life that Mama hasn't been beside me in the front. I just don't understand."*

After crossing the state line, I looked into the rearview mirror at Mama. "Wanna stop at the rest area just up ahead?"

"If you don't mind."

"If I don't mind? Of course I don't mind." The strangest feeling came over me, one I'd just as soon forget. While in the restroom I asked again, "Why aren't you sitting in the front with me?"

"Like I said earlier, with his condition, Papa is better off in the front."

"But Mama, what about your claustrophobia?" As I waited for another answer, the sight of Mama's frightening paleness and hunched-over shoulders pierced like a dagger through my body. A strange uneasiness penetrated my soul just before the evil one lowered the blinders once again.

"Well, we ain't making time in here," I announced rudely, tormenting myself inside for saying it. *Jesus? Where did that come from? What in the world made me say such a cruel thing to Mama? Jesus, what is happening to me? Please, I beg You, help me.'*

"You're right. I'm finished in here. Let's go," Mama said.

"Well, that didn't take long. What is it, Mama? Are you alright?"

"Gotta go, Papa. We need to get there before dark." Mama simply brushed off those cruel words I'd spoken as if I'd never said 'em. By the time we reached our destination, the orange light in the dash was staying on longer and longer. Here we were, strangers from another state, hundreds of miles from home and having car trouble, and anger began to boil within my soul. The only problem I'd uncovered was not being able to turn the outside mirror.

"Daddy, did you have this problem the last time you drove the car?"

"No honey. It worked just fine for me."

"Well, I guess it's my fault. I did something to cause it to not work, right? Everything's my fault here lately." I was speaking hatefully to Daddy, too. As my soul churned with deep humiliation, the evil one continued nibbling at my mind, using each and every word that formed as stones of destruction.

"Now wait a minute." I was startled by the tone of Daddy's voice. "I didn't say that. All I said was it worked fine for me the last time I drove the car."

"Don't argue with her, Papa, let's just see if we can find a place to help us."

Pushing the evil one back to one side, I did the best I could to carry on this conversation. "Daddy, let's stop at that BP station, maybe they can help fix it. What do you think?" I was trying desperately to use a different, more pleasant tone of voice.

Pulling into the station, I asked. "Sir, excuse me, could you take a look and advise me what to do about this mirror?"

"Yes, ma'am? What seems to be the problem? And how are you Sir, and you Ma'am," the mechanic said, nodding his head and tipping his cap to Mama seating in the back seat.

Then, turning back to me, he said, "Ma'am, go back to the light, turn left, follow that road about four miles, and you'll see a car dealership. They might be able to help you with this problem. They're open till nine, and their mechanics don't leave till seven."

"Thank you, Sir. How much do I owe you for your help?"

"Nothing, ma'am, just tell 'em Jim sent you."

I crawled back in the car and while driving away, Daddy waved at the service attendant as Mama piped in, "Sure was nice of him to help us and not charge the dickens out of us."

There it was exactly, where the man at the station had said. Before

I finished explaining the problem, this mechanic seemed to immediately know what to do. After examining the mechanisms, he adjusted a knob on the front driver door panel and all was back to normal.

"Sir, what did you just do?"

"Ma'am, somehow this knob had been turned off and in order to operate the mirror automatically you have to have it in the 'ON' position."

Talk about having egg on your face. *How, dear Jesus? How could I've been so stupid?* I asked as the raging animal inside me tried desperately to surface. It had become a constant struggle for me to suppress and push back the evil one's attempts to control my every thought, move, and entire being. If only I had something I could hit! Yes, that's it, a punching bag would be perfect for venting the anger, bitterness and awkwardness that seemed to engulf my soul, not to mention the frustrations of not understanding.

I thanked the young man for showing me the problem, fixing it, then asked how much the charge would be. "No charge, ma'am. Y'all have a nice visit while here, and tell your friends about us."

"Well, I guess it's time now to try and find the Swete Motel, while it's still light. Seems like I saw one when we first drove into town. I bet that was it." Approaching the entranceway, Daddy said, "Hmm, I'm not quite sure about this. Doesn't look too inviting."

"Well, it's just for one night, and I'm sure we can manage. Mama? What do you think about it?" I asked.

"It's up to you. Doesn't matter to me. Whatever you say is fine with me."

"Well, we'll be closer to Ruthann, Mama. We can meet and eat together and not waste much driving time. Okay, let's see how much they'll charge, and if it's within reason we'll stay." This was totally my decision. I was determined to stay so we could be close to Ruthann.

"Here, here's my card," Mama said.

"No, you keep your money, Mama. I'll pay for it. Besides, it's really a business trip anyway. We'll be attending the rally and signing up another rep. Thank you just the same, but this one's on me, okay?" Mama frowned, shook her head and said, "Okay, that's fine with me, then."

After I checked us in, Mama began getting out her and Daddy's medicines. Daddy had to take eighteen pills a day, not to mention breathing his inhalers two to three times when needed. Then, between Mama taking 120 mg of heart medicine three times a day and making sure her nitroglycerin prescription was up to date, she hoped she hadn't forgotten any. "Shug, I'm thankful you're healthy, 'cause I don't think I could keep up with another set of medications."

"Honey, this trip has nearly worn me out, and I'm even surprised that your mother is considering going with you to the rally. She's had a hard day, too. However, if I can't stay at Ruthann's house while y'all attend, then just bring me back here. What about it, Mama, are you going with them tonight?"

"Sure, Papa, as long as I have my heavenly dust, I'm just fine. My question is, will you be all right by yourself at the house?"

My parents were the most concerned people over each other I'd ever seen. *Dear Lord, if only Charles' and my relationship . . .*

30

Split Seconds

HE MANAGER SAID, "The only double bedrooms available are upstairs."

"But sir, my dad's on a cane and recouping from hip surgery, and my mom has a severe heart condition and is unable to climb stairs. Don't you have anything, anything at all downstairs?" I pleaded.

"Nope, sorry. Ma'am, if I were the owner I'd give you the one on the corner. However, she isn't here, and I don't have the right to. Take it or leave it. Then again, you might try the Holiday Inn about five miles from here. I know they're equipped for handicapped customers."

"Well, I sort of wanted to be close to my cousin, and this is the closest. Well, I'll just have to help 'em upstairs when we return tonight I guess."

Returning to the car, I explained what the manager had said. "Oh well, sounds like you've already made the arrangements to stay here. Don't worry about us, we'll do just fine." After hearing this, I knew I'd again done the wrong thing. But, with my stubborn nature and not wanting to admit I'd made a mistake (although my inner feelings knew otherwise) the evil one continued persuading his spirits to rule as I struggled to talk to Jesus.

Parking near the base of the stairs, I popped the trunk lid and retrieved our overnight cases. By the time I shut the lid and turned to help them up the stairs, Mama yelled down, "What's taking you so long?"

Oh, thank You Jesus. Mama's feeling better already and beginning to joke some. At least that's what the evil one lead me to believe. As we entered the musty room, the phone began to ring. Motioning it was Ruthann, Mama hollered from the bathroom, "Go ahead and talk to her while I get Papa settled and we take some powders for our headaches."

Headaches? Hmm . . . first I knew about them having headaches. "She said to c'mon over and we'd go out and eat someplace." All I had on my mind was the rally and signing up another representative. Then, all of a sudden, Mama jumped up and said, "Okay, we're ready. Let's go find Ruthann's place."

"Mama? Are you sure you and Daddy are up to it? You just mentioned having headaches. Don't you want to rest a spell?"

"Shug? I'll be resting later and . . ."

"So will I, honey, let's go ahead before it gets any later. We don't need to rush. We need to visit some — remember?"

Trying to be polite, I forced some concern. "Mama, are you sure you feel up to attending the rally?"

"We came down for it, and besides, I'll be resting soon." The evil one had such strong blinders around my ears, eyes, and mind that Mama's remark passed right over my head.

Oh, what a pretty little place. Ruthann had her mama's touch all right. The flowers were so full of color. Swinging the back door open here she came just a holler'n, "Hey Papa. Jeannette, why are you driving? I just knowd Papa'd be driving."

Mama rolled out of the backseat and opened Daddy's door as he replied, "Ruthann, I'm still not quite up to it yet. I've driven the truck some, but on a long trip like this, I thought it best for Jeannette to drive."

We went inside and before we even could sit down Mama began telling of my embarrassing episode at the car dealership. She was laughing so hard that she could hardly get it out quick enough. Even Daddy started laughing. She told Ruthann that she'd never seen my face redder than it was at that point. They laughed and laughed. This six-footer felt like a two-footer all over again.

On this particular day, this was more than an embarrassing moment.

I felt like I was on the threshold of a dark enclosure with no way to escape. I was on a roller coaster ride that was leading to total and complete destruction, and I had no control over it. None! I felt my cries for help were not being heard. As I searched and pondered and looked here and yonder, I was screaming for help but no one was there.

They finally stopped laughing and began talking about food. "We can go in my old jalopy. Ah, c'mon, it'll get us there and back," Ruthann said. "I promise."

"That's okay," Mama said. "Let's go in the Lincoln. With Papa's hip and all, it'll be better for him."

We passed the dealership on the way and the laughing started all over again. "Jeannette, what school did you say you graduated from, and were you paying attention when he told you where the 'ON' knob was?" I tried to be a good sport and laughed right along with them, but inside I was humiliated. "Let's just drop it, okay?" Well, this was NOT the thing to say.

"Hey look, Papa, we could've gotten a room there instead of at that motel," Mama said.

"Yes. I told Jeannette on the phone that's where Ronald stays when he comes down. I told her about the motel, 'cause she insisted on staying close to my house." I began to feel frustrated. I hadn't wanted my parents to know of my insistence. However, through the innocent character of my cousin, their eyes were opened to the truth. *Oh Jesus, if only I'd been honest with Mama and Daddy from the start, I should've told them my thinking that by staying close to Ruthann we'd have more time for visiting 'cause we hardly ever got a chance to see each other anymore. And yet, in Your sovereign way, just this once, You let my true colors shine, didn't You? Jesus, for a split second, I felt peace within my soul 'cause I'd been caught. For a split second, I was free of the evil one's lying and conniving ways. Dear Jesus, for this split second, I thank You.*

I noticed Mama's white, powdered-looking face. "Mama, are you feeling okay?"

"I'm fine. Don't mind me, Shug, I'm just fine."

She was quiet, not like herself at all. Oh, she'd pipe up every now and then, but something was different about Mama, and I couldn't figure out what. I really didn't try too hard. I was afraid that it would spoil the night's activities. (I was still thinking of myself and not of others, especially Mama, the one I loved more than life itself.) After supper, as we were approaching Ruthann's, I asked, "Hey Papa, are you going with us?"

"Why don't you all take me back to the mote . . . "

"Nonsense, you ain't staying at no motel. You're staying right here at my house and that's final," Ruthann insisted.

"Honey, give me your number again just in case. I don't see I'll need it, but just in case I do." As I reached to give Dad my cellular number, Mama spoke of needing to re-fuel her nerve medicine, her snuff which she so often called her "heavenly dust." Soon we were ready to head for the rally.

"Let's go in Mama's car, Ruthann."

"No, I insist on driving mine, and besides, I know where to go."

I didn't think we would ever get there. I've never seen so many cars in my life. From the time we got to North Myrtle, it was bumper to bumper all the way to South Myrtle. Arriving about thirty minutes late, there wasn't anywhere to park. I explained Mama's handicap to the desk clerk who said it'd be fine to park at the lower end of the fire lane as long as I put the handicap sticker in plain view — preferably over the rearview mirror.

We entered the auditorium, which was packed full of representatives. One rep in particular had an innocent way of bringing laugher and smiles to our faces. Folks like this are so special. *Thank You, Jesus, for Mama.* I came out of my trance, looked over and saw Mama wearing her favorite red culottes and rose-embroidered pullover sweater. A big smile brightened her recently wrinkled face as she leaned over and whispered to Ruthann, "Now there's an honest man. Why, I can tell just by the way he's presenting himself that he's a good person. I like him." She was clapping, but her shoulders had dropped and she seemed to be forcing herself to sit up straight.

The rally was soon over, and we waited till nearly all had left. Mama didn't like crowds. She said it was like being closed in and not being able to catch a breath of fresh air. Ruthann recognized a few folks and said seeing them helped make the trip worthwhile.

Just before leaving for the trip back to Ruthann's home, she drove us around the beach area and even drove into the parking lot of a new mall where everyone was shopping.

"Oh, No!" Ruthann shouted.

"What is it?" I asked.

"Hold on to your hats," Ruthann said while bracing herself in a firm position.

"Why?" Mama asked from the back seat.

"Another car has driven in since we came in and has blocked our exit. I've got to cross this cement isle so we can get out of here. So, hold on and brace yourself, it might be a bumpy one." *Oh no, Jesus. Mama doesn't need this with her heart condition. Please, please don't let it jar her too bad — please.*

Ruthann got up speed and nearly went airborne in her little car. Not being able to say Mama's name plainly when growing up, Ruthann along with other relatives in the family always pronounced Mama's name with a "z" in the middle instead of an "s." "Boy, that was a rough one. Is everyone okay? Jeannette? Druzilla?"

Ruthann instantly looked in the rear view mirror and I turned toward the back seat just as Mama answered us both, "Yes," clearing her throat and speaking quietly, "I'm okay."

Ruthann turned on the overhead light and asked me to look in her satchel and hand her a little white pill in a silver wrapper. She said she had a headache and needed to take something before driving back to her house.

I searched the best I knew how but couldn't find it. "Are you sure it's in here?"

"Yes. I have several aspirins in there."

"Here, Mama, see if you can find it." I passed the satchel back to her. Mom didn't argue as she reached out for the heavy satchel and searched for the silver wrapper.

"Thanks, Druzilla. Jeannette's still so shook up over the mirror that she's not seeing straight. She better get those eyes peeled before driving home tomorrow so she won't make any more mistakes." Laughter broke out again. I just sat there hoping they'd soon hush.

With the slamming of the screen door and the turning of the wooden door's key, Daddy's voice rang out hoarsely, "Uh, what time is it?"

"Papa, you were sleeping, weren't you?"

"No, just resting my eyes. Did you all have a good time? Well, Mama, how did you enjoy the trip?"

"It was different, Papa. It was different." I noticed Mama's words were somewhat strange.

"Well, Jeannette, you'd better get your paperwork out and sign me up now cause I need to get to bed. Five o'clock comes mighty early, and I need to be at work by six," Ruthann said. After the papers were all signed, we said our good-byes and headed to the motel. The next morning, I awakened to find Mama sitting in the chair. She just sat there saying not a word as she looked around the room and over at Daddy. Then she saw me looking at her.

"Good morning, Shug, did you sleep good?" she asked with a strange look on her face. I didn't pay much attention to it as the evil one let the thought drift over my head.

"Yes ma'am, did you?"

"Ump, huh."

"How long have you been up, Mama?"

"Ump, I couldn't sleep. These walls are sort of thin, and I heard nearly every move our neighbors made. Doors slamming and kids screaming and lots of movement downstairs and beside us too. Sure is a noisy place. Papa slept restless. Tossed and turned nearly the whole night long."

"But, Mama, you didn't get much rest then, did you?"

"Yes, I slept some."

"Well, I could sleep all day long but guess I'd better get up. Papa needs waking so we can go and get something to eat. You need to take your medicines." Just for a split second, I was concerned and I really did care.

"Shug, why don't you go and find us something. All I want is an egg biscuit without mayonnaise."

"Um, I'm not asleep," Daddy said. "Let's see, that will be fine with me too, except, I *do* want mayonnaise."

"Are you sure that's all you want? Mama, you never eat eggs, are you sure?"

"Yes, now get going and hurry on back. We need to get dressed and on the road before too much longer."

It was only 8:30 A.M. and Mama always slept till around nine or nine-thirty due to her heart condition. Again, I didn't think anything of it. I found a fast food restaurant, ordered and returned as soon as I could.

"Shug? I didn't want mayonnaise."

"I'm sorry. Here, let me scrape it off."

"No, never mind. I'll eat it anyway."

We ate and were soon on the road and headed home. As we traveled, Mama asked from the backseat if we'd mind listening to the cassette tape of her boyfriends, The Statler Brothers. "I know you heard 'em coming down yesterday, but I'd really like to hear 'em again — if you don't mind."

"I don't mind Mama, do you Daddy?"

Just as the gospel tape finished Mama asked, "Does anyone remember seeing me take my heart pill this morning?"

"I was getting yours and Daddy's order for breakfast, and you didn't take anything before I left."

"Papa? Did you see me take my medicine?"

"I know you took a pill, Mama, but you didn't tell me what it was. Don't you remember?"

"Oh, well, maybe I did."

"Why, are you not feeling well?"

"I'm okay, I reckon. Don't worry, I'm okay."

Then, she asked me to put the instrumental gospel tape in. After a while Daddy asked if we wouldn't mind turning the volume down some. Having only one ear, he was getting a headache and would like some quietness.

"Oh sure, Papa, no problem." Mama nodded her approval. We stopped at a spanish restaurant at the state line around noon. Not being able to read the menu or speak their language, we managed to order toasted cheese sandwiches and glasses of water. Soon, we were back on the road and decided to stop at the North Carolina rest area before heading toward Dunn.

I parked close to the entrance without having to use the handicap sticker, "Mom, you go ahead, I'll wait here for you and Daddy."

"Honey? I don't need to go. You go ahead with your mother."

"No. Neither of you has to go with me. I'll be just fine."

That was the first time in my life Mama's gone in alone. Papa and I sat patiently in the car and waited for her return as the mid-evening sun peeped through those tall oak trees on this warm day in May. I realized that Mama was looking kind of pale. I wondered if she was feeling OK or was she really *not* okay. I didn't ask. I was too self-centered at the time to ask.

It was getting on toward suppertime. I really don't remember the subject nor the comment I made to Mama, but Papa's comment to me still rings in my ears. Mama had said something that really peeved me, and I backtalked her in the most evil-minded way.

"Jeannette, don't you dare talk to your mother that way!" I felt flushed all over, silenced by my horror over slashing out. For several miles, silence continued. Not a word was spoken. Then, I heard these words coming from Mama and I've never forgotten them: "I don't know my daughter."

With my right hand on the steering wheel, I began rubbing my forehead with my left hand and thinking, *I don't know her either, Mama. Oh God, I don't know Your daughter either. Oh Mama, if only I could talk to you. I mean, if only I could tell you of the prayers I've prayed for Jesus to help me and He hasn't. If only I could speak the words I long to speak from the depths of my soul. Oh, Mama if only you knew of the tangled web the evil one has on me. If only, Mama, if only. Dear Jesus, what is happening to me? Why, oh why haven't You answered and helped me. And there's Papa, dear Jesus. His health ain't no good either. Oh, Jesus, I'm scared, dear Lord, I'm so scared. I've been running away instead of running toward You. Please, please help me."*

But it wasn't time. It was my will for His help. Right now, help me *right now*, not later; but *right now* — this was my will. I demand You to help me right now. He didn't. I felt just out of reach, just at arm's length of His wonderful grace. I was here and He was there, and so were Mama and Daddy. I couldn't, for the life of me, open up and talk to them like we used to talk many years ago. The evil one had a hold on me and really was messing up my mind. He kept telling me I was grown. I could do what I wanted to when I wanted to and nobody had a right to tell me any different, and that especially included parents. *And yet, Lord, You didn't stop the evil one from creeping into my life.*

Jesus, You know Mama stopped going to church because Daddy couldn't walk far due to his breathing and because of her heart condition. Anytime a force of air from a fan, an air conditioner, the change of weather — whether it be from the blistering heat to a raw cold — would cause Mama's heart to act up by bringing on an angina attack. Just because they didn't attend their dearly beloved church didn't keep 'em from reading Your Holy Word. And it didn't keep them from conversing with Brother Rogers and from loving the body of Christ. Lord, they didn't use that as an excuse not to worship You, but I know I did. Please, Dear Lord I pray, bless my parents, and protect them from the evil one.

I kept wondering why Jesus hadn't stopped me from falling into a pit of no return as the anger and bitterness continued to eat my soul alive. The evil one had my mind so confused that I continued lashing out to God on this homeward journey. Years of unclaimed emotions filled my spirit of not knowing what to do or how to act as I began standing at the threshold, ready to burst into a mighty volcanic eruption. What seemed so right was so deadly wrong.

Mama knew I was in trouble and yet she graciously prepared herself to carry out God's plan with perfection.

31

Touched by the Master's Hand

WE ARRIVED IN Dunn around four o'clock on Friday afternoon. Mama enjoyed eating at a local steak house there, so we decided to stop for supper. They'd just opened and, as we walked inside and through the line, Mama seemed almost addle-minded. I turned to ask what she was gonna eat and saw that her face was as white as a sheet.

"I don't know. Nothing seems good. I'm really not hungry, but guess I do need to eat something."

"How about some cream potatoes, Mama?"

Daddy had already gotten his steak and salad while Mama was just moseying around as if in a daze. This was very unlike her.

"Here Mama, try some of these potatoes. They may help you feel better. They're not real heavy, and won't lay heavy on your stomach."

"Well, I'll try and eat some."

She managed only a few mouthfuls with a half glass of water.

After the waitress brought the bill, we gathered our things and headed for the checkout. Daddy reached in his back left pant pocket for his billfold while Mama and I headed for the corridor.

Approaching the doorway and leaning into the door to push, Mama said, "My, this door sure is heavy isn't it?" I reached to help just when it nearly knocked us both down. "They need to put an automatic door opener on this — it's nearly impossible to open," I said.

On the way home, Mama didn't have much to say. As Daddy

conversed over the not-so-satisfying meal, I every now and then looked in the rearview mirror at Mama. *Jesus, what could be wrong with her. Mama's shoulders are slumping lower and lower as though she's in some sort of discomfort. And she's so pale looking, as if there's no blood in her face whatsoever."*

"Mama? Are you feeling okay?" Daddy asked after catching a glimpse in his visor mirror overhead.

"Yes. Um, hum."

"Honey? Do you mind if Jeannette swings by the drugstore to pick up my prescription that Dr. Ashley called in?"

"No, that'll be just fine, Papa, then you won't have to go tomorrow."

We arrived home a little after six o'clock. Mama checked the answering machine to discover that Tracey had called, leaving a grocery list and announcing that she was in need of her afternoon toddy.

"Jeannette, here, let me give you some money to go to the Clixie and get Tracey's supplies. Be sure and get enough to last her up to three weeks."

"Three weeks supply? Do you know how much that will cost?"

"Tracey won't mind paying you once she finds out how much you got her."

"I'll pay for it — you keep your money for later, Mama."

"Well . . ." she just trailed off, not even giving me an argument. That was worrisome.

Paying some, but not really that much attention to her, I went ahead and wrote down the items Tracey wanted and gathered my things for the trip up.

"Would you like to ride with me, Mama?"

"No, not this time. I'm a little tired. I'll walk out with you though and go out to the shop where Papa and Paul are."

I decided to let the Lincoln rest and crawled into my old '90 Buick. I can't explain the feeling that came over me just before I started the motor. I sat in the car for five minutes, watching Mama as she walked out to the shop. She was wearing her favorite teal polyester pants that were loose around her stomach, a cream-colored pullover sweater with red roses embroidered down each side, and her tiny white tennis shoes. All I saw was her back the whole time she walked, and she was talking to Papa and Paul. I remember she leaned over to her right, hands in her pockets, and spit, then she went back to talking.

I love her so much, dear Lord. I love the pure ground Mama walks on. I must go to get those groceries and yet, why am I looking at her so enticingly, as if . . . I didn't let myself finish that thought. I put the gearshift in reverse, backed out of the driveway, and headed toward Raleigh.

Sure enough, Tracey was delighted to get all that toddy and an ample supply of groceries. "Jeannette, what in the world possessed you to buy so much?"

"It was Mama's idea."

"Please thank Dru for me. She always seems to know exactly what I need. How was your trip?" I put away Tracey's groceries and visited with her some, then I excused myself to head back home. She told me she'd call Mama later to thank her personally, then she told me to be careful.

On the drive home, all was going well when suddenly I thought of Aunt Hattie. I hadn't thought of her since she passed away back in 1991. Out of the blue, her name flashed before my eyes like a streak of lightning. As I arrived at the intersection stoplight at Tryon Road, a white dove flew across the windshield and fell down beside my right fender.

Strange, I thought, as I slowly pulled off. I remember hoping I hadn't run over him, and when I looked into the rearview mirror there was no dove to be seen. At home, I found Papa sitting in his favorite recliner in the den and Mama in the blue rocker Daddy had bought her for Christmas last year. Her propped-up feet were somewhat swollen.

"Tracey just called thanking me for all those supplies. Now there's a lady. You don't find 'em like that any more. Yes, she's a fine lady."

"It's been two whole days since I've been on the computer. Think I'll go and play. Y'all gonna join me?" I asked.

"Shug, you go ahead. Don't stay too long. Come back in here and visit with us some, okay?"

It seemed like minutes, but it had been nearly two hours when I heard Mama say, "Shug? The Miss Universe Pageant is coming on. Won't you leave that computer alone and come and watch it with Papa and me?"

"I'll be there in a minute, Mama."

"Shug? It's ten o'clock. Please leave that computer alone and come and visit with us some . . ."

"In a minute, in just a minute . . ."

"Shug? It's ten twenty. Please, come and visit with Papa and me and watch the pageant."

"In a min . . . OKAY, I'll be right there . . . in a min . . ."

I quit where I was and went into the den and sat in Grandma Ferrell's rocking chair. Mama was still setting in the blue rocker.

"Mama?"

"Huh?"

"Don't your feet hurt? They seem swollen pretty badly."

Daddy spoke, "I asked her if she didn't want to go to the doctor and she refused. She kept saying she'd be all right. Just let her get a good night's sleep and she would be just fine."

"Mama? Daddy? I pray to Jesus everyday to bless y'all. I love you so much. I don't know what I'd do without you."

"Shug, we love you too."

"No, really, I mean it. Mama, I thank Jesus everyday for you both."

"Shug, we pray for you too, every day. Always lean on and trust in Him. We might not always be here — but remember we'll be just a thought away. For love never . . ." I butted in, "Well, let me get back to the computer and finish the records. I'm getting Ruthann put in and re-evaluating the business."

Soon Mama came on in the living room and started playing her favorite video game. Sometimes we'd play it together. But tonight I was busy on the computer with the business, and she played it alone. She was still pale but there seemed to be a little more color in her face than there had been this afternoon at the restaurant in Dunn.

Just before Daddy came in, Mama began playing the keyboard she'd saved for and bought with her own money just before Christmas last year.

She had always wanted to learn to play by ear, so one day she ordered little stick-on notes. I came home late from work one night and was in my bedroom changing clothes when I heard the prettiest music coming from the living room. It was Mama, she was playing by ear. I just stood there, in the gracefulness of the moment and quietly listened. *Please Jesus, please help me to remember this special time in Mama's life — her playing by ear.* I remembered how only three months earlier I had witnessed Mama's playing by ear on her very own Christmas present to herself. I was so overwhelmed that I grabbed the camera and took her picture.

Mama had played several songs and was playing a few gospel tunes by ear when Daddy came in and sat down on the swivel chair beside the keyboard. Mama had just finished playing *"Where The Roses Never Fade"* and was just starting another when, all of a sudden she crossed her right leg over her left leg and slumped onto the keyboard beneath her. Her glasses fell from her face and she lay still upon the instrument. I jumped and ran to her side as Daddy shouted, "Doll, *D-o-l-l,* Drusilla, answer me *D-r-u-s-i-l-l-a?*"

"Mama?" Gently I took hold of her shoulders and pulled her back. She fell into my arms. I pulled her off the stool as best I could and laid her across the living room floor, starting CPR while Daddy continued to call her name.

"Oh dear Jesus, what has happened to Mama? Dear sweet Jesus, honey, you gotta call for help. I can't get up, and I can't get down there to help you. My hip — my hip won't let me."

"One-one thousand, two-one thousand, three-one thousand." Then, I'd stop and breathe into mama's mouth. "One-one thousand, two-one thousand, three-one thousand." I kept repeating the procedure I'd learned from a course I'd taken at the local technical college a few years earlier. Only this time, it wasn't on a rubber doll, it was on a real person — my dear, beloved Mama.

"Daddy, you can help. Press here on Mama's chest while I go and call 911."

"This is 911, may I help you?"

"This is Jeannette Ferrell, and my mom has had a heart attack, and we need the rescue squad immediately!"

"Ms. Ferrell, calm down and give me some information."

"Don't you understand? My Mama had a heart attack and we need the rescue squad right now!"

"Calm down and tell me where are you located, Ms. Ferrell."

It was all up to me. Daddy couldn't help much, and now this operator at the emergency center wouldn't cooperate. She just kept asking questions.

"What's the date of birth of the patient, and what time did this happen and what state was she in at this time?" It seemed like hours passed as I tried so hard to get the EMS here. She continued not wanting to listen to my urgency. "Look, I need to get back in there and continue CPR. Dad isn't doing well either, and I can't take care of both of 'em. Please, p-l-e-a-s-e, help me. I need you now. I'll turn the porch light on so you'll know which house it is. The one on the corner at Hill Top. Please, please hurry."

I was barely able to get the phone back on the hook because I was shaking so badly. I ran and fell down again on the floor beside Mama and continued CPR. "Jesus," I spoke aloud and didn't care who was listening, "Please, please help Daddy and me. One-one thousand, two-one thousand, please! We need your help NOW! Don't say no like you have to me in the past. Please, help me and Daddy NOW!" No, no, no, no, no, no, this can't be happening. No, no no, Jesus; No! Not now; no, no, no, no.

It seemed like an eternity before the rescue squad arrived. When they finally did come, forty minutes later, I was told that all ambulances were on call and they managed to free this one up from Harnett County. Daddy wanted to ride with her, but they told him it'd be best if he rode with me to help calm me down. As they put Mama in the ambulance, I told the paramedic that Mama's wish was to never go to Memorial but rather be carried to Rex Hospital. Turning he said, "You do want your mother to live, don't you? We're carrying her to Memorial."

"NO. Mama made me promise to NEVER have anyone carry her to Memorial — ever again. NO, you carry her to Rex hospital — do you hear me?"

"Ma'am, like I said, we are carrying her to Memorial."

Knowing there was no time to lose, I nodded, turned, and went back inside to find Daddy struggling for air.

"Daddy, don't worry. Jesus will take care of Mama. Are all your pills in your container? Let's get Mama's list of things she's allergic to and take it with us."

Just before leaving the house, Daddy reminded me, "Honey, don't forget her billfold. It has a list of her medical insurance and other needs. Let's go now. Time's a wasting and we need to be there should she call for us."

I finished gathering as much as I could while Daddy got his sweater and went to the car. I made sure all the lights were off and the central air conditioner was turned back and closed the door behind me.

Still in shock, I began repeating the Lord's prayer over and over again until Daddy asked me to stop. He said I was getting on his nerves. *Jesus? I'll never stop saying Your precious prayer. Please, please hear our prayer and let Mama be okay when we get to Memorial.*

"Honey, I overheard what the attendant said to you. Mama will understand. You did your best NOT to have her carried to Memorial." Daddy soothed me. Then, with a sob he said, "What are we gonna do without Mama?"

"Daddy, don't talk like that. Mama's gonna be okay. Just you wait and see, she's gonna be okay. She's just gotta be. We love her so much. Jesus will take care of her till we get there. Mama's gonna be okay." *Please, please Jesus, please . . .*

An intern met us at the emergency door and asked if we were the relatives of Mrs. Ferrell. After the preliminary questions and finding out that Mama was in really bad shape, Daddy and I were asked to step into a tiny room where the hospital chaplain would join us.

"We don't need a chaplain. What are they talking about? Mama's gonna be just fine. Jesus will take care of her, and she's gonna be just fine," I insisted to Daddy.

"Shish, honey. It's just precaution. Let's go along with 'em. Shish," he repeated as he patted me on my right hand. "Just calm down. I can't take you and Mama both, so just calm down and continue praying."

He reached for another puff of his inhaler. The following forty-eight hours were unforgettable.

* * *

Mama was still holding on and seemed to be showing some signs of improvement. The doctors insisted her movements were just reflexes, but *I* knew better. I raised the bottom covers to rub Mama's feet just once more, and to see if the swelling had gone down and if they were cold. Mama always had cold feet. I touched the bottom of her tiny feet and she moved them. Finally, a ray of hope. This was the first time she'd moved since Friday night before the attack.

"Daddy, did you see that?"

"What, honey?"

"Quick, call for the nurse and let her see."

"Don't get your hopes up, folks. It's just reflexes." The on-call doctor said.

They don't know my Mama. She's strong, and I've never known her to ever give up. On Sunday evening, Jane, a friend of the family was visiting Mama. Jane turned with streams of tears flowing down her cheeks and said, "Mama Ferrell is saying, 'I love you', Jeannette. I think she's looking at you and saying those words."

Immediately she stepped to one side, and I walked over to Mama's right side. I watched her eyes actually follow my movement. I looked at her lips. Yes, Jane was right! Mama was saying, as best she could, "*I love you, I love you, I love you.*" I felt her hazel green eyes piercing clean down to my inner soul. I just stood there, slowly putting my right hand on Mama's right hand, and gently squeezed. Looking down into her eyes, I spoke some words she hadn't heard earnestly from me in quite some time, "I love you too, Mama. I love you *so* much." Daddy once told me I had to be strong and that crying was a sign of weakness, but it was all I could do to hold back the tears.

The nurse pulled out a metal stool from under the corner sink and motioned for me to sit. The evil one seemed to be losing his grip on me somewhat as I struggled with my sincere compassion and my attempt to control my heartfelt sorrow for my beloved Mama. Jane was quietly whispering to the night nurse. I couldn't stand it any longer, and the tears began to flow violently. In spite of what Daddy had told me, I just couldn't help it. I'd taken all I could. *This is my mama. Dear Jesus, this is my dear, sweet, loving Mama.* For the first time in my entire life, I broke down and openly wept. Jane knelt down, put her arms around me, and held me close as the night nurse reached and held us both. How I wished it was Mama holding me. All I ever wanted was for Mama to hold me close and not let go — *ever*!

Instantly, it felt like the floodgates of heaven opened. Although Mama lay motionless on the hospital bed, I strongly felt her arms wrapped around me, through the presence of Jane. Those shackles that Satan was holding onto were being loosened as Jesus Himself showered me with His everlasting arms of *love!*

* * *

Since Mama's attack on the seventeenth, Daddy and I spent most of our time at the hospital, hoping and praying for a miracle. This is what it would take for Mama to come home. According to the doctors, Mama went so long without oxygen during her heart attack that her brain was dead.

How could this be? Mama's so active and so alert. She's had a heart attack. It has nothing to do with her brain. I struggled with thoughts of Mama being a vegetable for the rest of her life. She'd made Daddy and me promise to never put her on life support, saying that if she didn't have any quality of life left, she'd rather pass on than live in an unknowing state.

On Tuesday, the doctor had just finished examining Mama when Dad and I walked in. He asked for permission to do one more brain scan to be sure what he'd told us earlier was indeed true. While he continued to discuss Mama's condition right there in her room, Daddy walked over and put his right hand on Mama's left shoulder. Miraculously, Mama moved it as if to say for us NOT to have it done — or was it just another reflex motion? Daddy looked up at me, I looked at the doctor, and he looked at Mama with a raised eyebrow. Then he turned to me and asked about the scan. Not to Daddy, but to me. Daddy didn't butt in, as if he, too, didn't know what to say.

"Sir? I did everything I knew to do. I immediately started giving Mama CPR, and then I called 911 not once, but twice. It took them forty minutes to respond to my calls."

"Jeannette? May I call you by your first name?" I nodded. "You probably saved your mother's life. She wouldn't be alive if it hadn't been for you. Miracles still happen. It's just that this scan will show us the extent of the damage and if there's anything at all left that we might be able to do to help her." I probably said wrong, knowing how terrified Mama was to be closed in tight places, but I agreed to them doing one more brain scan. Daddy glanced over at me but said nothing.

* * *

The following Friday, May 24, 1996, was just another day visiting Mama at the hospital. But Daddy and I had spent Thursday night there.

Around lunchtime, I noticed Daddy getting the weak trembles. Was it his sugar dropping? Wasn't he eating properly? Was he using the inhaler too often? I asked the nurses if they happened to have an extra wheelchair around. He was just too shaken up to walk, and his hip was hurting after a restless night in those not-so-comfortable waiting room chairs. *Jesus, please, tell me what is happening with Daddy. Mama would know instantly what to do, but I'm so inexperienced, and I'm afraid I'll not make another right decision — ever again. Jesus, I don't feel I can take much more.*

I went down to the cafeteria, got some sandwiches, and brought them back to Daddy. He ate them with a Diet Coke. Later in the afternoon, Cousin Richard came up to visit a friend of his and stepped in to check on Mama. Daddy asked Richard if he'd mind taking him home so he could rest a bit. I promised I'd be on shortly — before dark.

Before Daddy left, he and I went in to see Mama. We stayed longer than normal as Daddy continued patting her arms and loving her and kissing her on the lips while Mama just lay there without any movement at all. The doctor said if her brain was active that she'd be talking and laughing with us. He said that all her vital signs were normal and that we'd soon have to decide what to do. As far as they were concerned, Mama could live in this state for a long, long time.

Daddy slowly sat back down in the wheelchair and rested a bit. Then he rose once more, rubbed Mama's arms and gently placed his left hand on her forehead. He leaned down and kissed her once again on her soft, rosy lips, hoping for some kind of response.

"I love you, darling. Do you hear me? I love you, Doll. I love you. Dear sweet Jesus, I love you." Still, no movement at all — only a silent stillness prevailed. Just about that time two hospital chaplains came into Mama's small ICU room. *Jesus, why're they here? Mama's okay. She's gonna be just fine.* I turned to the young chaplain saying, "I can't wait to get to heaven and ask Eve why in the world she took a bite of that forbidden fruit." Anger was raging deep within my soul. As I turned back toward my parents, he asked for a moment of prayer. Afterward, he excused himself, leaving us alone. Once more, it was just the three of us, as it had been for all my forty-eight years.

Daddy leaned down, hugged Mama, kissed her on the lips one last time and told her that he'd see her later. He told her that Richard was taking him home, and if she needed him to have the nurses call and he'd be right by her side.

After Daddy left, I went over and got one of those pink pre-moistened sticks. I opened the wrapper and placed it on Mama's lips. When I took it away, there was no response. I went to the door and asked the nurses if they had any more, as that was the last one I could find. They didn't. Back in the room, I moistened a wash cloth and wiped Mama's lips with it. Then I dribbled a few drops of water onto another wash cloth and patted her face and forehead.

It was just me and Mama and nobody else. I walked over to the right side of the bed and just stood there looking down at my loving mother. A sudden urge came upon me to kneel and pray. *But how, Jesus? How do I do this?* Knowing I wasn't righteous enough to bow beside Mama's bed, I turned and took two, maybe three steps, till I was in front of the sink in Mama's tiny hospital room. My arthritic knees crackled on the way down as I lowered myself onto the cold tile floor below. In a squatting position at first, I began to recite the 23rd Psalm — out loud so Mama could hear me. I wanted her to know that I loved her, and I wanted her to hear her daughter praying.

Guilt and shame pierced my soul. I knew I had no control over Mama's living or dying. *Oh, dear sweet Jesus — I don't want her to die! What will I do without Mama? I love her so much — more than words. Lord? I love the pure ground Mama walks on, yet look how I've treated her over the last years — and especially the last few months. And just last week, those harsh words coming out of my mouth that I had no control over, and the times I've prayed to You for help. Well! I think its time to come clean. I'll do it the only way I know. Dear Lord, I've been away from You for quite some time. I've heard Mama and Daddy pray, but Lord, I really don't know how. All I can do is be truly and completely honest with You as best I know how.*

Jesus, I know I can't ask You not to let the unbearable happen 'cause You are the One and only true God. You know best. Dear Lord, You know the desires of my heart, but it isn't going to be my will be done, heavenly Father. As hard as it is for me to say this, I know from deep within that it's Your will be done."

After unloading my burdens and confessing all my shame over letting the evil one seduce me, I laid everything at His feet. A moment of silence came from deep within my soul.

* * *

I couldn't wipe away the tears fast enough. Then, miraculously, I heard a sound coming from Mama's way. I stood up slowly, holding onto the sink in front of me. I saw Mama's tongue licking her lips. Slowly moving toward her, I saw her open her eyes as she began to make a gurgling noise. Then she tried to clear her throat as she looked up near the ceiling.

As I reached the cold metal bed-rails, Mama licked her lips, swallowed three times, and then Mama began *smiling!* I was so elated I was speechless. *She's gonna be all right. Mama's coming home, thank You Jesus.*

But then I realized that Mama was seeing something or someone upon that ceiling. Her smile — that sweet, pure smile on her face — was so radiant, so peaceful, so loving and innocent and kind and so very, very happy!

I could hardly believe my eyes. The room darkened, and thunder rumbled just outside the window. A brilliant light descended from the top eastern corner of that intensive care room. This magnificent light lowered a transparent golden glow as it hovered over Mama's frail body. I didn't know what was happening. I just stood there and witnessed the most beautiful, breathtaking event I've ever seen. I watched in amazement as Mama's soul literally lifted out of her body, *passed right before my eyes*, and went upward toward *the Heavenly Light*.

The *Light* was so piercingly bright. I would have been blinded if I'd looked within its depth. All I could see were radiant beams that shown brightly from the whiter-than-white light. As this was taking place, I remember thinking, *Lord, I want to go, please let me go and leave it all behind*. Then a firm yet gentle voice from the left-hand corner of Mama's bed spoke, "It's not your time yet. It's not your time yet. It's not your time yet."

Just before the halo descended, I was filled with a warm sensation from the top of my head to the soles of my feet. An electrifying power seemed to erase my sins. I actually felt the chains Satan had on me melt away as Christ's mighty force continued piercing through my body like healing waters overflowing a river's bank. I knew beyond a shadow that it came only from Jesus Himself. His mercy and grace pierced my entire sinful body, and my mind was completely cleansed by His heavenly touch.

The halo that carried my sins away flowed peacefully toward the bright heavenly light. Then the curtains were drawn as the light faded back toward the eastern corner of the room where it had first appeared only moments earlier. At four-twelve in the evening of May 24th, I knew *beyond a shadow of any doubt* that I had been gracefully touched by my *Master's Hand*.

The room returned to normal. I looked down at Mama, slowly removing my right hand from the bed rails and gently placing it on her soft right arm. I felt a slight warmth at first. Then the slow coolness began creeping under my fingertips up toward her chest. I let my eyes drift up to Mama's face. I was astonished by her expression. Her head was thrown back and her mouth was wide open. Mama's skin was covered with a brilliant golden color and her hazel green eyes were wide open. I didn't know I was supposed to close Mamas' eyes and shut her mouth and tilt her head back down on the soft, white pillow. I was too caught up in the most speechless moment of my life.

I turned and opened the big, heavy wooden door and walked slowly out of Mama's room. I walked through the intensive care unit, down the corridor and into the waiting room. As I reached the exit door, the receptionist called to me. She had another list of callers who had inquired about Mama. As I stopped to heed her call, Uncle Lawrence and Aunt Sally came in from the Lake to see how Mama was doing.

"Jeannette, how's Druzilla?"

"She's gone. Jesus came and took Mama home."

"Can I see her?"

"Sure. I have to call Daddy. Please excuse me." A lady at the desk asked, "Are you all right?" I began nodding and *smiling*.

"Daddy, I've got to tell you something, and I don't know how."

"Honey? What is it?"

"Jesus just came and got Mama, just moments ago." There was silence from the other end of the phone.

"Why didn't I stay? I should've been there with her. Honey, are you all right?"

"I'll be home after a while, Daddy. Uncle Lawrence and Aunt Sally just arrived as I came to call you. I was with Mama, Daddy. She wasn't alone. Jane wanted me to call her. I'm sure she'll ride with me home so don't worry. I'm okay. It'll be a while — up to an hour."

"Honey, send the house key with Lawrence, and you come on home as soon as you can. My Papa and Grandma Ferrell both died in my arms. I should have stayed with Drusilla as she passed too. I should have stayed there with you. No matter about my health, I could've stayed one more hour. I should've stayed just a little while longer."

"Daddy, it wasn't meant to be. I was with Mama, and that's the way Jesus wanted it to be. Daddy, I witnessed Mama's homecoming, and it was breathtaking. It was the most beautiful thing I have ever seen in my life. Jesus released the shackles from my body, and I actually felt the chains as they slid down my legs and across my feet and the warmth that was left behind. And, Daddy, through sanctification I was purified by the touch of His wonderful loving hands. The same ones you and Mama experienced many years ago. Dad, I repented at that very moment, and I am walking with Jesus again.

"I'm glad Richard is there with you, Daddy and Uncle Lawrence will be on shortly. Do you have your pills?"

"Yes. I took the heart and the diabetic pills on the way home. Don't you worry about me now. You go ahead and take care of matters there and get home as soon as you can. And honey, I love you. It's just you and me now and don't worry, Jesus will take care of us. You hear? Jesus will always take care of His children, and He will never leave us and He doesn't put on us more than we can stand. Thank you for calling on Richard's car phone, and honey, do be careful driving home."

I know in my heart that Mama laid down her life for me. She knew the turmoil I was in. Mama knew Satan had a hold on me. Jesus not only granted Mama's request back in 1995, of her asking to go Home before Daddy. But, He also allowed Mama to give up her life so I could live.

I nearly lost my soul as God granted the request I made back in the seventies. When I asked for living a little in the world, I did not know the impact or the devastation that it would bring to my parents. I was actually standing on the threshold of disclaiming all my morals and my family's love for Christ.

32

Reforming Grace

THE FIRST PERSOn I met when I arrived home from the hospital was Reverend Rogers. I was so happy I could hardly keep my feet on the ground. I grabbed hold of his hand and shook it vigorously while sharing about that wonderful event I had just witnessed. I know he must've thought I was insane as his blue eyes peered into mine and he forced a half-smile upon his clean-shaven face. I don't believe he expected to see me this joyful. After all, Mama had just passed away two hours earlier.

I couldn't help it. It was like a river that had burst through its dam. I was so amazingly overwhelmed by Mama's homegoing that I didn't want to let it end. Entering the den, I found Daddy in his favorite blue recliner talking to a neighbor. He tried to stand in his weakened condition. I rushed to his side, reaching for a hug as we embraced and wept together. As the house began to fill with folks, I spoke of smelling something good. Nodding his head, blowing his nose and wiping his eyes, he mentioned that Clara and Rachel were having supper for us. It wasn't long until Clara came handing Daddy a big plate of food, including a homemade biscuit with a slab of ham inside. "Umm, thank you Clara. Now, that sure looks good, but you know I'm not hungry one bit."

"John, now you know you've gotta eat, especially with your diabetes and all those pills you take. Please, try a little something. You know what Drusilla would say, 'Papa, it ain't my cooking, but it'll do, and it's good for you.'"

A tear fell from his eye as he looked up at Clara and smiled. Turning to me, she insisted I follow her to the kitchen. "I'm, not hungry either, Clara," I insisted, but once I'd consumed the first mouthful, it wasn't long until I'd devoured three plates full and downed two glasses of iced tea. "Clara, I apologize. I've never done this before."

"Shish, Jeannette. You and John both are worn out and hungry. You've spent every waking moment with your Mama. You're exhausted, and Jesus knew it was time for *all* of you to be fed. He provided the place for Drusilla, and He's provided us for you and John. I've never seen any family as close as you all were."

"That's right, Clara," Rachel agreed. "Whenever I saw one, I'd see the other two — unless Jeannette was working. I even remember many occasions, after Jeannette had worked those twelve hours. She and Drusilla would have to take something to Tracey, and this was at nine o'clock at night. Dedication and love, pure and simple, that's all it was."

"But Rachel, it's a way of life — our life together. I'd have it no other way — *Oh no*, Rachel!"

"Jeannette, what is it?"

"How am I gonna tell Tracey about Mama? I can't — but I've got to. No, I can't. I know, I'll call Betty and ask her to go over and tell her. I can't leave Daddy. I need . . . "

* * *

After the funeral, the house was so different. The rooms that not so long ago were full of laughter and kidding and carrying on had become dreary and empty, inhabited by days full of yearning for our loved one. Each day simply dragged by, with me not wanting to believe what had happened. I was totally in shock, yet I knew I was the only one left to take care of Daddy. Although he had gone through loss before, I was definitely not ready for the desolation that followed Mama's passing. "Daddy, why did Jesus take Mama?" I asked late one June day, tears flowing down my face.

"Honey, we shouldn't question the Lord's will. We must accept it and go on. It's gonna be hard 'cause your Mama did *everything* for us. She was a good soul, bless her heart. She went the extra mile for us, honey. She was a good trooper in every way. It's just you and me now with Jesus, and we will survive. Yes, it's different and it'll never be the same again. Just continue to believe and live the Christian way and, one day, we will be together again. That's what the Bible says, and with all my heart I believe."

"But Daddy, I don't know how to do anything. Mama did all the cooking, all the washing of the clothes, all the canning, all the freezing, took care of all your medicines and appointments. Mama even read the paper for me and told me what was going on. It's been twenty years since I've cooked!"

"Don't you ever think you can't cook, honey. You might be out of practice but you can cook things just as good as your mother could. I'm so proud of you, the way you've held up and taken charge."

"It wasn't me, Daddy. I think Jesus had an angel with me 'cause I've never been down this road before like you have."

"I've never lost a mate before and that's different. Yes, I lost my Mama and Papa but loosing Drusilla — well, I know Jesus knew what He was doing, but I miss her, honey. I miss Drusilla so much. She was my partner, my best friend — I know you only understand from a child's point of view, but honey, your mother was my soul mate." Tears overwhelmed him, forcing Daddy to use his inhaler to open up his airways. *Oh dear Jesus, please help us. We're so lost without Mama.*

* * *

A few weeks later I remembered Dr. Burney's comments about not wanting Mama to drive due to never knowing when a "spell" would hit. I never did question him about these so-called spells, because I didn't want to know. I couldn't face living without her (I was running from reality). She was always so lively and so loving.

How could this be, living without Mama? *Dear Jesus, You've got the very best. Please, let me hear from her every now and then, please.* I'd pray as

I buried my head in the covers so Daddy couldn't hear my cries of grief. I had to be strong for his sake as Mama's words rang ever so clearly in my mind.

The housework really wasn't as important as Daddy was. He often told me to let it go and just come and sit so he could talk to me. At times it seemed like Daddy was trying to replace Mama with me. Memories came flooding back of Mama sharing with me about Daddy's demands on her while she tried to keep the housework going. All he wanted was for her to drop everything and just sit and talk. When she wasn't available, it wasn't long until he'd say, "Mama? Where are you? I can't see you?" Mama would get angry over this. It would get on her nerves so badly that she'd just buckle up and not even answer him.

And now Daddy had a few things he wanted to share with me and I didn't want to listen. I was afraid he was trying to set me up for his own homegoing, and I surely wasn't ready for that.

Toward the end of the summer of 1997, I began noticing an unusual change in Daddy. The shoulders of his six-foot-one structure seemed to be a little more humped. He seemed to need his inhaler more often, and he began visiting the doctors a little more frequent. He also began needing help with feeding. He was unable to hold a fork because of the severe shaking caused by his Parkinson's Disease. Not long ago Daddy's hands were strong and mighty, yet full of gentleness. With his breathing being worse, he was unable to bathe himself. In the summer months, I'd place a fan in the bedroom as he sat on the cloth plaid chair. I made sure the water wasn't too hot or too cold. Not being able to use scented soap, I'd simply moisten the washcloth, wash his upper body and his lower limbs. I'd excuse myself as he washed his privates. (In the Old Testament, Leviticus 18:6 reads, "None of you shall approach to any that is near to kin to him, to uncover their nakedness; I am the LORD.")

I realized that a heavy decision needed to be made concerning Daddy's health. I knelt beside my bed one night and earnestly prayed for Christ's help. I prayed for His answer to come clearly for my own understanding.

* * *

On August 19, 1996, a little over two months after that electrifying moment of Mama's heavenly journey, I dreamed of Isaiah 13:18, "Their bows shall also dash the young men to pieces . . . "

When I talked to Daddy about this, he suggested I not only pray about it but I might consider mentioning it to Reverend Matthew Rogers.

Because of my distant feelings about my former church, I just settled for the prayer part and waited. However, as the days and weeks followed, I grew increasingly unsettled. This strange feeling kept nagging at the very pit of my stomach and before long, the urgency to kneel at an altar became unbearable.

As my once home church came into focus, I began hesitating and asking Jesus, *You know You're not asking me to go there. Somebody might see me, and then what on earth would I do?* "The very idea of going to the altar — c'mon now Jeannette, you know good'n well somebody's gonna see you —" the other inner voice kept trying to inch me away.

It wasn't long before the inevitable happened. The Holy Spirit encased my mind, and I found myself leaving the office and driving toward my *old* church. Shaking like a leaf doesn't come close to describing the shape I was in.

The parking lot was full of cars. I looked around and realized the preacher's car was gone. At least I didn't have to face him. Praying God's protective shield to cover me so I'd not be seen, I entered the side doors. Walking toward the large sanctuary, I heard some ladies laughing in the kitchen area. *Oh dear Jesus, please don't let them see me. Please!*

As I knelt in front of the altar that morning, I humbled myself before my Creator. *Lord? It's just me. It's always been the three of us, and now it's just Daddy and me.* My heart was so full of the heaviness of taking care of him and trying desperately to console him in Mama's absence while still trying to deal with my own grief, which at times became almost unbearable. We did everything and had gone everywhere together. The three of us had enjoyed life together.

In the midst of those releasing moments, the hand of Jesus comforted me. I wiped away floodgates of tears as He filled my soul with wonderful hugs of love. Rising and making sure no one was looking, I turned and walked back down the hallway and out the side doors. That crisp fall morning in November 1996, I drove around to where Mama was laid to rest, knelt, and asked God to bless her soul.

Driving back to the office, I felt an urge to turn on the radio. *"Burdens Are Lifted At Calvary,"* was playing as I realized my prayers were heard. Soon afterward, a hymnal message, *"God Will Take Care of You"* appeared in my mind, forming a warm peace within my soul.

* * *

With this newness of Christ in my soul, everything was so beautiful and alive. The ground, the trees, the flowers, even the grass beneath my feet were full of color, as though all I had to do was reach out and touch any of it to become consumed with its entire being. I felt so close to Jesus. I began searching for a church where I could express my feelings and not be ashamed. Jane began telling me of her church and their teachings from the King James Bible. She said that the Trinity was taught, and that God's word was honored as the Truth.

I had been raised on this Truth. I began visiting this small church in the country, which proved to be an entirely different environment than I'd ever experienced. It felt *good* to raise my hands in Jesus' name. It felt *good* to go to the altar, confess my sins, and ask for forgiveness. It felt *good* to be able to talk openly about Him with others. I grasped everything that came along pertaining to His Word. I was so overjoyed that I simply couldn't stand myself.

When I was asked to teach children's Sunday school, I accepted, only to find the child in me coming out with happiness. When asked to participate in some musicals, I accepted, only to find hidden talents coming out while I lifted praises to the King. When asked to join in the ladies parlor for the evening prayer services, I accepted, only to find out, once again, that Jesus answers prayers.

But in spite of all my happiness, there was a gray cloud at home. Daddy didn't leave anything to the imagination when pointing out his feelings about my attending this country church.

"Honey, your mother and I wanted you to attend our home church.

I don't understand why you insist on going to another."

"But Daddy, Jane and her husband speak highly of it, and I really like it. Yes, it's different than your church. They do things a little differently there and yes, it is a smaller congregation, but Daddy, I'm going, and that's exactly what you and Mama wanted — for me to go to church and get involved."

"Oh dear Jesus, you are right, honey. You are attending, and I can't argue with you on that. It's just that I wish you were attending our home church in Fuquay." I knew all too well where Daddy was coming from, and the more he talked about it the more determined I was to resist. I didn't know at the time why I kept buckling, but it wasn't long until my insistence paid off.

It was the second week in September. Daddy had asked fervently for me to stay home with him that evening. He said over and over that it was so lonely there by himself and that my being gone just made it worse. I knew where he was coming from. I was having a hard enough time dealing with my own loneliness, not to mention having to deal with his as well. Nevertheless, this one time, I butted heads with Daddy and went to church despite his razor-sharp words of despair.

The strangest urge filled my body when I entered the prayer room that evening. Before I knew it, I was sitting among the thirteen in attendance, and in the only chair left in the tiny classroom. Each member was involved in his or her own prayer request. I silently prayed, *Dear Jesus, please give me an answer. Should I quit work and stay home with Daddy?*

During the closing of the prayer meeting, I felt a warm sensation throughout my body, and instantly knew I was being touched by a heavenly being. I saw a bright, radiant flash of light. From it sounded a pure baritone voice I recognized from just a few months earlier. Within the words of the sweet and earnest closing prayer, I knew immediately God's answer. Pushing the chair away from the table and with a puzzled look on her face, Miss Mabel asked, "Jeannette, what is it? You have the most beautiful expression on your face."

"Yes you do. Please share it with us before we leave," Miss Linda said.

"Ladies, Jesus answered a prayer of mine just now and it came like a flash as you were closing. It was similar to the flash I witnessed when He took Mama home to be with Him."

"What?" Their eyes broadened with amazement. "Well praise the Lord, tell us all about it!"

"No, not until I share it with Daddy. I'll share it with you next week." I could hardly wait for the service to be over. I probably should've left right then, before they started, but I didn't. When I arrived home around 8:15, Daddy called to me with enthusiasm. I thought it was just his relief over my being back until . . .

"Honey, what is it? Your face is radiant. Are you feeling all right? Did everything go okay at your church? Please, tell me what is it that's so different about you." As I began explaining about the incident in as much detail as I could, Daddy's face lit up like a firecracker.

"It was Jesus that spoke to you, wasn't it, honey?"

"Yes Sir, it was. He told me that it was time for me to quit work and be here at home with you, and that He would take care of us both." Tears of joy began forming in his eyes as Daddy lifted his frail arms to hug me, while giving thanks to Jesus for bringing his daughter back home safely.

Although Jesus had given me the answer to quit work, I dragged my feet. Nearly three weeks passed, until I really couldn't stand the guilt and discomfort that were forcing me to make a move. Was it Jesus, or the evil one trying to creep in again and mess with my mind? Struggling with this, I lifted the same question to Him, and that very night Jesus' answer was so strong that it woke me up. The urgency was so forceful that I got up in the middle of the night, wrote out my resignation, and gave it to the department supervisor the very next morning. After receiving it, Rebecca said to me, "Jeannette, you're different. Although you have worked here over eighteen years, you are a child of God. Your face tells it all, and you really don't belong here anymore. I pray for you to go in peace." Arrangements were made, and I left work to take care of my beloved daddy.

* * *

As I walked in this new path, trying so hard to make our sad home a happy one, one day Daddy happened to mention that happiness came from within. Adjusting to just the two of us, I began to notice a happier side to Daddy. How gentle he was in stepping in and bringing forth a smile or speaking an uplifting word of wisdom that only came from the Lord after years of experience.

Grocery shopping, picking up medicine, preparing three meals a day, washing and running errands for Tracey became my weekly routine. However, Paul was Daddy's right arm. Daddy used to share with me about taking Paul under his wing and teaching him everything he knew, from running a newspaper route to using his hands with wood and the skills of the trade. Anything from making a simple shelf to making cabinets or framing and trimming out houses. Even doing some plumbing and painting too.

"Honey, if you ever need anyone to do things around the house, and I happen to not be here, just call Paul. He'll do it for you, and it won't cost you an arm and a leg." Daddy loved Paul and often said that he was like a son to him.

Every Friday morning, Daddy looked forward to an old friend bringing those Sunday sermon tapes from Rev. Rogers, a kind-hearted old soul, hair of silver and small, slanted eyes that reminded you of Roy Rogers. He was such a dedicated man of God, always thinking of others. He was such a delight, always finding the good in people just like Mama used to do. Never once did we hear him say a negative word about anybody.

It was Daddy's continuing remarks, along with studying of God's word, that brought me to confessing to Daddy about my personal feelings concerning Mama. Ah, it felt so good to finally be able to open up and tell Daddy the truth. He just lay there in bed, the oxygen machine seeming to rise and fall as it pumped fresh air into his weakened body. Daddy just listened and didn't speak a word. He gave me time to stammer and stutter and finally, I was able to get it all out, including the raging jealousy that had consumed me for so long.

"Daddy, I didn't feel I could talk to Mama. I was so envious of her. She was so talented and witty . . . I could never compete. She always knew exactly what, when, and how to say just the right thing. You and

Mama were always there with protection. Daddy, do you think Mama will ever forgive me? Do you think Jesus will ever forgive me?"

"Honey, your mother loved you, as Jesus does, unconditionally. It was you who turned away. We both knew you were in trouble. She and I talked about the changes in you. We knew you were under pressure at work. We knew you were going through some mighty rough times and that you wanted desperately to make the telemarketing job work so you could stay here with us. Honey, we knew what your intentions were, and yet, though we tried to help, you wouldn't let us. You were grown, and you thought you had all the answers. We knew you were hurting, and we felt your turmoil and the pain of not knowing which way to turn.

"Mama sees your change, Honey. I truly believe in my heart that she is watching over you and me. Someday both of us will be watching over you, if it's the good Lord's will."

"Thank you, Daddy. Thank you so much for letting me talk. I've been wanting to talk for such a long time, but the old devil kept putting obstacles in my path."

"Your mother and I know about the world and the way things are. We've had many experiences, sometimes they were life-threatening. You know, we even wondered if we were too protective of you. You always did have a strong will, however. Mama and I often prayed for Jesus to melt that stubbornness. We knew there was coming a day when you would be left alone, totally alone. Your mother often told me that our prayers would be answered one day. However, God's touch wouldn't come until you asked for His assistance.

"Daddy?"

"Huh?"

I adjusted the oxygen tube that had slipped to one side and fluffed up the three stacked pillows under his head. "Daddy, may I tell you something that I firmly believe in my heart?"

He nodded.

"Daddy, I believe without a shadow of a doubt that Mama laid down her life for me. I was in the worst sort of way. You are so wise and strong. I see the difficulties you have in rising each morning and the struggle you have in breathing. Daddy, I feel very strongly that Jesus is using you to guide and direct me into staying on the right path.

"I know you haven't approved my attending the church down the road. Although you've supported me in my decisions, I'm gradually learning that no matter — right or wrong – you too are there for me, just like Jesus is. Daddy, I've never experienced a personal walk with Him as y'all did. I've been so scared to walk alone. I've dreaded, ever since I can remember, not having you or Mama here."

"Honey, say no more."

"But Daddy, I have so much more to say."

"Honey, say the rest to Jesus. It's not for my ears to hear, but for His."

"But Daddy?" He halfway raised up from those layered pillows, reached out his arms, and motioned for me to come close. Pulling in a chair from the hall, I sat closely beside him. With moist eyes he said, "Honey, Mama and I are welcoming you back into the sheltering arms of Jesus. Welcome home." What a peace overcame me, and what a joy flooded my soul! Immediately I knew that Mama had forgiven me for the way I'd treated her just before her attack and for pushing her to the utmost limit, and that Jesus was all around us. I melted in Daddy's arms and received the best hugs of love I'd ever experienced.

For the first time in my life, my hard-core of stubbornness was over-taken by a warm sense of humbling, comforting peace. I wept openly with my father in submissive sincerity. I did not run to my room to hide. Instead, I was running toward Jesus through the comforting arms of not only Daddy but also the spiritual arms of Mama.

"Your mother and I knew there would come a day when we would be going home and you'd be left all alone," Daddy shared. "Our question to Jesus was, had we trained you how to live the right way? Had we taught you how to handle situations by praying and waiting on Him? Honey, the best advice I could ever give you is to always go to Jesus about everything. Don't rely on people. They can sometimes lead you astray without you even realizing it. The only person that you can really talk to, really be in joy with and cry with, is Jesus. One of the gospel songs I liked singing with you and Mama is 'What a Friend We Have in Jesus.' It's among my favorites. And yes, honey, one day I too will be with your mother as the song says, 'where the roses never fade.' But until that time, I'm right here with you.

"And honey, try to remember not to be too hasty or too eager in making decisions. Always pray before acting. Let Jesus be your friend, and only trust the ones He sends your way. I know that He is the only one you can trust. If you happen to need some personal assistance, I recommend you call our home pastor. Reverend Rogers will not lead you wrong.

"I know how you feel about that church you're attending, and I've got a gut feeling that the only reason is that you're letting others influence you."

"Daddy? What are you saying? You don't believe I truly like attending?"

"That's not what I said. You probably won't understand what I'm saying until after I'm gone."

"What do you mean, after you're gone? Daddy, you aren't going anywhere — no! Not you too. I need you, Daddy." Tears began to roll again in my desperate attempt in getting Daddy to fight harder to stay with me, knowing I had no control over the Lord's work. I just could not bare the raw fact of being left here all alone.

"Now, now, gather yourself together. I'm not going anywhere just yet. But, to get back to our conversation about that other church, I'm still praying that some day you'll return to your home church."

"I really like attending this church, Daddy, and it's totally different from yours. They aren't afraid to raise their hands in recognition of Jesus. They aren't afraid to say 'Amen' during a sermon in response to statements from the Bible. Daddy, it's okay to go to the front altar and kneel when the Holy Ghost leads."

"Listen to the way you are talking."

"What's wrong with the way I'm talking?"

"Honey, I have always been taught that when in the Lord's house, you are to be quiet and show respect with silence. If the Holy Ghost appears, it will be in the entirety of the congregation and only at the end of the service, when the preacher opens the church for acceptance. This is the only time one shows any openness. The rest of the time is spent in a personal manner with yourself and your Master. No one else is involved. You surely do not make a spectacle of yourself by lifting your hands or kneeling at an altar or especially by saying 'Amen' out loud. I'm not saying that kneeling is not right. Honey, when you are truly led by the Holy Ghost, kneeling is the proper thing to do. But, it is to be done in the proper way.

"I've visited the church you're attending. I've seen the actions of dear Christian people. I'm not saying they aren't believers. I'm just saying to be careful, in what you say, in how you present yourself to others, and what you pray for. Sometimes Jesus answers our prayers in ways that might not be exactly what we expected. Why, just look at what happened when you asked Him to let you live in the world! Look back at your marriage. Not that I probably wouldn't've done the same thing you did. What Charles did was very immoral and extremely disrespectful for all. Anyway, I know perfectly well that the church is just a building. However, when this building is acknowledged as being a place to worship God, I feel like I am walking as close as I can to sacred ground here on earth."

I slid off the chair, knelt and laid my head on Daddy's chest, trying not to put much weight on him knowing his weakened condition.

"Daddy? May I pray?"

"Yes, I'd like that very much."

Dear Jesus, help us. Help Daddy to help me. We miss Mama so much. We feel so empty without her. Jesus, You've got the very best with You. She's so full of life and she'll keep you smiling cause you see, Lord, Mama's so full of love. Jesus, bless Daddy. Help him to feel better. Help him to be able to breathe easier. And Lord, help me understand and to listen and not hold it in, ever again. It hurts, Jesus. My tears began to flow, as water falls from the highest mountain ranges.

Lord, I pray for guidance and protection from the ways of the world. I pray for friends and loved ones both near and far. I thank You, Jesus, for my salvation and for my parents and for my being brought up in this, Your Christian Home. . . About the same time, we both reached for a tissue and in closing, we recited the 23rd Psalm together. The warm sensation that engulfed my body as we prayed that day felt as though Christ Himself was present in our midst.

33

Hugs from Heaven

ON WEDNESDAY EVENING after supper, I got the bills down from the hopper and began sorting them.

"Honey, would you like for me to come help you tonight?" Daddy asked.

"Sure, if you're up to it. Nothing would tickle me better. It'd be like old times, us doing it together again." It'd been nearly six months since Daddy had had the strength to sit at the table and take care of the business of running a home.

I watched out of the corner of my eye as he slowly raised himself from the recliner and grabbed his walker. First he balanced himself, then he aligned the oxygen tube so it wouldn't get caught as he walked. He gathered it between the palm of his left hand and the top of the walker, then he proceeded toward the kitchen. Pulling out the chair where I used to sit when Mama was with us, he pushed the walker to one side and pulled the oxygen cord up and across his lap. His pants just hung on his tall thin body. Just last week we'd used the ice pick to make three more holes in his belt.

"Honey, when you write the check, go ahead and record it in the books, and place it with the statement and give it to me. I'll put it in the envelope, place a stamp and one of my return stickers on it, and then I'll give it back to you to lick for sealing," he said laughing. We took care of business, reminisced a little, spoke of the current events, and had a wonderful daddy-daughter moment together.

The following Wednesday, Daddy said, "Please, honey. Please come and sit with me. We don't have to talk. Just your presence and being able to look at you is all I want. Please, won't you come and just sit for a minute?" Not understanding the nature of Daddy's insistence and feeling so closed in and never having any time to myself, I thought, *Dear Jesus, I ain't Mama.* Before I knew it, I'd blurted this out, and Daddy had heard it.

I'd never expressed these feelings verbally before. I'd always managed to suppress the frustration, the shame and the festering anger that once seemed to encase my very soul. That restlessness and rage that was once controllable (by an inner being that *did* control me) was now out in the open. On an impulse, I simply exploded.

"Daddy, I'm sorry you heard that. I need to get away for a while. Just bear with me, and I'll be back home before you know it."

"Jeannette, I can't stay by myself."

"I'll only be gone for about an hour. If you want, I'll call Paul and see if he can come and sit with you."

"No. I'll be okay for an hour — maybe."

"Now Daddy, don't go and put another guilt trip on me. I don't think I can take much more. I'm doing all I can — please don't." He started crying. I slammed the back door. I ran through the den and down the hallway, and I didn't stop until I reached my bedroom and slammed that door, too. I remember clenching my fists and hitting the bed covers as hard as I could, flexing tighter and tighter until I began shaking and falling onto the bedspread Mama had helped pick out. Pretty soon I heard a tapping at the bedroom door.

"Honey, please. Oh God, I'm sorry if I upset you. I love you. Please don't pay me any attention. Please come out and let's talk about this. You're acting . . ."

"Don't. Please, just don't." I couldn't stand to face him or God or anybody at that moment. I was so hurt and angered and felt like the whole world was on my shoulders and there was nowhere to go. *God, why did You let this happen? I wasn't able to grieve for Mama and now I'm facing yet another heartbreak of Daddy's homegoing too.* The pain became nearly unbearable, slicing into my soul like a razor's edge.

"Honey, please come out. I'm sorry. I promise I won't say anything again. Dear Jesus in heaven knows I didn't meant to upset you. All I wanted was for you to come and sit with me."

I opened the door slowly, so full of guilt for the way I'd acted that I just scooted between the wall and Daddy, hurried back toward the den and abruptly sat on the couch — right where Mama use to sit, right where Daddy wanted me to sit — in a stubborn kind of way.

"Honey, get your things and go on to the mall. I'll go and lie down while you're gone. I'll be all right. Go ahead. It'll do you good to get away some. I know I'm a burden on you, and you can't live your life. I'm so proud of you, and Mama is too."

This simply broke my heart. I fought to hold back the tears, but they flowed uncontrollably.

"Daddy, I'm sorry. I don't know what gets into me at times. I'm trying so hard to do things right. I'm trying so hard to be strong, and I'm trying so hard to please you. Daddy, I'm not Mama and I'll never be her. I don't have the personality she had. Oh how I've wished I did. She used to tell me that there was nothing at all like her in me, and you know something Daddy? She was right. Daddy, I've been your little girl for fifty-one years, and I'm just scared. I know one day I will be left here all alone without you or Mama's shelter. Just me and Jesus is all it'll be; just me and Jesus. I'm sorry I yelled at you. I truly didn't mean to. I'm so sorry I've disappointed you." Tears poured from my overflowing soul.

"Don't say that, honey. You are not a disappointment to me. Never have been and never will be. I'm proud of the way you've picked up and gone on taking care of the house and me. I know you didn't know how to do a lot of things. Oh honey, I don't guess I tell you enough. I wasn't brought up to say I love you a lot. We young'uns just knew Papa and Mama loved us from the way they took care of us, and we had chores to do and if we didn't do 'em, then we had to deal with Papa. I learned early not to let him deal with me. Only a few times I remember told me he loved me, but his love showed in his actions louder than having to go around speaking it. And Mama? Well, she too told me she loved me in actions. She knew the way I liked my biscuits and the way I like other things. Every once in a while, even after I was a grown man, Mama would grab my britches leg and pull me down to where she was seated and give me a kiss on the cheek.

"Honey, your mother had ways of showing her love, too. We were a tight-knit family. I love you so much. It's just that I'm afraid something will happen to you out there on the road, and then what in God's name will I do?"

"Don't worry, Daddy. Jesus is going to take care of you and me. He always has with this family, and He always will. It's just that I never knew how to trust Him before Mama passed. I'd never really ever walked with Him or talked with Him. I'm learning, Daddy, that you and I both are safe in His sheltering arms of love."

An hour or two passed, and Daddy and I were back on pleasant terms again. Sure enough, he went to bed and insisted I go. While driving along the highway, my cell phone rang. I froze when I saw it was from our home number. Slowing from the forty-five speed limit, I hesitantly answered.

"Hey honey."

"Hey Daddy, what is it? Is something wrong?" I was in a near panic.

"No, I just wanted to hear your voice and to tell you, I Love You."

"I Love you, too, Daddy. I love you too."

I really didn't have anything to do at the mall. It was just a place I'd chosen just to get out and browse around, hopefully to let off some steam. I wasn't even gone an hour. Walking and talking to Jesus each step of the way, I felt an urge to turn around and go home. It would tickle him that I was home earlier. After all, Daddy was grieving, too, and I had to be humble and let him know in a grown up way how I felt so Jesus could heal us both *together* — not separately as before. Words from the Bible came rushing in like a tornado: "*I can do all things through Christ which strengtheneth me,*" Philippians 4:13 and "*I will never leave thee, nor forsake thee,*" Hebrews 13:5b.

On the way back, a stoplight caught me at the southern end of Tryon Road. Sitting and thinking about these Scriptures and letting the Holy Ghost filter in, a dove flew past my windshield and dropped down beside the right fender of the Mercury. Instantly Mama's homegoing flashed brilliantly before my eyes. Startled by the loud shrieking of horns exploding around me, I was awakened to the reality of life and headed home to a loving, God-fearing daddy.

Daddy's breathing worsened over the holidays of 1998. With my insistence, he finally agreed to call Dr. Ashley and make an appointment; but only after the first of the year. He said that he wanted us to have as good a Christmas as possible.

In mid-January 1999, Daddy was hospitalized with a breathing attack. The oxygen hadn't been strong enough, and Dr. Ashley thought it best Daddy get some bed rest as he tried a new kind of medicine. The day Daddy was released from the hospital Dr. Ashley came in and sat in a green metal chair at the end of the bed. Over his gold rimmed glasses — and in front of Daddy — he looked straight into my eyes and asked, "Do you want me to put him in a nursing facility or do you want me to send him home with you?" Stunned, but without hesitation, I said, "Nursing home? No way! Daddy's coming home with me as I've always promised."

"John, I'll leave instructions at the nurses desk, and you're free to leave anytime you wish."

That was it. Just like that. *Jesus, what kind of daughter did he think I was to let my daddy go to a nursing home? He had always said, as Mama had, that he hoped You would see to it that he never had to be put in one. Lord, my conscience would never rest if I allowed it to happen, provided I could prevent it.*

I've already gone against Mama's wishes about being transported to the Medical Center when she had her attack in 1996. Jesus, you know I promised her she'd go to Rex — and I failed. You know I wrestled with it for many months afterwards, until Daddy told me it just wasn't meant to be. Even her doctor was out of the country and well, the medic did ask me if I wanted my Mama to live. Jesus, why did Dr. Ashley ask me that question about the nursing home anyway?

* * *

February 5, 1999 was such a beautiful spring-filled morning. I was fixin' breakfast when I heard Daddy and his walker coming down the hall. "What's this I smell this morning?"

"Hey, Daddy. Thought I'd get an early start with the wash. Weathermen say it's gonna be a pretty day and up in the sixties. Good time to hang sheets out on the line."

"Umm! I always did like crawling into freshly aired sheets."

"Honey, if we have any milk left, put a dab or two in the coffee for me this morning. Like I used to tell your Mother, I like my coffee white and sweet." He chuckled from his corner of the den. After washing up the breakfast dishes, I made my way in and out of the utility room with the dried clothes and was putting in the last load when Daddy called out. It was such an unusual sound that I raced in to see what it was. To my surprise, Daddy was gasping for air.

"Daddy? What is it — please tell me. Are you all right?"

Coughing and hacking, he finally got his breath, but he was as white as a ghost.

"Don't mind me, I'm fine," he croaked, clearing his throat. "I guess I got strangled over that last swallow of coffee. I guess it went down the wrong way or something. I'm okay, honey. I'm gonna be just fine. You go ahead and finish the washing and come in here and sit with me."

"Daddy. I'm in and out. Can't you see? I don't have time to come in and sit with you. Its such a pretty day and all, I thought I'd get the house cleaned up for the weekend before it turns cold again." I ran into the utility room to check on the washer, which sometimes would hang up in mid-stream.

"What do you feel like you could eat for dinner, Daddy?"

"I'm not really hungry, honey. I know I need to eat a little . . . what are you eating?"

"Now Daddy, you know good 'en well I'm eating what I always eat — mayonnaise and peanut butter sandwiches."

"Well, I guess. Fix me one too."

"Are you sure?"

"Yes, I reckon."

Just as we finished, here came some friends for a visit. "I just don't think I'm up to visitors, honey. See if they would mind coming back."

I should've picked up on Daddy's remark. He'd never said anything like that before.

I went out on the porch to greet them. Explaining about Daddy not feeling up to company, they seemed to understand and said they'd be more than happy to come back another day. Just as I finished, I heard a loud commotion. I opened the storm door and heard Daddy talking loudly.

"Honey, it's okay. Let 'em come in for a while."

"Daddy, are you sure?" He nodded. After they had left Daddy said, "Honey, I didn't think I was gonna make it through."

"Daddy, what are you talking about?"

"I need to use the portable commode, honey. I can't hold it much longer."

"Sure, Daddy. Here, let me help you."

Trying to stand him up in his weakened condition, I suddenly realized how much weight he'd lost just in the last few weeks.

After Daddy finished his task on the portable commode, I raised him up and placed himself back in his favorite recliner. I then turned to get the oxygen cord out from under him when I noticed he was fast asleep. Assuming he was exhausted from his recent ordeal, I went and sat down on the couch. But something kept nagging at me until I looked up and saw how red-faced he was. He seemed to be in an unconscious state.

"Daddy, D-a-d-d-y??? Speak to me, Daddy!" I began vigorously rubbing his right arm and shaking him while reaching for the phone to call 911.

"This is 911 emergency, may I ask whose calling?"

"This is Jeannette Ferrell and I'm calling about my daddy. He's unconscious and I can't wake him up. I'm rubbing his right arm and calling him name but there's no response. None at all! Please help. Please, somebody help me!"

"Jeannette, keep talking and keep rubbing his arm. Maybe he's asleep. You did say he was hard of hearing. Is his hearing aid in?"

"N . . . n . . . no . . . he has no need of a hearing aid. Send someone out to help me, please! No Jesus, no. No, no, no — not again. No, not daddy too! Nooo!"

"Jeannette, someone is on the way." About that time, Daddy began clearing the gurgling that was coming from his throat and chest. He opened his eyes. A bronze halo formed around his pure white face that was, just seconds earlier, blood red.

"Hey honey," he said, as though he hadn't seen me for a long time. "Who are you talking to in such a disturbing voice?"

"It's the emergency service, Daddy. I couldn't wake you up and you scared me to death."

"I'm all right. Call them back and tell them not to come. I'm gonna be just fine now. Everything's gonna be just fine."

"Daddy? Are you sure you're gonna be okay?"

Raising his head and looking directly into my eyes, Daddy began nodding and smiling like I've never seen before. I forced my mind *NOT* to think back to the day when Mama passed away . . .

At two o'clock daddy had another urge to use the portable com-mode, except this time he didn't have the strength to get back to his favorite blue cloth recliner. He kept leaning over, going back into an unconscious state.

"D-a-d-d-y" I yelled. I needed to call 911 again. That phone might as well have been ten miles away, 'cause I couldn't hold him up and reach for the foot-away phone. Finally in a desperate move, I let go just long enough to grab it and pressed the redial button. This time they knew to come and to get here quickly.

"Daddy, repeat after me . . ." Somewhere, sometime, I remembered somebody telling me to have a person repeat things — that sometimes it helped to revitalize them, to keep them in a conscious state.

"Daddy? Do you hear me?"

"Umm, ah huh."

"Dad, Say 'A, B, C'."

"Aaaa, Beee, Ceee."

"Daddy, Say, '1, 2, 3'."

"oooonnnneee, ttttwwwwooooo, tttthhhhhhhrrrrrreeee" in nearly a whisper.

"D-a-d-d-y. Do you still hear me???"

"Ummm."

"Daddy, your oxygen isn't in your nose. Here, let me help put it back in. You need it to breathe, Daddy. Do you hear me?"

"Ah."

Dear Jesus, where are they? What is taking 'em so long to get here? Why did I let Daddy talk me out of letting them come earlier? Why?

"Daddy? I love you!"

"I . . . I . . . I Love, love, you . . ."

* * *

After Daddy's funeral, realization began to set in that life's decisions were now totally left upon my shoulders. I didn't turn away. This time, I turned toward Christ for help. He not only listened; He answered.

While writing this book, I've discovered that I didn't know true happiness and contented peace within my soul until I walked through darkness and loneliness, anger and jealously and envy, and been touched by the devilish ways of entangled lies, dishonesty and untrustworthiness. I did not know true spiritual love of Christ until I experienced the love of the world. I did not know true repentance until I went through difficult times and nearly ruined my life.

Born and raised in a Christian home,
I knew not of the worldly things;
God granting me a special request,
As I slipped into *no* true rest.

Years came and went and I dug deeper,
Into a place where no light was to be;
Crying and praying didn't seem to help,
Believing Jesus had turned His back on me.

Through purification I was sanctified,
As I witnessed Mama's breathtaking event;
And instantly knew of God's healing touch,
As He accepted this sinner's earnest repent.

"I want to go," I asked to go and leave it all behind.
When I heard Christ's gentle, yet firm voice say,
"It's not your time yet. It's not your time yet.
It's not your time yet."

Another death, Daddy's time approached,
Two years, eight months, twelve days away;
I cried out from the depths of my soul,
The churning of *all* the hurts and hates.

Oh why, oh why, are they taken away,
As I am left here all alone;
There will never be in my life again,
Anyone to supplant the confidants that are gone.

I search, I wonder, I go here and yonder,
With my heart seeming nearly to burst;
Looking for someone, searching for someone,
And learning there's no one to trust.

320

My heart yearns as my soul is torn,
From these deep-rooted death pains;
No one to talk to, no one to listen,
As some seem to think I'm insane.

I've struggled so hard fighting that sign,
The sign of the beast to say the least;
As I prayed, I knew God's answer would come,
His sign for me would be from the East.

Now I know the dreams I had,
Those dreams were meant for me;
How blinded I was to the reality of *Love*,
That could've destroyed the sign of the beast.

As I have come to realize the one to trust,
From friends who seemed touched from above;
With Mama's homegoing and Daddy's daily walk,
They both are flourishing with His Eternal *Love*.

For it is Jesus,
The Truth and the Light;
The Holy One Who has set me free.

— *Jeannette Yvonne Ferrell*
February 27, 2000

34

The Lighted Path

RETURNING SOME DISHES to my former church after Daddy passed, I turned and upon leaving the building I ran into the secretary who invited me to attend the upcoming Sunday services. I smiled and brought to her attention that I was now a member of another place of worship. She most graciously reminded me that I still had a membership there. While small-talking, my thoughts turned inward. *Oh Jesus, You know how often I've wanted to return but felt I couldn't. You know how often I've shunned these very people who appear to love me nearly as much as my parents.*

I caught somewhere in our conversation that the letter of transfer had actually never occurred. Though puzzled at this, another warm sensation began filtering into my soul. It was as though the heavenly gates themselves opened just enough so I could witness the smiles upon Mama and Daddy's faces. Once again His hand provided a way; and with an eager heart to walk in His light, this time I followed.

In the days of my youth, a Sunday school teacher once asked the class to memorize John 3:16. This verse has brought many comforting moments, as I clung to Christ's words of long ago, especially during my wayward days. Through purification, I was sanctified and forgiven of all my sinful ways. Although trials and tribulations of life continue, I've been inspired to share with you encouraging words to never give up. There is always hope.

There is one thing left in this world that is *free for the asking*, and that is Jesus Christ. "Behold, I stand at the door, and knock . . ." Through the miraculous cleansing of my wretched mind, I am now walking in *The Lighted Path*.

Through generations of my ancestry, our families were raised on God's Holy Word. Today I am ever in thankful prayer to Him for my parents who stood firm on the solid rock and made ours a Christian home where Faith, Hope, and Love lived. One day I, too, will join them and bow down, rejoicing and praising our Heavenly Father in His complete serenity of Eternal Life.

* * *

Those old familiar Scriptures that I was raised on are much more meaningful now than ever before. *"Let not your heart be troubled;"* *"Let brotherly love continue . . . ";* *". . . and all ye shall hear of wars and rumors of wars . . .";* *"and we know that all things work together for good. . . ."* Then there's The Romans Road, that I always knew existed but never really comprehended until that moment in time when I was touched by my Master's hand: *". . . though your sins be as scarlet, they shall be as white as snow . . ."*

In the millennium year of 2000, on June 17, the day before Daddy would have turned seventy-seven, I dreamed of Isaiah 16. By now I was aware of the position of each book in the Bible and quickly found the chapter. The head notes read, "Judgments of nations." Realizing that Babylon was the city, I wondered if the dream was in some way signifying our own country and a possible future downslide of events.

After all, when the United States was founded, this nation family was not only raised on God's Holy Word, but it also used the Bible religiously for every situation life brought. That's how I was raised, but for a while I lost my way. I didn't go to the Bible for answers, nor did I seek Christian advice. Instead, my stubborn nature caused the angel of darkness to enter in. I relied on myself, and discovered in the process that I had left God out. As earnest repentance was prayed, the angel of darkness vanished and God's Holy Spirit dwelled within my soul — protecting it with His armor and filling me with His glorious light.

To all who have lost loved ones, and to all who experienced the horrifying attack on America Tuesday, September 11, 2001, here's a reminder:

As the sun rises and sets on each day following, the stillness of the night's air seems to produce a silhouette of possible uncertainties. But we have hope. God's Holy Word remains, reminding us that *Love Never Dies!*

Dreams from God

All Biblical scriptures came from the King James Bible.

JUNE 1984

Page 218   *Psalm 150:1*   "PRAISE ye the Lord. Praise God in his sanctuary; praise him in the firmament of his power.

2: Praise him for his mighty acts: praise him according to his excellent greatness.

3: Praise him with the sound of the trumpet; praise him with the psaltery and harp.

4: Praise him with the timbrel and dance: praise him with stringed instruments and organs.

5: Praise him upon the loud cymbals: praise him upon the high sounding cymbals.

6: Let every thing that hath breath praise the Lord. Praise ye the Lord.

SEPTEMBER 21, 1986

Page 225   *Isaiah 10*   Isaiah was called a major prophet from the size and importance of the book. This entire book contains prophetic oracles, sermons, hymns, narrative, and autobiography.

These Chapters include:

Calling of the Gentiles	Covetousness of Rulers
Parable of the Vineyard	Isaiah's Vision of the Lord
Christ Being Promised	Kingdom and Birth of Christ
Judgments for Pride	Christ's Peaceable Kingdom
Thanksgiving of the Faithful	A Triumph over Babylon

NOVEMBER 1990

Page 274   *Proverbs 4–12*   Emphasis is on the fact that the right life is not merely moral, but one lived toward God. Sharp contrasts are drawn between wisdom and folly, righteousness and sin.

Jeannette Yvonne Ferrell

These Chapter's include:

Wisdom's Fruits
Mischiefs of Whoredom
Wisdom's Eternity —
  She Keepeth Open House
Sundry Proverbs
Their Contrary Vices

Keep the Heart
True and False wisdom
Proverbs of Solomon
Moral Virtues

FEBRUARY 1, 1993

Page 282 *Jeremiah* 1–11   Jeremiah was called "the weeping prophet," devoted to his people but receiving only insults. Protesting against the low spiritual state of the Jews, he foretold their captivity and restoration, and lived to see the judgments fall. Surrounding nations also came under his survey, and in the far distance, Messiah's kingdom.

These Chapter's include:

Man's Unkindness
Israel's Confession of Sin
The Prophet Lamenteth
Vain Confidence of the
  Disobedient
Jeremiah Proclaimeth Anew
  with a Touch of God's
  Covenant

Judah Worse than Israel
Judah Called to Repentance
God's Judgements on the Jews
Impenitency of the People
Trust in God

ℬible 𝒬uotes

King James Version

Page 411   *John 3:16:*   **For God so loved the world,** that he gave his only begotten Son, that whosoever believeth in him should not perish, but have everlasting life.

John 14:1: **Let not your heart be troubled**; ye believe in God, believe also in me.

2: In my Father's house are many mansions: if it *were* not so, I would have told you. I go to prepare a place for you.

3: And if I go and prepare a place for you, I will come again, and receive you unto myself: that where I am, there ye may be also.

4: And whither I go ye know, and the way ye know.

5: Thomas saith unto him, Lord, we know not whither thou goest; and how can we know the way?

6: Jesus saith unto him, I am the way, the truth, and the life: no man cometh unto the Father, but by me.

Hebrew 13:1: **"Let brotherly love continue."**

2: Be not forgetful to entertain strangers: for thereby some have entertained angels unawares.

3: Remember them that are in bonds, as bound with them; *and* them which suffer adversity, as being yourselves also in the body.

4: Marriage is honourable in all, and the bed undefiled; but whoremongers and adulterers God will not judge.

5: Let *your* conversation *be* without covetousness: *and be* content with such things as ye have: for he hath said, I will never leave thee, nor forsake thee.

6: So that we may boldly say, The Lord *is* my helper, and I will not fear what man shall do unto me.

7: Remember them which have the rule over you, who have spoken unto you the word of God: whose faith follow, considering the end of *their* conversation.

8: Jesus Christ, the same yesterday, and to day, and for ever.

9: Be not carried about with divers and strange doctrines. For *it is* a good thing that the heart be established with grace; not with meats, which have not profited them that have been occupied therein.

Matthew 24:6: **And ye shall hear of wars and rumours of wars**: see that ye be not troubled: for all these things must come to pass, but the end is not yet.

Romans 8:28: **And we know that all things work together for good** to them that love God, to them who are the called according to *his* purpose.

The Roman Road   Page 412

Romans 3:10: As it is written, There is none righteous, no, not one.
    23: For all have sinned, and come short of the glory of God:
    12: Wherefore, as by one man sin entered into the world, and death by sin; and so death passed upon all men, for that all have sinned.

Romans 6:23: For the wages of sin is death; but the gift of God is eternal life through Jesus Christ our Lord.

Romans 5:8: But God commendeth his love toward us, in that, while we were yet sinners, Christ died for us.

Romans 10:9: That if thou shalt confess with thy mouth the Lord Jesus, and shall believe in thine heart that God hath raised him from the dead, thou shalt be saved.
    10: For with the heart man believeth unto righteousness; and with the mouth confession is made unto salvation.
    11: For the scripture saith, Whosoever believeth on him shall not be ashamed.
    12: For there is no difference between the Jew and the Greek: for the same Lord over all is rich unto all that call upon him.
    13: For whosoever shall call upon the name of the Lord shall be saved.

I John 1:9: If we confess our sins, He is faithful and just to forgive us our sins, and to cleanse us from all unrighteousness.

Revelation 3:20: Behold, **I stand at the door, and knock**: if any man hear my voice, and open the door, I will come in to him, and will sup with him, and he with me.
    21: To him that overcometh will I grant to sit with me in my throne, even as I also overcame, and am set down with my Father in his throne.

Isaiah 1:18: Come now, and let us reason together, saith the LORD: **"though your sins be as scarlet, they shall be as white as snow;"** though they be red like crimson, they shall be as wool.